Gallica
Volume 29

VIOLENCE AND THE WRITING OF HISTORY IN THE MEDIEVAL FRANCOPHONE WORLD

Gallica

ISSN 1749–091X

General Editor: Sarah Kay

Gallica aims to provide a forum for the best current work in medieval and Renaissance French studies. Literary studies are particularly welcome and preference is given to works written in English, although publication in French is not excluded.

Proposals or queries should be sent in the first instance to the editor, or to the publisher, at the addresses given below; all submissions receive prompt and informed consideration.

Professor Sarah Kay, Department of French, New York University, 13–19 University Place, 6th floor, New York, NY 10003, USA

The Editorial Director, Gallica, Boydell & Brewer Ltd., PO Box 9, Woodbridge, Suffolk IP12 3DF, UK

Previously published titles in this series are listed at the end of this volume.

VIOLENCE AND THE WRITING OF HISTORY IN THE MEDIEVAL FRANCOPHONE WORLD

Edited by

Noah D. Guynn
and
Zrinka Stahuljak

D. S. BREWER

© Contributors 2013

All Rights Reserved. Except as permitted under current legislation no part of this work may be photocopied, stored in a retrieval system, published, performed in public, adapted, broadcast, transmitted, recorded or reproduced in any form or by any means, without the prior permission of the copyright owner

First published 2013
D. S. Brewer, Cambridge

ISBN 978–1–84384–337–5

D. S. Brewer is an imprint of Boydell & Brewer Ltd
PO Box 9, Woodbridge, Suffolk IP12 3DF, UK
and of Boydell & Brewer Inc.
668 Mt Hope Avenue, Rochester, NY 14620–2731, USA
website: www.boydellandbrewer.com

A CIP catalogue record for this title is available
from the British Library

The publisher has no responsibility for the continued existence or accuracy of URLs for external or third-party internet websites referred to in this book, and does not guarantee that any content on such websites is, or will remain, accurate or appropriate

Papers used by Boydell & Brewer Ltd are natural, recyclable products made from wood grown in sustainable forests

This publication is printed on acid-free paper

Printed and bound in the United States of America by Publishers Graphics, LLC on sustainably sourced paper.

CONTENTS

List of Illustrations	vii
List of Contributors	ix
Acknowledgments	xi

Introduction
1. Historicity, Violence, and the Medieval Francophone World: *Mémoire Hystérisée*
   Noah D. Guynn and Zrinka Stahuljak — 1

Part I. Theorizing Violence
2. Violence, History, and the Old French Epic of Revolt
   Andrew Cowell — 19

3. Rhetoric, Providence, and Violence in Villehardouin's *La conquête de Constantinople*
   Noah D. Guynn — 35

Part II. Institutions and Subversions
4. Vice, Tyranny, Violence, and the Usurpation of Flanders (1071) in Flemish Historiography from 1093 to 1294
   Jeff Rider — 55

5. Marvelous Feats: Humor, Trickery, and Violence in the *History of the Counts of Guines and Lords of Ardres* of Lambert of Ardres
   Leah Shopkow — 71

6. Dismembered Borders and Treasonous Bodies in Anglo-Norman Historiography
   Matthew Fisher — 83

7. The Good, the Bad, and the Beautiful: Violence in the *Canso de la Crozada*
   Karen Sullivan — 99

Part III. Gender and Sexuality

8. Political Violence and Sexual Violation in the Work of Benoît de Sainte-Maure
   David Rollo — 117

9. The Sexuality of History: The Demise of Hugh Despenser, Roger Mortimer, and Richard II in Jean Le Bel, Jean Froissart, and Jean d'Outremeuse
   Zrinka Stahuljak — 133

Part IV. Trauma, Memory, and Healing

10. "Guerre ne sert que de tourment": Remembering War in the Poetic Correspondence of Charles d'Orléans
    Deborah McGrady — 151

11. Commemorating the Chivalric Hero: Text, Image, Violence, and Memory in the *Livre des faits de messire Jacques de Lalaing*
    Rosalind Brown-Grant — 169

12. Coming Communities in Medieval Francophone Writing about the Orient
    Simon Gaunt — 187

Index — 203

ILLUSTRATIONS

Fig 1. Paris, BnF fr. 16830, fol. 1r. The author depicted as Toison d'Or, Jean Le Fèvre de Saint-Rémy, king of arms of the Burgundian Order of the Golden Fleece. Reproduced by kind permission of the Bibliothèque nationale de France, Paris. — 174

Fig. 2. Paris, BnF fr. 16830, fol. 31r. Lalaing displays his arms before combat begins at the Nancy joust. Reproduced by kind permission of the Bibliothèque nationale de France, Paris. — 180

Fig. 3. Paris, BnF fr. 16830, fol. 157v. Lalaing among the ranks of Burgundian knights pitted against their Ghentish foe in the battle for the Pont d'Espierres. Reproduced by kind permission of the Bibliothèque nationale de France, Paris. — 182

Fig. 4. Paris, BnF fr. 16830, fol. 202r. The death of Lalaing at the siege of Poeke in the Ghent War. Reproduced by kind permission of the Bibliothèque nationale de France, Paris. — 183

CONTRIBUTORS

Rosalind Brown-Grant is Professor of Late Medieval French Literature at the University of Leeds. She is the author of *Christine de Pizan and the Moral Defence of Women: Reading Beyond Gender* (Cambridge University Press, 1999) and *French Romance of the Later Middle Ages: Gender, Morality, and Desire* (Oxford University Press, 2008). She is currently co-organizer of the international research network Text/Image Relations in Late Medieval French Culture (14th–16th centuries): http://textimagerelations.wordpress.com.

Andrew Cowell is Professor of French and Linguistics at the University of Colorado. He is the author of *At Play in the Tavern: Signs, Coins, and Bodies in the Middle Ages* (University of Michigan Press, 1999) and *The Medieval Warrior Aristocracy: Gifts, Violence, Performance, and the Sacred* (D. S. Brewer, 2007), as well as works on Native American languages, traditional narrative, and culture. His current work on the Middle Ages focuses on space, subjectivity, and identity.

Simon Gaunt is Professor of French Language and Literature at King's College London. His books include *Love and Death in Medieval French and Occitan Courtly Literature: Martyrs to Love* (Oxford University Press, 2006) and *The Cambridge Companion to Medieval French Literature* (Cambridge University Press, 2008), which he edited with Sarah Kay. A book on Marco Polo is forthcoming.

Noah D. Guynn is Associate Professor of French at the University of California, Davis. He is the author of *Allegory and Sexual Ethics in the High Middle Ages* (Palgrave Macmillan, 2007) and is currently writing a book on ethics, politics and religion in late medieval and early modern French farce.

Matthew Fisher is Assistant Professor of English at the University of California, Los Angeles. He is the author of *Scribal Authorship and the Writing of History in Medieval England* (Ohio State University Press, 2012) and is currently writing a book on the aesthetics and politics of forgetting in later medieval England.

Deborah McGrady is Associate Professor and Chair of French at the University of Virginia. She is the author of *Controlling Readers: Guillaume de Machaut and His Late Medieval Audience* (University of Toronto Press,

2006), and co-editor of *A Companion to Guillaume de Machaut* (Brill, 2012) and *Christine de Pizan: A Casebook* (Routledge, 2003). She is currently completing a book on late medieval patronage dynamics.

Jeff Rider is Professor of Romance Languages and Literatures and Medieval Studies at Wesleyan University and author of *God's Scribe: The Historiographical Art of Galbert of Bruges* (Catholic University of America Press, 2001). Most recently, he has co-edited *The Inner Life of Women in Medieval Romance Literature: Grief, Guilt, and Hypocrisy* (Palgrave Macmillan, 2011), co-edited and co-translated *Le Lai du conseil* (Liverpool Online Series of Critical Editions of French Texts, 2013), and translated Galbert of Bruges, *The Murder, Betrayal, and Assassination of the Glorious Count Charles of Flanders* (Yale University Press, 2013).

David Rollo is Associate Professor of English at the University of Southern California. He is the author of *Historical Fabrication, Ethnic Fable, and French Romance in Twelfth-Century England* (French Forum, 1998), *Glamorous Sorcery: Magic and Literacy in the High Middle Ages* (University of Minnesota Press, 2000), *Kiss My Relics: Hermaphroditic Fictions of the Middle Ages* (University of Chicago Press, 2011), and *Alain de Lille's "De planctu Naturae": A New Translation from the Latin* (forthcoming). Before taking an appointment in English he taught French for twelve years to the rank of Professor.

Leah Shopkow is Associate Professor of History at Indiana University, Bloomington. She is the author of *History and Community: Norman Historical Writing in the Eleventh and Twelfth Centuries* (Catholic University of America Press, 1997), translator of *History of the Counts of Guines and Lords of Ardres* by Lambert of Ardres (University of Pennsylvania Press, 2001), and is currently completing an edition and translation of the *Chronicle of Andres* by William of Andres.

Zrinka Stahuljak is Associate Professor of French and Comparative Literature at the University of California, Los Angeles. She is the author of *Bloodless Genealogies of the French Middle Ages* (University Press of Florida, 2005) and *Pornographic Archaeology: Medicine, Medievalism, and the Invention of the French Nation* (University of Pennsylvania Press, 2013), co-author of *Thinking Through Chrétien de Troyes* (D. S. Brewer, 2011), and co-editor of *Minima Memoria: Essays in the Wake of Jean-François Lyotard* (Stanford University Press, 2007).

Karen Sullivan is Irma Brandeis Professor of Romance Literature and Culture at Bard College. She is the author of *The Inner Lives of Medieval Inquisitors* (University of Chicago Press, 2011), *Truth and the Heretic: Crises of Knowledge in Medieval French Literature* (University of Chicago Press, 2005), and *The Interrogation of Joan of Arc* (University of Minnesota Press, 1999). She is currently writing a book about the perceived dangers of Arthurian romance.

ACKNOWLEDGMENTS

The editors wish to express their gratitude to Peggy McCracken for inspiring them to pursue this project; to Sarah Kay, Elspeth Ferguson, and Caroline Palmer for supporting it from its inception; to the anonymous reader for the press for offering many useful suggestions for improvements; and to Sharron Wood for copyediting the manuscript.

The editors also wish to acknowledge the University of California, Davis and the Center for Medieval and Renaissance Studies at the University of California, Los Angeles for providing crucial funding support.

1

Introduction
Historicity, Violence, and the Medieval Francophone World: *Mémoire Hystérisée*

NOAH D. GUYNN AND ZRINKA STAHULJAK

> This infinite passage through violence is what is called history.
> Jacques Derrida, *Writing and Difference*

In the 1869 preface to his *Histoire de France* (1833–67), the great Romantic historian Jules Michelet declares that, prior to the composition of his magnum opus, France "avait des annales, et non point une histoire" [had annals but not a history].[1] In his view, annals are to history as mere facts are to life itself: while the former do little more than compile information about great men, pivotal events, and dominant institutions, the latter captures the national spirit and life in its totality: "la vie historique ... en toutes ses voies, toutes ses formes, tous ses éléments" [historical life ... with all its paths, all its forms, all its elements] (p. iii). Positing history "comme *résurrection de la vie intégrale*" [as the *resurrection of the whole of life*] (p. iv), he proposes a set of obligations for the historian: he must penetrate beneath the "surface" of past events in order to access France's social, cultural, and political endeavors in their "infini détail" [infinite detail] (p. i); embrace "l'unité vivante des éléments naturels et géographiques qui l'ont constituée" [the living unity of the natural and geographical elements that constituted her] (p. i); delve into the "sources primitives" (p. i) that abound in her manuscript collections and archives; and study the somatic, humoral, and pathological conditions of the population, thereby apprehending France itself "comme une personne" [as a person] (p. xxiii). History is thus, for Michelet, *national*, *total*, *organicist* history. He conceives of the past as a body in which each of the organs – geography, climate, institutions, laws, health, morals, ideas – is necessary for

---

[1] Jules Michelet, "Préface de 1869," in *Histoire de France*, in *Œuvres complètes*, vol. 1 (Paris: Flammarion, 1893–98), p. i [pp. i–xlv]. All translations are ours unless otherwise indicated.

creating and sustaining the life of the people. Rather than dissecting that body with a scalpel, severing its constitutive parts from the whole, the historian must instead look upon it with a loving, all-encompassing gaze, merging its parts into a global vision of "la vie historique" and then fusing with it completely: "L'histoire, l'historien, se mêlent en ce regard" [History and the historian merge in this respect] (p. ix).

Though Michelet's notion of the past as "vie intégrale" anticipates the endeavors of esteemed successors (including practitioners of *l'histoire totale* such as Lucien Febvre and Fernand Braudel), his totalizing claims about, and delirious fixations with, the past have also been a source of considerable anxiety. As Pierre Nora reminds us, Michelet's private journals reveal that he didn't merely study history but was actually sickened by it, was rendered quite literally "malade de l'Histoire."[2] Not only did he regularly fall ill from overwork, but he also experienced a range of psychosomatic symptoms brought on by an emotional surrender to the past: he fainted upon entering the Musée des Monuments Français, fearing that the statues of great men would come to life; he had hallucinatory visions in which the dead rose up from the dusty parchments housed in the Archives Nationales; and he bled profusely from the nose while writing about the September Massacres.[3] These episodes have earned him the reputation of having "hystericized" history, of giving in to "l'hystérie identitaire," a compulsive overidentification with, and somaticization of, his intellectual object (p. 6). Yet many scholars would agree with Nora that Michelet was also a paradigmatic historian, as he was the first to conceive of the past as an integral whole: "Michelet presents the strange, troubling case of an exemplary, absolute, referential historical memory that at the same time is rooted in a totally pathological and hystericized memory" (pp. 6–7). For Nora, Michelet's "mémoire hystérisée" is disconcerting precisely because it intertwines things that modern historians strive assiduously to disentangle: exemplary, national, total history and individual, compulsive, morbid subjectivity.

But what else does Michelet's *mémoire hystérisée* unsettle, and what else can it tell us about historiography in the West? Is it possible that Romantic history isn't merely subjective, overwrought, and diseased – the antithesis, therefore, of modern critical detachment? Does it perhaps also suggest the risks, biases, and blind spots inherent in *all* historical methodologies, past and present? And what should we make of Michelet's repudiation of the work of his predecessors, the post-Revolutionary "pléïade historique" (p. ii) whose work he dismisses as mere annals? What motivates his critique of his predecessors – or, for that matter, our own rejection of "this neurotic,

---

[2] Pierre Nora, "Michelet, ou l'hystérie identitaire," *L'esprit créateur* 46.2 (2006): 6 [6–14]. Nora cites Roland Barthes, who refers to "Michelet, malade d'histoire" in *Michelet* (1953; Paris: Seuil, 1995), p. 13.
[3] See Nora, "Michelet," 6.

visceral, shadowy Michelet" (Nora, "Michelet," 6)? Does the authorization (and professionalization) of modern history require a decisive break with, or "othering" of, earlier historiographical methods? What kind of faith should we place in our own methods if we know that sooner or later they will be dismissed in favor of other modes of historical analysis? And, finally, what should we do with premodern historical narratives – sources that Michelet valued a great deal but that have often been considered the unscientific, unreliable, extravagant "other" of modern historical inquiry?

These questions are of considerable urgency, since, to quote Donald R. Kelley (who in turn cites Michel de Certeau), "the study of history is ... one of the latest, if not the last, of Western mythical constructions by which we try to make sense of the largely unknown and perhaps ultimately unknowable world beyond our small cultural horizons."[4] Though history is unquestionably *a* – if not *the* – dominant epistemology of Western modernity (for Hegel and Sartre, it is the very bedrock of phenomenology),[5] it has acquired its authority by recounting its disciplinary history as the progressive repudiation of pseudohistorical and protohistorical epistemologies of the past: "According to an old and familiar story, history emerged from myth and purged itself gradually of legendary features until it gained full enlightenment in the age of Machiavelli and Guicciardini – or perhaps Voltaire and Gibbon, or perhaps Mommsen and Ranke, or perhaps the 'new' economic, social, and cultural histories of this century, and so on" (Kelley, p. 1). Does our faith in the explanatory powers of history require a continual process of disenchantment – a periodic shedding of outmoded methods and genres that is, according to de Certeau, "a uniquely Western trait" (p. 4)? For that matter, what kind of faith should we have in a discipline that claims to access the truth of the past by discrediting the means by which the past was remembered *in the past*?

Focusing on authors who wrote in French or lived in the medieval francophone world (areas in which French was a dominant, prestige, or bridge language), the chapters in this volume propose a different – and hopefully more integral – relationship with historiographies of the medieval past.[6]

---

[4] Donald R. Kelley, *Faces of History: Historical Inquiry from Herodotus to Herder* (New Haven, CT: Yale University Press, 1998), p. 1, citing Michel de Certeau, *The Writing of History*, trans. Tom Conley (New York: Columbia University Press, 1988): "History is probably our myth" (p. 21).

[5] See Eric Hirsch and Charles Stewart, "Introduction: Ethnographies of Historicity," *History and Anthropology* 16.3 (2005): 264–65 [261–74]. As Hirsch and Stewart note, Claude Lévi-Strauss criticized Sartre for his "inability to recognize that history is merely one limited way of looking at the world" (265).

[6] For a useful introduction to this world and the place of historiography in it, see Keith Busby, "Vernacular Literature and the Writing of History in Medieval Francophonia," in *Imagining the Past in France: History in Manuscript Painting: 1250–1500*, ed. Elizabeth Morrison and Anne D. Hedeman (Los Angeles: Getty Museum, 2010), pp. 27–41.

Specifically, we aim to study how medieval writers commemorated violent events (torture, dismemberment, fights, uprisings, executions, rapes, murders, assassinations, beatings, battles, wars, crusades), and how they in turn transformed a violent past into a usable one (a past that unifies the historian's audience, shapes their beliefs and perceptions of reality, and motivates individual and collective actions). Building on pioneering work on medieval historical representation by scholars in literature, history, and linguistics,[7] this project stands in stark contrast to a tendency prevalent among modern scholars to reify and instrumentalize medieval narrative history – that is, to use *annales*, *chronicae*, and *historiae* as sources of factual data and to evaluate that data for accuracy before incorporating it into recognizably modern forms of historical narrative, argument, or analysis. Little attempt is made to understand medieval historiographical methods and styles on their own terms or to situate texts within a set of rhetorical, interpretive, and cultural practices – sometimes, as John O. Ward has shown, at the expense of compromising factual accuracy.[8] By contrast, the contributors to this volume strive to demonstrate how knowledge of the medieval past can be enhanced by fearlessly encountering medieval modes of historical representation and consciousness, by reading medieval historical texts as much as possible on their own terms, and by acknowledging – and resisting – the desire to subject them to modern conceptions of historical intelligibility.

[7] See especially *The Medieval Chronicle*, a yearbook founded in 1999 and published by Rodopi, as well as these monographs: Peter F. Ainsworth, *Jean Froissart and the Fabric of History: Truth, Myth, and Fiction in the "Chroniques"* (Oxford: Clarendon, 1990); Jean Blacker, *The Faces of Time: Portrayal of the Past in Old French and Latin Historical Narrative of the Anglo-Norman Regnum* (Austin: University of Texas Press, 1994); Dominique Boutet, *Formes littéraires et conscience historique aux origines de la littérature française, 1100–1250* (Paris: Presses Universitaires de France, 1999); Peter Damian-Grint, *The New Historians of the Twelfth-Century Renaissance: Authorising History in the Vernacular Revolution* (Woodbridge, UK: Boydell, 1999); Bernard Guenée, *Histoire et culture historique dans l'Occident médiéval* (Paris: Aubier Montaigne, 1980); Sophie Marnette, *Narrateur et points de vue dans la littérature française médiévale: Une approche linguistique* (Bern: Peter Lang, 1998); Monika Otter, *Inventiones: Fiction and Referentiality in Twelfth-Century English Historical Writing* (Chapel Hill: University of North Carolina Press, 1996); David Rollo, *Historical Fabrication, Ethnic Fable, and French Romance in Twelfth-Century England* (Lexington, KY: French Forum, 1998); Gabrielle M. Spiegel, *Romancing the Past: The Rise of Vernacular Prose Historiography in Thirteenth-Century France* (Berkeley: University of California Press, 1993); Michel Zink, *Froissart et le temps* (Paris: Presses Universitaires de France, 1998).

[8] See John O. Ward, "Some Principles of Rhetorical Historiography in the Twelfth Century," in *Classical Rhetoric and Medieval Historiography*, ed. Ernst Breisach (Kalamazoo, MI: Medieval Institute Publications, 1985), pp. 103–65. For Ward, "any assessment of the factual basis of a learned twelfth-century narrative can only proceed from a firm grasp of the rhetorical purpose and techniques of the medieval historian in question, and, thus, much modern scholarship on important aspects of the first crusade, for example, is built upon sand" (p. 106).

This undertaking has certain features in common with "posthistorical" criticism, a new movement in medieval literary studies that boldly challenges the long-unquestioned assumption that responsible scholarship must begin by situating texts within the social and political contexts that determine their meaning. In their preface to *The Post-Historical Middle Ages*, Sylvia Federico and Elizabeth Scala argue that the "critical edge" given to historicism in the 1980s and 1990s has dulled considerably over time. They call upon medievalists to hone that edge, not (as their title may initially seem to imply) by abandoning history as a mode of textual and cultural analysis, but rather by refusing to see it as the ground of analysis or its teleological fulfillment. We should notice "the multiple histories that inform a text in contradictory ways," they assert, and should "remain open to the stakes of our present engagement with the past."[9] Though he is in some ways critical of Federico and Scala's project, Paul Strohm echoes their call for scholars to refine their "appreciation of the unruly multiplicity of ways in which history can manifest itself within a text" and of the "complex embeddedness" of a text "in historical process."[10] In his view, historicism should struggle to avoid the tendency to "'read through' the text to its supposed historical 'meaning'" (p. 386), and he therefore endorses Maura Nolan's claim (in her contribution to *The Post-Historical Middle Ages*) that "historicism after historicism" should attend first and foremost to formal devices, "allow[ing] for the strange, the exceptional, the weird, and the outsized, and accept[ing] the notion that such oddities are endemic to art."[11]

As Strohm and Nolan urge, the contributors to the present volume remain invested in the project of recovering the textual traces of medieval lived experience, even as we strive to move beyond a version of historicism that does little more than match texts to flat, static contexts. On the one hand, we deploy the methods of cultural studies to *historicize* medieval historiographical genres and to speculate about the material and institutional forces that shaped them. On the other hand, we *hystericize* those genres: we study them as textual remainders of modes of historical consciousness rather than as more or less flawed repositories of historical data; we draw attention to their disconcertingly foreign modes of commemorating the past and their stubborn resistance to intellectual totalization; and we attend simultaneously to factual indices and textual effects, even when the latter obscure the former

---

[9] Sylvia Federico and Elizabeth Scala, "Introduction: Getting Post-Historical," in *The Post-Historical Middle Ages*, ed. Federico and Scala (New York: Palgrave Macmillan, 2009), pp. 5, 7.

[10] Paul Strohm, "Historicity without Historicism?" *postmedieval* 1.3 (2010): 382 [380–91]. Responses to Strohm's review have been posted at http://postmedieval-forum.com.

[11] Maura Nolan, "Historicism after Historicism," in *The Post-Historical Middle Ages*, ed. Federico and Scala, p. 84 [63–86].

through blatantly phantasmal, overtly stylized depictions of the past. In short, we are interested in the kinds of cultural phenomena that anthropologists Eric Hirsch and Charles Stewart call *historicity*: not "an objectively determinable aspect of historical descriptions," but rather "a human situation in flow, where versions of the past and future (of persons, collectives or things) assume present form in relation to events, political needs, available cultural forms and emotional dispositions" (262).

Inspired by this relativist, constructivist notion of historicity, we asked our contributors to reflect on the following sorts of questions. How do medieval historical conventions and methods, rhetorics and styles function, and what kinds of cultural and ideological needs do they fulfill? How do medieval historians select and authorize specific forms of testimony and modes of representation? How, when, and why do they differentiate (or fail to differentiate) between real events and fictional narratives? How do they situate historical events within ethical, religious, and political schemes, and how do they use those schemes to persuade readers of the veracity of their claims? How do historical facts (*res factae*) and factual reporting (*scriptum rerum*) relate to other reality constructions, including fictional narratives (*res fictae*) and sublime, transcendent truth (*veritas*)? Most specifically, how do writers emanating from the medieval francophone world commemorate violent events (whether factual, partially factual, or nonfactual), and how do they use that violence to mold historical and ideological consciousness?

Since the relationships between and among historiography and violence, *la francophonie* and *le Moyen Âge* call out for elucidation, we will attempt to theorize them here before allowing our contributors to guide us through their more detailed explorations of the questions posed above. To begin with, we wish to observe that in the medieval and modern West historiography and violence are virtually coefficient terms. They are yoked together not only by the kinds of events that have captured the imaginations of historians and their audiences, but also by the cultural invention of historical knowledge. As de Certeau has argued, this is particularly true of "modern Western history," which is constituted through forceful, violent acts of "othering": a "discourse of separation" that severs historians from their object of inquiry and establishes "intelligibility ... through a relation with the other" (p. 2). Simultaneously invoking and dispelling Michelet's hallucinatory visions, de Certeau describes history as a textual "sepulcher" or "haven" inhabited by ghosts who "can neither speak nor do harm anymore" and who are remembered on the condition that they "remain *forever silent*" (p. 2). This "silence of the other" instills in historians and their audiences a desire for a past that simultaneously invites and thwarts intellectual mastery – again, shades of Michelet. Unlike his Romantic predecessor, however, de Certeau avers that the modern historian cultivates a violent, rather than loving, relationship with an embodied past: history "forces the silent body to speak," and "the violence of the body reaches the written page only through absence, through the intermediary of documents that the historian has been able to see on the sands from which a presence has since been washed away, and through a murmur that lets us hear – but from afar – the unknown immensity that seduces and menaces our knowledge" (p. 3). Though de Certeau is referring here to *historical violence* (the social upheavals that gave Michelet nosebleeds and awakened his fear of the dead), he is equally interested in *historiographical violence*: acts of reclamation, narrativization, and periodization that dissect the past and then reassemble it according to principles of relevance, causality, and temporality; the creation of intellectual and disciplinary categories and frameworks that brutally separate "what can be *understood*" from "what must be *forgotten* in order to obtain the representation of a present intelligibility" (p. 4); and, finally, the return of history's repressed in the form of new historiographies that annihilate older ones and resurrect forgotten corners of the past in the name of greater truth.

An anxious awareness of the mutual entailment of violence and historiography was, however, endemic to Western cultures long before Michelet. Herodotus and Thucydides were both obsessed with war and its causes, even if they demonstrated profoundly different approaches and styles, the former "a cosmopolitan and compulsive tourist," the latter "a practical and committed man of affairs."[12] Roman historians were themselves fascinated by the aggression inherent in legislative and legal processes and the violence that arose when those processes failed to contain or canalize political tensions.[13] If Roman intellectuals subsumed history to the art of rhetoric and conceived of historians as "exornatores rerum" [ornamenters of things done] rather than "tantummodo narratores" [mere relaters of facts],[14] it may be in part because, as Jody Enders has shown, the canons of Roman rhetoric were "built upon ... violent originary narrative[s]."[15] Christian historians differ markedly from their pagan counterparts in taking sacred history and its revelations of divine love and grace as their starting point. And yet they, too, usually conceive of history as a record of human brutality. For Augustine, Cain's murder of Abel inaugurates the struggle between the earthly city and the City of God, a struggle that characterizes secular history as a whole; for Orosius, history is a record of unremitting depravity and carnage that can be redeemed only by Christ; and, for the ninth-century chronicler Freculph of Lisieux, the project of history is "to describe the fortunes of war, the ruin of kings and the miseries

---

[12] Kelley, *Faces of History*, p. 2.

[13] As Joy Connolly writes, "Romulus' legendary founding act of fratricide turns out to be emblematic of politics in Roman historiography." See "Virtue and Violence: The Historians on Politics," in *The Cambridge Companion to the Roman Historians*, ed. Andrew Feldherr (Cambridge: Cambridge University Press, 2009), p. 190 [181–94].

[14] Cicero, *De oratore*, 2.12.54, ed. E. W. Sutton (Cambridge, MA: Loeb Classical Library, Harvard University Press, 1967), p. 236.

[15] Jody Enders, *The Medieval Theater of Cruelty: Rhetoric, Memory, Violence* (Ithaca, NY: Cornell University Press, 1999), p. 16.

of their subjects."[16] It would be a mistake to imagine that the premodern world was somehow more violent or more preoccupied with violence than the modern, genocidal one is. We therefore hasten to agree with Peter Haidu that the technological advances of modernity have not been accompanied by "greater sophistication in the understanding or management of violence."[17] And yet Haidu is also right to acknowledge, first, that "the use of force in forms we consider violent was a social norm in medieval society: society was unimaginable without its presence" (p. 3); and, second, that modern ideologies and aesthetics of violence – if not modern technologies and historiographies of violence – are in large measure founded on "bases laid down in the Middle Ages" (p. 195). A major goal of this book is to demonstrate not only that violence was indeed pervasive in the medieval world but also that depictions of a violent past were endowed with tremendous cultural and ideological weight.

Of course, violence is not a singular phenomenon, and nor can it be viewed from a singular perspective. This volume is therefore divided into four parts, which are devoted to the following topics treated in nonexclusive ways: Theorizing Violence; Institutions and Subversions; Gender and Sexuality; and Trauma, Memory, and Healing. Part I, which includes chapters by Andrew Cowell and Noah D. Guynn, seeks to theorize violence in terms of, on the one hand, violent actions and social relations, and, on the other, rhetorical language and narrative representation. Cowell investigates the Old French epic of revolt using anthropological scholarship on the gift to critique the notion of a historical and theoretical opposition between gift giving and violence. Like gift giving, violence can be reciprocal; conversely, gift giving can be quite hostile; and both are socially regulated through their relationship to the sacred. Nonreciprocal violence subverts this order, as the transgressor, an individual, attempts to appropriate the sacred for himself, causing social and political disturbances that can only be rectified by reinforcing networks of reciprocity. Cowell thus resituates heroic violence within a context of social reciprocity and rereads the *chansons de geste* as social histories used to contain or restrict hostility.

Like Cowell, Guynn is interested in the ideological uses of historical narrative, though his principal emphasis is on the language of historiography.

---

[16] See Beryl Smalley, *Historians in the Middle Ages* (New York: Charles Scribner's Sons, 1974), pp. 44–45, citation at p. 45.

[17] Peter Haidu, *The Subject of Violence: The Song of Roland and the Birth of the State* (Bloomington: Indiana University Press, 1993), p. 4. Cf. Robert Muchembled, *A History of Violence*, trans. Jean Birrell (Cambridge: Polity Press, 2012), which argues that murder rates in Western Europe declined significantly from the thirteenth century through the twentieth as new models for the social and behavioral control of unmarried men were developed. Even as violence disappeared from social spaces, however, national governments sought to mobilize male aggression to achieve lawful political and military goals.

Specifically, he examines the relationship between rhetorical history and the justification of a morally and religiously fraught course of events: the diversion of the Fourth Crusade to Zara and Constantinople and the founding of the Latin Empire, specifically as these events are reported by Geoffroy de Villehardouin in *La conquête de Constantinople*. Though the religious justification of crusading is a familiar topic for medievalists, Guynn offers an innovative approach to the subject by addressing the persistence and necessity of doubt within providential rhetoric. He argues that, rather than attempting to exclude doubt from his narrative, Villehardouin repeatedly calls into question the believability of the events he commemorates in order to insist that God alone could have been their author. By reminding his readers that providential design is the only plausible explanation for the Crusade's outcomes, he illustrates an ideologically potent mode of textual reception and historical analysis.

Part II, "Institutions and Subversions," examines institutional violence, meaning concerted forms of aggression used to achieve political or religious goals and justified by historical modes of representation, as well as anti-institutional violence, meaning the subversion of social and political power through counternarratives and acts of resistance or revolt. Jeff Rider's chapter examines the first recorded rupture in the dynastic line of the Flemish counts and an inaugural moment for Flemish historiography: Robert the Frisian's usurpation of the county of Flanders and his assassination of Arnold III. For nearly three centuries, Flemish historians retold the story of this coup d'état and used the commemoration of its violence for exemplary, didactic purposes, notably as a mirror for princes. Lambert of Saint-Omer's *Liber Floridus*, with its portrait of Robert as a tyrant with an inner flaw, stands in contrast to the anonymous and influential *Flandria Generosa*, which focuses on the tyranny of Rachilda, widow of Baldwin VI and mother of Arnold III. Rider notes a shift that opposes two moral portraits of violent historical events, from the description of the ruler's flawed character to that of women's vices.

Leah Shopkow similarly focuses on the chastisement of the great and powerful, turning to Lambert of Ardres's *History of the Counts of Guines and Lords of Ardres*. When this Lambert introduces comic details into otherwise serious reports of the wounding or killing of powerful lords, humor becomes a response to the violence of ruling elites and a form of comic relief for the powerless who suffer under their yoke. Lambert's history serves as a counterpoint to official Flemish histories and shows how comic writing can be used to subvert physical, institutional, and ideological power. Not content to impose modern tastes on medieval sources, Shopkow inquires into the nature of medieval jokes and draws parallels between humorous incidents in Lambert's history and the explosive, violent humor found in contemporary literary texts, notably French epics and fabliaux and Latin satires.

Matthew Fisher's reading of chronicles that depict the execution of traitors under Edward I is inspired by Michel Foucault's claim that law and order are constituted through acts of physical brutality, notably public ordeals, torture, and dismemberment. Yet, just as the violent exercise of power serves as a sign of Edward's sovereignty, the fragments of the traitors' tortured and butchered bodies signify in unanticipated ways. On the one hand, the symbolic display of severed body parts at each of the four points of the kingdom defines the geographical reach and terrifying power of the law, and official histories of these executions depict dismemberment as an inevitable, just punishment for treason. On the other hand, the body parts themselves have a certain degree of autonomy and can be interpreted as relics that sanctify the rebels' actions and as evidence of the actual instability of monarchic power, which asserts itself through violent actions but is also violently opposed.

Like Fisher, Karen Sullivan focuses her analysis of the *Canso de la Crozada*, an Occitan history of the Albigensian Crusade, on tensions between narratives and counternarratives. The authors of the *Canso* allow us to glimpse how each side in the conflict sought to invalidate and deplore the enemy's violence and to glorify their own. Indeed, the history makes clear that the Crusade's atrocities were only fully intelligible when they were associated with ethical and metaphysical claims. While the *Canso* condemns as unjust violence that aims at an unwarranted end or destroys bonds of kinship, allegiance, or faith, it also justifies violence that achieves moral or tactical goals that are perceived as legitimate. In some cases, the *Canso* aestheticizes legitimate violence through vivid, colorful descriptions of feats of knightly honor and valor. Ultimately, the *Canso* allows us to understand that violence without an ethical and metaphysical frame is historically irrelevant, and that violence is intelligible only insofar as it sustains or weakens an ideologically privileged ethos.

Part III engages with two categories of analysis – gender and sexuality – that are not often at the forefront of discussions of medieval historiography, yet are fundamental to narrative constructions and reconstructions of the historical past. Reading Benoît de Sainte-Maure's *Chronique des ducs de Normandie* alongside the poet's earlier *Roman de Troie*, David Rollo argues that the chronicle does not glorify William the Conqueror and the Plantagenet line, as has often been supposed. Instead, it subtly erodes Plantagenet claims to unbroken succession by drawing attention to specious genealogical claims and suspicions of illegitimacy. In *Troie*, Polyxena's violent death at the hands of Neoptolemus maintains the purity of Priam's line and prevents rape and bastardy; however, it also puts an end to Priam's line and casts doubt upon the Normans' claims to Trojan ancestry. Likewise, in the *Chronique*, Benoît offers an alternative account of William's conception, insinuating that William's mother Arlette may already have been pregnant with him when she was seduced by Duke Robert. Far from being a propagandist for the Angevin Empire, then, Benoît uses the physical violation of Polyxena's and Arlette's bodies as opportunities to insert alternative, censored narratives into an official history.

Zrinka Stahuljak's chapter also revisits received notions on the uses of gender and sexuality in medieval chronicles, focusing specifically on depictions of the execution of Hugh Despenser, Edward II's lover, in Jean Le Bel, Froissart, and Jean d'Outremeuse. Comparing Hugh's murder to the execution of Roger Mortimer, Queen Isabelle's lover, Stahuljak shows that historians of the Hundred Years War do not single out same-sex practices for punishment and moral condemnation. Rather, they indict any form of sexual compulsion, indiscretion, and excess that contributes to political instability in a moment of profound crisis. Even Edward's well-known punishment (a hot poker is thrust into his rectum) is not necessarily tied to the crime of sodomy, nor is sodomy alone deemed responsible for the damage done to the body politic. The contemporary fascination with reclaiming evidence of the violent suppression of same-sex practices in the late Middle Ages may therefore have obscured the actual ideological uses of sexuality and violence in medieval historical texts – uses that are more broadly political than scholars have sometimes acknowledged.

Finally, Part IV introduces an important new dimension to the reading of medieval violence by examining war as a traumatic event that is silenced and displaced, glorified and commemorated, or (in one particularly compelling case) recuperated and superseded with a gesture toward an imminent supra-community beyond conflict. Deborah McGrady advances the bold claim that late medieval poets, and Charles d'Orléans in particular, explored poetry's power to reshape history through the commemoration of violent conflict and through an acknowledgment of poetry's power to change the course of events. Though Charles d'Orléans depicted his twenty-five-year imprisonment in England as a form of love captivity, McGrady reads this aesthetic sublimation not as an avoidance of political engagement but rather as a silent witness to the complexities of peace negotiations, which were the condition sine qua non for Charles's release. The poet's secret lyric correspondence with the Duke of Burgundy reveals covert attempts (during Charles's captivity) to influence peace negotiations and eventually (after his liberation) overt attempts to specify the social and historical context of his earlier writings. This poetic collaboration is revealed to be a collaboration for peace as well, since Charles used his personal manuscript (BnF, MS fr. 25458) to transform wartime trauma into a monument to friendship and alliance beyond political divisions.

Rosalind Brown-Grant turns our attention to chivalric biographies, a genre dedicated to the commemoration and exemplification of knightly conduct. She focuses on the anonymous *Livre des faits de messire Jacques de Lalaing*, which describes a Burgundian hero who was accidentally killed at the age of thirty-two when he received a blow to the head from a rebounding fragment of a wooden mantle from a bombard. The earliest extant manuscript (BnF MS fr. 16830) contains eighteen miniatures that, together with the narrative, strive to give sense to a life that was ended unintentionally and without achieving any sort of chivalric purpose. In attempting to give to the whole more coherence than the sum of its episodes, the narrative creates dissonance between Lalaing's celebrated life of chivalric violence and the randomness of his death by the very violence that chivalric biography claims to have mastered. The images fill in the gaps, however, reframing the hero's violent acts as the ultimate realization of knightly identity and community and recuperating his accidental death as an occasion for the literary immortalization of an exemplary chivalric career. The text thus invites future generations to imitate Lalaing's example and perpetuate his violent legacy.

Simon Gaunt's chapter comes last in the volume because it explores the perpetually deferred moment of a coming community, a utopian world that Marco Polo associates with the empire of the Great Mongol. Gaunt challenges the claim of much medieval postcolonial scholarship that certain key texts posit Europe's intellectual, cultural, and religious superiority and/or impose a binary view of Western Christian civilization and its others. Marco's *Devisement du monde* belies this claim by demonstrating a remarkable attention and openness to difference and by troubling an inherently violent account of the medieval "clash of civilizations." Marco sees in Kublai Khan's Mongol Empire an alternative form of government and community in which the obstacles created by linguistic differences are surmounted with a shared currency. Only communities that do not partake of the same monetary regime are defined in absolute terms by their linguistic singularity. By setting its value at will, Kublai Khan makes paper money the distinctive marker of Mongol sovereignty; and by imposing its use, he creates networks of symbolic exchange out of which a community can be built. Shared currency serves as a symbolic language that transcends linguistic difference, and the Mongol Empire becomes, for Marco, an alternative symbolic order in which violent conflict yields to shared values. The *Devisement* also constitutes French, or rather the Franco-Italian literary koine that Marco used, as a shared language that mediates various forms of linguistic and cultural difference, including French, Italian, and Mongolian.

The issue of the language of historical representation and the specific status of the vernacular in communicating historical knowledge is, of course, a foremost concern of this volume. The chapters described above study works emanating from the surprisingly vast geographical area in which Gallo-Romance dialects were spoken. In general usage, the word "francophone" refers to an individual who uses French regardless of his or her native language, birthplace, residence, or nationality. In postcolonial criticism and French studies, it also refers to cultures in which French has served as a language of colonization and currently serves as a language of cultural expression emancipated from the hegemonic dictates of metropolitan, "hexagonal" France. Much of modern francophone literature reflects the multilingualism and transnationalism of the postcolonial world and seeks to disrupt, pluralize, or transcend the linguistic categories linked to modern

European nation-states. For many, "francophone" has been a vexed term, as it has been perceived to atomize the field of French studies and to threaten the purity and prestige of hexagonal culture. Others equate the term with a second-class, ghettoized subdiscipline that is defined solely by its identitarian politics. Confronted with these attitudes, many scholars are now seeking to critique "a polarized, imbalanced, even falsely dichotomized view of the relationship between France and its former colonies or current dependencies" and to move toward a globalized conception of the francophone world that relies on "a more flexible approach to intersections and interdependencies."[18] The term "francophone" is thus being used to transcend hexagonal limitations and to imply the nonexclusive use of the French language in cultures that are either bilingual or multilingual.

We intend for the concept of "the medieval francophone world" to register the massive geographical and intercultural reach of French dialects in the medieval world without in any way implying that the sharing of a common linguistic matrix produces unifying, consolidating, or centralizing effects. In the period that this volume spans, from the Norman Conquest through the fifteenth century, and especially after the thirteenth-century eclipse of literary Occitan, French was unquestionably the dominant vernacular language of cultural and literary production in Western Europe. As Sharon Kinoshita argues, it was also in many ways a major "Mediterranean vernacular": it not only served as a lingua franca that enabled communication between merchants, pilgrims, and other travelers in southern Europe and the Middle East but was also the language that authors in those regions used "to reach an 'international' readership" and to "cultivate the political favor of a specifically French [i.e., francophone] audience."[19] Indeed, Old French was the language of political elites not only in northern France but also in England, Occitania, Naples, Sicily, the Latin Empire, and elsewhere and was therefore intimately associated with an ideology of geographical and political expansion. Old French is, to quote Kinoshita, "extraterritorial *avant la lettre*," meaning that it expresses myriad forms of cultural identification and political allegiance. It has little to do with national imaginings or an ideology of French unity, as Romance philologists repeatedly argued. On the contrary, the diverse forms of Old French utterly disrupt the philological fantasy of an underlying linguistic essence of nationhood and indicate a multilingual,

---

[18] Charles Forsdick, "Between 'French' and 'Francophone': French Studies and the Postcolonial Turn," *French Studies* 59.4 (2005): 529 [523–30].

[19] Sharon Kinoshita, "Worlding Medieval French," in *French Global: A New Approach to Literary History*, ed. Christie McDonald and Susan Rubin Suleiman (New York: Columbia University Press, 2010), p. 7 [3–20]. Kinoshita cites two historical texts, *La fleur des histoires de la terre d'Orient*, written by the Prince of Armenia and presented to Pope Clement IV in 1307, and *La geste des Chiprois*, a history of Cyprus.

decentered vector of cultural production and exchange in which "dominant" and "peripheral" are dynamically related and interconnected.

Though the contributors to this volume discount the nineteenth century's preoccupation with the transcendent spirit of the nation, we share a desire to expand notions of historical relevance beyond the mere reporting of events toward a broader conception of "la vie historique ... en toutes ses voies, toutes ses formes, tous ses éléments." Our specific goal is to discern and revalue the broad social, cultural, and political significance of medieval historiography's often conspicuously unreliable, biased, and anachronistic depictions of the past. Rejecting the claim that the Middle Ages somehow lacked the ability to perceive and represent diachronic change, we propose instead to read medieval historical narratives as self-conscious modes of reflecting on the practical and conceptual challenges that the past poses to the present. As Margreta de Grazia argues, there are dangers intrinsic to the claim that Italian humanism's discovery of anachronism marked a radical, "epoch-making" shift and its corollary proposition, that the Middle Ages could conceive of the past only as it "flowed into the present in a continuous tradition of *Latinitas*."[20] Modern scholars have interpreted the supposed inability of medieval intellectuals "to differentiate the world of the present-subject from that of the past-object" not just as "a violation of the basic principle of epistemology" but, more seriously, as an "ethical failure," a "reduction of the other to the same [that] constitutes an effacement of the other" (pp. 13–14). And yet the notion of the historical naïveté of the Middle Ages, which imposes modern, linear, absolute concepts of time on premodern texts, could itself been seen as a failure of historical imagination and an erasure of the alterity of the past. Indeed, de Grazia interprets references to the "diachronic innocence" of the Middle Ages as disciplinary maneuvers used to signify the modern scholar's power to control, if not actually to totalize, his or her intellectual object.[21] By rendering history as a teleological unfolding that leads inexorably to a moment of intellectual awakening (whether in Dante, Petrarch, or Valla) at which time and history are finally grasped for what they truly are, modern historians repeat the gestures of a Whig history they otherwise repudiate.

What if, following de Grazia's lead, we were to "[loosen] chronology's hold on historical thought" and "remove the stigma from anachronism or turn that stigma to advantage," acknowledging that "chronology is only one way by which the past can be related to the present" (p. 32)? What might we discover by working in the instability of multiple, parallel temporalities

---

[20] Margreta de Grazia, "Anachronism," in *Cultural Reformations: Medieval and Renaissance in Literary History*, ed. Brian Cummings and James Simpson (Oxford: Oxford University Press, 2010), pp. 26, 29 [13–32].

[21] See de Grazia, "Anachronism," p. 30, citing Thomas Greene, *The Light in Troy: Imitation and Discovery in Renaissance Poetry* (New Haven, CT: Yale University Press, 1982), p. 30.

and striving to understand not what really happened or how things actually were (history as events and conditions fixed in memory and stripped of their contingencies and indeterminacies) but how the past acquired significance in medieval cultures through processes of textual mediation, rhetorical elaboration, and visual translation?[22] Could we perhaps see the anachronisms of medieval historiography as evidence that the past can never be captured or reclaimed but can only be made relevant to the present by being invested with intellectual, affective, and ideological energies and by being shaped in accordance with available textual and visual cultural forms?

For medieval historians, the past that gets remembered is often a cruel, brutal one, and their tendency to view history as a record of inexorable, inevitable violence suggests the pervasiveness and broad relevance of violence in their world. The methods of medieval historiography are aggressive, too: events are matched to narrative forms, visual representations, and dominant ideologies in order to justify – and in some cases to motivate – violent actions. And yet there is tremendous intellectual, cultural, and perhaps even ethical richness to be found in the work of medieval historians and their supposed ignorance of cognitive distance. If, as de Certeau argues, the violence of modern Western history lies in the creation of a "discourse of separation" that violently subjugates the past even as it constructs the illusion of scientific detachment, no such separation can be found in medieval historiography, which instead blatantly appropriates the past to meet the ideological needs of the present and draws attention to its own inherently violent rhetorical methods. In so doing, medieval historiography prefigures Walter Benjamin's critique of historicism and exemplifies his injunction, "We must attain to a conception of history that is in keeping with this insight," namely that the "'state of emergency' in which we live is not the exception but the rule."[23] Only by accepting that history is not a rational, teleological process oriented toward the future can this state of emergency be acknowledged as the underlying assumption of all historical writing – an assumption whose beginning is necessarily hysterical and anachronistic because its interest in the past always begins in the present. Though the distinctive traits of medieval historical methods have been retroactively constructed as its conceptual and ethical defects, that gesture has its own epistemological and ethical flaws. By conceiving of historicity as culturally and historically contingent modes of representation and by striving to understand the complex, often self-conscious relationship between historicity and violence in medieval historical narra-

---

[22] For a particularly fine exploration of visual translation, see Anne D. Hedeman, "Presenting the Past: Visual Translation in Thirteenth- to Fifteenth-Century France," in *Imagining the Past*, ed. Morrison and Hedeman, pp. 69–85.

[23] Walter Benjamin, "Theses on the Philosophy of History," in *Illuminations*, ed. Hannah Arendt, trans. Harry Zohn (New York: Schocken Books, 1969), p. 257 [253–64].

tives, we hope to achieve greater understanding not only of these supposedly "defective" narratives and their historical and cultural significance but also of the challenges they pose to our own intellectually and ideologically coercive conceptions of the past.

PART I
THEORIZING VIOLENCE

2

Violence, History, and the Old French Epic of Revolt

Andrew Cowell

A number of scholars of literature, history, and anthropology have recognized that the old distinction made by Marcel Mauss and Claude Lévi-Strauss between gift giving and violence is no longer tenable.[1] Lévi-Strauss suggested that the opposition between gift and violence was largely homologous with the opposition between friend and enemy. More recently, however, scholars have noted that gift giving often includes highly aggressive elements, while violence can be a socially constrained and regulated tactic that can be understood as a form of reciprocity that is not always dissimilar from the reciprocity of gift giving.[2]

---

[1] See Claude Lévi-Strauss, *The Elementary Structures of Kinship*, trans. James Harle Bell (Boston: Beacon Press, 1969); Lévi-Strauss, *Introduction to the Works of Marcel Mauss*, trans. Felicity Baker (London: Routledge and Kegan Paul, 1987); Marcel Mauss, *The Gift: Forms and Functions of Exchange in Archaic Societies*, trans. Ian Cunnison (New York: Norton, 1967).

[2] Among anthropologists, see Jacques Godbout, *The World of the Gift*, trans. Donald Winker (Montreal: McGill-Queen's University Press, 1998); Maurice Godelier, *The Enigma of the Gift*, trans. Nora Scott (Chicago: University of Chicago Press, 1999); Annette B. Weiner, *Inalienable Possessions: The Paradox of Keeping-While-Giving* (Berkeley: University of California Press, 1992). Among historians, see Stephen D. White, *Custom, Kinship, and Gifts to Saints: The Laudatio Parentum in Western France, 1050–1150* (Chapel Hill: University of North Carolina Press, 1988); White, "Stratégie rhétorique dans la Conventio d'Hugues de Lusignan," in *Histoire et société: Mélanges offerts à Georges Duby*, 4 vols, *Le couple, l'ami et le prochain*, vol. 1 (Aix-en-Provence: Publications de l'Université de Provence, 1992), pp. 147–58; White, "The Politics of Anger," in *Anger's Past: The Social Uses of an Emotion in the Middle Ages*, ed. Barbara Rosenwein (Ithaca, NY: Cornell University Press, 1998), pp. 127–52; Donald J. Kagay and L. J. Andrew Villalon, eds., *The Final Argument: The Imprint of Violence on Society in Medieval and Early Modern Europe* (Woodbridge, UK: Boydell, 1998); Richard Kaeuper, *Chivalry and Violence in Medieval Europe* (Oxford: Oxford University Press, 1999); David Nirenberg, *Communities of Violence: Persecution of Minorities in the Middle Ages* (Princeton, NJ: Princeton University Press, 1996). Among literary scholars, see Sarah Kay, *The "Chansons de geste" in the Age of Romance: Political Fictions* (Oxford: Clarendon, 1995), Andrew

At the same time, it has also been recognized that both forms of reciprocity need to be understood in the light of a concept of the sacred. In particular, practices of socially regulated reciprocity – giving and violent taking – can only be fully understood if analyzed in relation to certain sacred "kept" items that individuals and groups seek to keep out of circulation, such as the ceremonial Sacred Pipe of certain Native American tribes or relics held by medieval churches and monasteries.[3] These kept items are essential to the authority, legitimacy, or identity of the possessor. Within the realm of Mediterranean studies, the same argument is made using the terms "honor" (associated with both gifts and violence) and "grace" (associated with the sacred). The pursuit of honor can only be understood – and controlled – within the framework of grace.[4]

This line of analysis sees socially regulated, reciprocal gift giving and violent taking as fundamentally similar. The analysis also makes clear that both gift giving and violence can be transgressive if practiced outside normal tactics of reciprocity in ways that challenge the ability of the recipients to respond and maintain reciprocal relationships. The overwhelming, nonreciprocable gift is one example. Similarly, violence that seeks to annihilate the opponent or the resources with which the opponent can respond – as opposed to taking noble captives for ransom, for example – would be nonreciprocable. Thus in place of gift versus violence we find an opposition of tactical, socially constrained reciprocity versus antireciprocal, extreme aggression.

Of course, nearly all forms of taking and giving are competitive to some degree and risk spinning out of control. This is why in all societies certain rites, ceremonies, individuals, or institutions associated with the sacred have a special duty to intervene and prevent confrontations that threaten social order and reciprocity from spiraling out of control. In North African Berber society the game of honor is fundamentally regulated by the intervening power of holy men; and, in Melanesia, the ultra-acquisitive "Big Man" ultimately faces

---

Cowell, *The Medieval Warrior Aristocracy: Gifts, Violence, Performance, and the Sacred* (Cambridge: D. S. Brewer, 2007).

[3] See Godelier, *The Enigma of the Gift*; Weiner, *Inalienable Possessions*; White, *Custom, Kinship and Gifts to Saints*; Cowell, *The Medieval Warrior Aristocracy*; Sarah Kay, "The Life of the Dead Body: Death and the Sacred in the *Chansons de geste*," *Yale French Studies* 86 (1994): 94–108; and Kay, "Singularity and Spectrality: Desire and Death in *Girart de Roussillon*," *Olifant* 22 (1998–2003): 11–38.

[4] See J. G. Peristiany, ed., *Honour and Shame: The Values of Mediterranean Society* (Chicago: University of Chicago Press, 1966), for original studies of honor, and J. G. Peristiany and Julian Pitt-Rivers, eds., *Honor and Grace in Anthropology* (Cambridge: Cambridge University Press, 1992), for more recent studies of the importance of grace. A broad summary of the debate can be found in Peregrine Horden and Nicholas Purcell, *The Corrupting Sea: A Study of Mediterranean History* (Oxford: Blackwell, 2000), pp. 485–523. The latter source largely ignores the issue of grace and the sacred, however, and also focuses on nonaristocratic forms of honor.

the need to give away all his accumulated wealth in a social ceremony that mocks and caricatures his desire for transcendence.[5]

With this understanding of the role of the sacred, we can say that the fundamental indicator of antireciprocal gift giving and/or violence is its refusal to operate within the anchoring structure of socially accepted forms and values of the sacred. Indeed, this antireciprocity very often specifically targets sacred "kept" items. To give an overwhelming, unreciprocable gift to a king means to claim a status superior to that of the monarch, and thus an equal or even superior access to the sacred represented by the crown. Socially and symbolically, this is an act that is as devastating as an attack on the king's person. Similarly, thefts of relics during the Middle Ages could produce crises of authority for the victims of such acts.[6]

Given the focus of this volume, in the remainder of my discussion I will turn primarily to the issue of reciprocal as opposed to extreme violence. The preceding introduction obviously suggests that this is a theoretically ill-advised move, unless we reformulate the very definitions of "gift" and "violence" within the new understanding of reciprocity and the sacred elaborated above. Indeed, it is fair to ask whether the terms "gift" and "violence" are even theoretically useful at this point. One must recognize, however, that they were conceptually crucial terms in the Middle Ages (as well as in the current world), and understanding why they were so useful is therefore crucial. As a point of departure for the rest of this discussion, I propose that the distinction lies specifically in the difference between direct engagement with the body and social persona of another (violence) and an indirect engagement mediated by symbolic objects (gifts). This difference is one of mechanism, not of deontology. On the other hand, we can recognize two different kinds of violence – reciprocal and antireciprocal – that have two different deontological statuses. I want to show in the following analysis how the medieval French Epic of Revolt explores these forms, their relationship, and the often-tenuous boundary between them. In particular, the epics focus on two related problems: the abuse of sacred authority for individual goals and the attempt to claim access to the sacred by those not socially authorized to do so. In both cases participants seek to engage in nonreciprocal violence and, furthermore, they employ strategies that attempt to "sacralize" this violence and thus legitimate it. Meanwhile, the epics depict the surrounding society as it attempts to desacralize this same violence through strategies of intervention that enforce reciprocity. To better understand this claim we must

---

[5] On these cases, see Cécile Barraud, Daniel de Coppet, André Iteanu, and Raymond Jamous, *Of Relations and the Dead: Four Societies Viewed from the Angle of Their Exchange*, trans. Stephen J. Suffern (Oxford: Berg, 1994), pp. 91–96, 44–46.

[6] Patrick Geary, "Sacred Commodities: The Circulation of Medieval Relics," in *The Social Life of Things*, ed. Arjun Appadurai (Cambridge: Cambridge University Press), pp. 169–91.

first consider more carefully the theoretical connections between antireciprocal violence and the sacred.

Reciprocity, Violence, and the Writing of History

Reciprocity is the basis of sociality itself. Likewise, a shared understanding of the sacred becomes indispensable for the imagination of a single social community held together in networks of reciprocity. Yet certain elements of medieval society, especially within the Church and surrounding the crusading movement, sought in the eleventh and twelfth centuries to establish new, more radical social distinctions based specifically on religious grounds.[7] They sought to radically exclude Cathars, Jews, and – most importantly for the epic – Muslims from "society" and reciprocity by emphasizing these groups' radical outsiderness in relationship to the Christian concept of the sacred. Of course, as David Nirenberg has argued in *Communities of Violence*, there were also alternative and competing discourses and practices surrounding religious minorities during this time, some of which were much more oriented toward reciprocity and accommodation. But in both Old French and Old Occitan epics there were strenuous attempts at "othering" in many of the texts. Both those texts that deal specifically with the Crusades and many epics in the cycles of William of Orange and Charlemagne are very focused on nonreciprocable violence, and they could be seen as encouraging or celebrating such events as the massacres in Jerusalem during the First Crusade and in Béziers during the Albigensian Crusade.[8] To the extent that these discourses

---

[7] See especially R. I. Moore, *The Formation of a Persecuting Society: Power and Deviance in Western Europe, 950–1250* (New York: Blackwell, 1987), but also Nirenberg, *Communities of Violence*, for a contrasting perspective. Nirenberg argues that the great majority of violence against minorities was low-grade and socially productive and constitutive, at least in Catalonia during the High Middle Ages. He further suggests that when the details of violent encounters between Christians and Jews in particular are examined carefully, this type of violence seems to have predominated throughout Western Europe during the Middle Ages. This situation is obviously in contrast to the extreme, antireciprocal forms of violence implicitly or explicitly advocated by some *chansons de geste*.

[8] A good recent guide to the Old French epic cycles is Luke Sunderland, *Old French Narrative Cycles: Heroism between Ethics and Morality* (Cambridge: D. S. Brewer, 2010). This study focuses particularly on the Cycle of William of Orange, examining it in terms of the sacrificial and sacral elements that characterize the majority of the nonrevolt epics. All of the key characters of this cycle – William, Vivien, Rainouart, Aymeri – are read in this way (see esp. p. 47). Cf. Sharon Kinoshita, *Medieval Boundaries: Rethinking Difference in Old French Literature* (Philadelphia: University of Pennsylvania Press, 2006), pp. 200–35, for examples of how even the Old Occitan account of the Albigensian Crusade is a hybrid text in which the discourse of sacralizing violence is contested. Kinoshita's book looks at these forms of contestation and subversion more generally throughout Old French literature.

of "othering" were successful, they established strict lines of difference and exclusion from the sacred as well as strict lines of nonreciprocity, opening Muslims in particular to antireciprocal, annihilating violence. Unlike in the Epic of Revolt, however, this violence is directed outward against an Other who is outside the realm of the society's sacred; indeed, it is practiced in the name of the sacred, and can be understood as "sacralized" violence.

But the "revolt" in the Epic of Revolt constitutes an attempt to "seize the sacred nomos" of the society, to use anthropologist Jacques Godbout's term (*The World of the Gift*, p. 143) – to gain direct access to the sacred or appropriate it for personal purposes. The plots typically focus not on the annihilation of perpetrators but on containing violence in order to maintain overall social cohesion. Specifically, there is an effort to convert or subvert the violence to a socially constrained, reciprocable form – in short, to suppress antireciprocal revolt. Thus, beyond their historiographical function, these texts should be understood as historico-theoretical studies of the *management* of violence, replete with motifs that explore the tenuous boundary between reciprocity and nonreciprocity. They depict efforts to desacralize violence and render it merely secular and reciprocable, at least within Christian society. Before looking at specific texts, we need to consider one other fact about violence in the Epic of Revolt. As the idea of nonreciprocity suggests, this violence is in a fundamental sense by and for the individual, not the society. The full implications of this seemingly obvious claim can be better understood through the concepts of individual integrity and the intransitive nature of the violence in question.

It is well known that medieval warrior aristocrats conceptualized and evaluated their social standing and their identity within society in terms of honor. Furthermore, the phenomena of honor and reciprocity were closely connected, in that failure to perform reciprocal obligations or retributive acts of violence led to loss of honor, while the performance of gift giving or plunder, to take two examples, increased honor. This leads us to the observation that reciprocity and honor were both performative phenomena that constantly needed maintenance, defense, and reiteration: honor can never rest on its laurels, for any failure to defend it leads to its loss.

Conversely, sacred truths within theology and sacrally authorized positions within society – whether saint, military martyr, royal line, a monastery founded by donation, or sacredly given land – were conceptualized in transcendent terms: at least in theory, they were not vulnerable to loss of status from performative challenges and could not be forced to engage in networks of horizontal reciprocity. In other words, the king was the king no matter how badly he performed as king, and a gift of land to a monastery was considered a permanent deposit not only with the monastery, but also with Heaven itself. Like the perfect tenth sphere of the heavens, these things did not "move," or at least were not supposed to move or enter into circulation within networks of earthly reciprocity. The relationships embodied in these items were vertical relationships to sacred authority, and the exchanges were vertical exchanges with the sacred.

To obtain such a social position – to performatively acquire honor so that one was in a position eligible to engage in such vertical relationships and exchanges with the sacred – was to attain a position of integrity, whereby one's identity could be authorized in a form that transcended the performative realm and the very need to perform. Integrity could be understood as an idealized position in which the individual is owed reciprocal obligations by all around and below him or her while maintaining the capacity to act, give, and take freely and overwhelmingly, such that the individual's gifts are nonreciprocable and the individual escapes a position of "horizontal" dependency in relation to others. It is from this position of integrity that an individual may engage in "vertical" exchanges in relation to the sacred, and in so doing stabilize his or her social position. This is the goal behind the act of "seizing the nomos" within one's society. One example of this process is the life of William the Conqueror, whose performances of ritual giving and violent taking culminated in an individual rising to a position of integrity from which he was able to lay claim to the crown of England and engage in a socially foundational act.

The pursuit of integrity necessarily involves the performance of violence, which advertises the *freedom* of the individual, the self-orientation of his or her motivations, and his or her nondependency on external restraints or obligations. Indeed, at its purest, this violence can be completely gratuitous, because in gratuity is complete freedom, complete nonconsideration of others. The anthropologist Glenn Bowman points out that the word "violence," though normally considered to be a "transitive" phenomenon in our culture (i.e., having a perpetrator and a victim), actually derives from Latin forms such as "violentus," meaning "full of force," or "violentia," meaning "vehemence." Thus the focus in Latin was actually on an "intransitive" quality of will and power, such that violence creates "integrities and identities" or "integral identities."[9] We can recognize in this etymological account of violence the reason why its use would be so appealing to an ambitious warrior aristocrat: it allows the display of an image of forcefulness, willfulness, and the outward projection of inward belief and motivation. In this glorification of intransitive will, the object or person on which that will is exercised can become virtually incidental.[10]

In contrast, cosmological violence against the other is defined by its funda-

---

[9] Glenn Bowman, "The Violence in Identity," in *Anthropology of Violence and Conflict*, ed. Bettina E. Schmidt and Ingo W. Schröder (London: Routledge, 2001), pp. 25–26, 27–28 [25–46].

[10] In a very interesting article on the Spanish bullfight as a forum for the expression of masculine honor and integrity, Garry Marvin makes a very similar point about the relationship between bull and bullfighter. See "Honor, Integrity, and the Problem of

mental transitivity – by the fact that it is directed against a foe who is depicted as outside networks of even potential reciprocity and thus a target for destruction. The redemption of Roland in the second half of *The Song of Roland* is inconceivable without the specific presence of the Muslims, against whom transitive violence is waged. *Roland* is an interesting case in that the first part of the text presents a figure whose largely individual-oriented pursuit of integrity is disastrous to his Frankish comrades. However, through a divine intervention at his death, his acts are reconfigured as sacrificial (and sacral), and they allow the previously squabbling and ambivalent Franks to attain the "national" unity needed to end all thoughts of exchange or reciprocity with the Muslims and instead pursue their utter destruction. As part of this reconfiguration, the stakes of the epic shift from issues of individual loyalty and honor in the first half of the text to religious and cosmological issues of Good and Evil in the second half, as Charlemagne defeats the Saracen king.

But an individual can pursue integrity and access to the *nomos* for purely individual or familial/clan purposes – illustrated most famously in medieval French literature by the rebel Raoul of Cambrai. Whereas a socially sanctioned foundational or sacrificial exchange with the sacred can be countenanced, or even seen as fundamentally necessary, attempts at such exchange and access in other contexts are inevitably seen as socially disastrous and in need of suppression. Another way of saying the same thing is to recognize that the *mechanisms* of the pursuit are the same in the case of William, Roland, or Raoul; and, in their moment-by-moment deployment of these mechanisms, they may all have been seen as admirable by their audiences, as powerful, willful individuals. However, the *deontological stakes* are presented or understood differently by the society and/or the texts. In Raoul's case, the pursuit of the *nomos* is presented as occurring outside socially sanctioned motivations for access to the sacred, and the *nomos* thus obtained would be socially disordering. This explains why Roland and Raoul – similar in so many ways – come to two very different ends.

Corresponding to these two different understandings of the relationship of the individual to the sacred are two different deontological valences of "reality" or "history" in the two types of texts. The foundational (William) or sacrificial (Roland) hero and the text that recounts his narrative should be understood as part of sacral History, meaning the cosmological realization and triumph of the sacred right and good (and capitalized here to distinguish it from the mere recounting of events). From the perspective of the warrior aristocracy, these texts are "History" itself, or at least they make this claim.

On the other hand, the individual epics of revolt always risk falling into mere "history" (in the modern sense, whereby historians attempt to provide

---

Violence in the Spanish Bullfight," in *The Anthropology of Violence*, ed. David Riches (Oxford: Basil Blackwell, 1986), pp. 118–35.

narratives of what happened in the past but do not normally attempt to show that it "had" to happen in this way – or was "made to" happen thusly – according to an unfolding divine teleology). In terms of the medieval context under discussion here, the latter is not history at all but simply narrative, *res gestis*. The Epic of Revolt largely escapes the cosmological framing that governs the epics of the Crusades, the royal cycle, and (to a lesser extent) the cycle of William of Orange. Their endings virtually always attempt to reincorporate the narrative into a sacred, cosmological discourse, but such gestures are usually fairly shallow and anticlimactic. These texts are virtual ethnographic studies of the warrior aristocracy, treasures of historical anthropology. We could say that they tell stories that are intimately aware of the sacred, its temptations, and its pitfalls. But, unlike the other epics of the twelfth and early thirteenth centuries, their narratives do not unfold *within*, nor do they ever get truly integrated *into*, the discourse of the sacred.

In the remainder of this chapter I will look more closely at three epics of revolt and explore the ways in which the integrity drive, nonreciprocity, and intransitive violence are represented. I will also examine the attempts within the texts to contain and re-embed the heroic violence within the realm of social reciprocity, as well as the ways in which the texts dramatize their own (usually failed) attempt to reintegrate the *res gestis* into a sacred discourse.

Girart de Roussillon and the Crisis of the *Nomos*

In its opening sections *Girart de Roussillon* takes great pains to establish a domain of French unity, centered on the secular leadership of Charles Martel and the religious leadership of the Pope. Charles is immediately qualified with the phrase "tal justise mellor non sai" [I know no better judge] (v. 45).[11] The Pope calls for a Crusade, exclaiming, "Baron, per Deu vos prai, annaz i *tuic*" [Barons, for the sake of God I pray that you *all* go there] (v. 73; emphasis added). Charles echoes this vision of unity, in which religious solidarity should also create political solidarity at the court: "Aicheste cort e Deu prodom ne giche!" [Let no nobleman abandon God in this court] (v. 91).

The opening thus sets up an expectation of cosmological, sacral violence directed against a non-Christian enemy. This expectation is not fulfilled, however; when Charles and Girart arrive in Constantinople, they meet the Greek emperor, who gives his two daughters in marriage to the two great Frenchmen. Charles, however, is chagrined to discover that the daughter given to Girart is more beautiful than the one given to him, and this incident leads to the wars and revolts that occupy the rest of the chanson: "Tornerent les regnes a mal escil" [The kingdom was devastated] (v. 264).

---

[11] *Girart de Roussillon*, ed. W. Mary Hackett (Paris: Picard, 1953). Parenthetical references will refer to verse and *laisse* numbers in this text. Translations are my own.

This incident must be understood in terms of the symbolic value system that undergirded the society of the warrior aristocracy. There is no indication that Charles's concerns are related to any personal, sexual desire for the other daughter. Rather, he perceives himself as the highest-ranking member of his society and believes that his wife should reflect this position by being the most beautiful and admired woman within that society. Thus, when the text notes of the daughter Elissent, who is intended for Girart, that her body is "covinent e virgenil" [charming and virginal] (v. 258) and that, on seeing her, "tans saives que gair'es chil / E qui de sa beltat non merevil" [even the wisest present were left dazzled / speechless by her beauty] (vv. 260–61), this depiction must be understood against the preceding reaction to Berta, who is intended for Charles, when "E latin e ebriu tot declarar ne pout nus om el munt sa par trobar" [(wise men) spoke in Latin and Hebrew declaring that no man could find one her equal in the world] (vv. 239–40). The silence of "the wisest men" that greets the arrival of the other sister clearly trumps the excited approval that greeted Berta: her sister Elissent's beauty is beyond words. Charlemagne recognizes the judgment of the "wise ones" and its implications for his honor in relation to Girart, and he immediately reacts with scorn for Berta. In terms of (in)transitivity, we could say that Charles actually has no desire for Elissent per se, but only for the symbolic capital associated with her, as an advertisement of his own honor. Indeed, to desire the woman herself would signal a loss of integrity – a compromising of inner-directed willfulness by sexual passion.

This dynamic is underlined by his concern with the issue of choice. He says, "Eu chausirai ... de ca meillor" [I will choose ... the best] (v. 346) and, later, "Eu cai causis" [I am the one who chooses here] (v. 370). He decides to impose his will, performing a symbolic act that will re-establish his sociopolitical precedence – and his honor. He is warned by all around him, including the Pope (l. 29), that this is unwise and will transgress the normal social constraints on what we might call "reciprocal" lordship. Nevertheless, he insists, and eventually Girart agrees to give up his rightful wife – but only in exchange for the guarantee of an allodial fief (l. 34). The fact that Charles must negotiate the exchange with Girart, rather than simply taking what he wants or being given what he wants free of constraints, symbolically establishes a complementary relationship and a rough equivalence of value and honor between the two men. Charles's desire to simply impose his will is thus thwarted: he says, "Non soufre par in sa reion" [He will suffer no peer in his realm] (v. 648; see also l. 113). As a result, he tells his council:

> Que ne preiçe un eu tote sa poigne
> Se Girart de sa terre fors ne redoigne,
> De Provence e d'Auverne e de Gascoigne.
> Ainc non vistes nul rei tanz maus ajoigne. (vv. 603–6)

[He did not value his power as much as an egg,
If he did not drive Girart from his lands
In Provence and Auvergne and Gascony.
Never have you seen a king so angry.]

Most generally, this series of scenes can be understood in terms of an initial gift – an act of reciprocity – from the Greek emperor, which Charles rejects. Subsequently, he also rejects relations of equivalence and reciprocity with his vassal. The court makes every effort to re-engage Charles in the socially established framework of reciprocity, while he continues to resist. Thus, at the beginning of this epic, it is actually Charles who revolts by trying to inject processes of sacrality and integrity into a relationship where this should not be at issue.

These events serve to create a very clear contrast between religious/cosmological strife, on the one hand, and honor-based, individually oriented strife, on the other. Crucial to this is the figure of the Pope, who is closely allied with Charles as long as the religio-cosmological issue predominates but then openly critiques his choices once the issue of personal honor – and especially integrity – comes into play. As in virtually all epics of revolt, the ruler is established as severely at fault in relation to his vassal, and the events are explicitly removed from the religio-cosmological realm and placed in the personal.

Once Charles begins his actual attack on Girart and his lands, the second key component of virtually all epics of revolt appears: the assignment of blame to the vassal for his resistance to the king, despite the king previously having been established as at fault. Charles attacks and seizes Roussillon through trickery, but he is then defeated in battle by Girart, who wins back his lands. This leads to escalating combat and violence, culminating in a great battle between Charles and Girart at Vaubeton. At this point there occurs a divine intervention, or what we might call a vertical intervention of the sacred against the honor system. Yet it is now Girart who refuses to respect the vertical intervention of religion against the advice of his councilors (ll. 178–83). Though at this point he has been wronged by Charles again and again, his own key vassal, Odilon, tells him:

> As en major pechat qu'eu non sai dire,
> Ne c'om no pot contar ne clers escrire.
> Ce ne pues tu neiar ne escondire
> Ne sies ses om liges e el tes sire;
> Nel pues cachar de canp, ne desconfire,
> Que n'as forfait ton feu, quin vou dreit dire. (vv. 3022–27)

> [I would not know how to express the sin that lies upon you,
> Nor could any man tell of it, or clerk write of it.
> You cannot deny or hide

> That you are his liegeman, and he your lord;
> You cannot drive him from the field of battle or defeat him,
> Without forfeiting your fief, according to the words of the law.]

In other words, despite the merely legal issues of right and wrong, and despite Charles's misappropriation of the *nomos*, Girart must not pursue integrity in the same way because of the threat it would pose to the social order. He is in the right on the level of horizontal (interpersonal) conflicts over honor, but in the wrong on the level of vertical relationships to the sacred.

The divine intervention continues (l. 182), and Charles momentarily cedes to this pressure, as does Girart, who offers sacred gifts to monasteries (l. 191). The two then jointly face a Saracen invasion (l. 199). Despite this, the intransitive nature of the violence practiced by both men remains at the forefront. When Girart comes to Charlemagne's aid,

> Ainc ne vistes nul rei qu'aisi rancur
> Quant Girarz s'ajostet, li cons, a lur.
> Ainz non vi tan baron, tan prou, si dur,
> Ne proeçe de conte qu'aisi mellur. (vv. 3296–99)

> [Never have you seen an angrier king
> Then when count Girart approached the enemy.
> Never had (Charles) seen a more skillful and hardy baron,
> Nor greater prowess from a count.]

This passage clearly shows that Charles is less concerned with the object of the violence that is occurring, or even the success of the battle against this object – even though it involves the archenemy Other, the Saracens – than with the particular way in which the violence is executed, by whom, and how. The focus of the description is adverbial and intransitive. The weakest verb/predicate adjective in the passage, ironically, is the one describing the actual encounter of the forces: Girart merely "approaches." The violence is as much in Charles's emotions and reactions as it is on the field.

Though the vast remainder of the text includes a good deal of actual violent combat, it is striking that, in comparison to a text such as *La chanson de Roland*, descriptions of actual battle occupy a relatively small portion of *Girart de Roussillon*. Rather, the text is full of many long and intense passages in which characters debate whether or not to respond violently to various provocations and exactly how much violence to use in their response. The violence is most intense in the characters' own wills, one might say, and in the arguments between allies about how to proceed. Charles and Girart both spend as much or more time strenuously arguing with their own followers about the need to push violence up to and beyond reciprocal limits as they do confronting each other, so that by the end of the text they look quite alike: despite being on the opposite sides of the battles, they both represent an improper assault on the social *nomos*, which both sets of followers attempt to restrain at crucial moments. This is the deeper battle and revolt within the text.

Renaut de Montauban and Sacred Closure

Renaut de Montauban is in many ways similar to *Girart de Roussillon* and includes the same two families: Girart's relatives end up in a battle with Charlemagne, a descendant of Charles Martel.[12] The epic is notable for the social unity and plenitude that dominate in the opening images: it begins at Pentecost, the time of the universal, united Church, and both Charlemagne and his enemy Buef d'Aigremont are conducting Pentecost ceremonies (ll. 5, 9). Moreover, the opening *laisses* focus primarily on Charlemagne's sending of a messenger to Buef to request his aid and fealty. Messengers are a key symbolic element of reciprocity in the epic. The actual subject of the message, however, is a threat from Charlemagne: if Buef does not immediately come to his court, Charlemagne will seek to seize all his lands. But Charlemagne's advisors continually urge him to employ what we could call "tactics of reciprocity" rather than impose crushing obligations and shame on Buef (vv. 112–20). Buef's advisors take the same tactic, specifically emphasizing that his fealty to his sovereign must outweigh any purely personal concerns with honor (ll. 7–8, 17). Moreover, the messenger, Charlemagne's son Lohiers, is told by *his* advisors as well not to allow personal concerns of honor to interfere with the mission (l. 9).

Despite all these strenuous efforts to contain the evolving struggle within the tactics of reciprocity, Buef rejects the discourse of fealty in favor of one centered on his own honor and integrity.[13] Like Charlemagne, he is unwilling to accept either dependency or equality and the reciprocity involved in each. A battle breaks out in the middle of his hall – a classic inappropriate locale for conflict, symbolizing the breakdown of sociality – and Buef kills the messenger, another classic medieval symbol of nonreciprocal intentions. In response, Charlemagne plans to assault Buef and asks for divine help in this endeavor (l. 29). Although such prayers are hardly uncommon in medieval epics, Charlemagne's attempt to invoke vertical, sacred aid for a crisis that is a result of his own inability to manage horizontal, secular affairs must be understood as a form of inappropriate use of the sacred *nomos*, as he

---

[12] *Renaut de Montauban*, ed. Jacques Thomas (Geneva: Droz, 1989). Translations are my own.

[13] See l. 7, vv. 303–5, where he echoes Roland's promise before the battle of Roncesvalles to lose "ne roncin ne somier" [neither nag nor packhorse] and l. 12, where he rejects advice of wise caution in favor of advertising his integrity and lack of fear, no matter the danger.

joins Buef in pursuing integrity over sociality. Charlemagne follows up on this prayer by promising Buef safe passage to his court, then betraying that (reciprocal) promise and ambushing and killing him. Not surprisingly, divine aid is conspicuously lacking for Charlemagne in the subsequent sections of the epic, as the text critiques his misuse of the *nomos*.

One final attempt is made to rein in the spiraling antireciprocal violence (ll. 58–61), but Bertolais, Charlemagne's nephew, and Renaut, Buef's nephew, get into a fight during the festivities. This leads to a battle in Charlemagne's hall (again), and Renaut kills Bertolais with a highly inappropriate weapon – a chess piece (l. 62). Symbolically, chess is a rule-bound game of reciprocal, socially constrained aggression. Using an element from that game to kill an opponent during a festival underlines the extreme antireciprocal attitude of Renaut and echoes the more general attempt of his uncle Charlemagne to misappropriate the social *nomos* for his private benefit. Later, just to make the nonreciprocal nature of the affairs clearer, there is another scene in which Charlemagne arranges a horse race, with his (sacred) crown offered as the prize. Renaut, with the aid of magic, manages to enter the race with his insuperable horse, Baiant, and win the prize. Then, when Charlemagne offers a gift in order to get his crown back (a classic instance of gift giving being understandable in relation to the sacred "kept"), Renaut refuses and chooses to keep the sacred crown (ll. 121–26). The relationship between nonreciprocity and sacral motivations on the part of Renaut could not be clearer in this classic attack on an opponent's sacred kept item.

Although Charlemagne eventually gets his crown back, the casualness with which he puts it to frivolous personal use is indicative of his problematic understanding of the social role of the sacred; he later tries to blackmail his barons into carrying out another of his questionable vendettas by threatening to give away the crown (l. 207). Eventually, it is his opponents who renounce their nonreciprocal violence, despite Charlemagne's continued stubbornness, and this opens the door for a sacred intervention to rein in the violence, leading to Charlemagne's ultimate capitulation to his baron's appeals for restraint and reciprocity, with Renaut departing on a pilgrimage.

Raoul de Cambrai and the Failure of History

Raoul de Cambrai is perhaps the best known of all Old French epics of revolt.[14] Here, the pursuit of the *nomos* is quite one-sided. Raoul is wronged by King Louis, who, unlike Charles Martel and Charlemagne, is not so much ambitious and overreaching as weak and conflicted. In response, Raoul decides to pursue his individual goals through a direct attack on and seizure

---

[14] *Raoul de Cambrai*, ed. Sarah Kay (Oxford: Clarendon, 1992).

of the *nomos*, largely as if neither the king nor any other overarching social or sacred constraints existed.[15] The themes of nonreciprocity and seizure of, or assault on, the sacred are rife in this text: there is a chess game which devolves into battle, with Raoul hurling the pieces in anger (vv. 482–503); there is an assault on the sacred in the form of an attack on the family nunnery of Raoul's opponents, the Vermandois family, leading to the burning alive of a number of nuns; and there is an effort at intervention and reconciliation. However, as in previous texts, a battle breaks out in the middle of the king's hall, with Raoul's relatives using table implements and furniture posts to attack their opponents (ll. 221–26). Raoul refuses all attempts at tactical intervention and desacralization of the conflict, as he follows his own will relentlessly in the pursuit of integrity. In the end, he and virtually all around him are destroyed, with little redemption.

We might briefly consider why that might be. In this text King Louis plays loosely with fiefs, giving them away at his whim, in the same way that Charlemagne played loosely with his crown in *Renaut de Montauban*. But Charlemagne seems to recognize the power of the crown – this is why he is tempted to abuse it and the sacred *nomos* more generally. Louis, on the other hand, seems not even to recognize the potential of the *nomos* and his role. More generally, it is as if there is no sacred anchor against which honor can be evaluated and constrained, and which would form the basis for a divine, vertical intervention in the strife. Thus Raoul desperately reaches for this *nomos* himself, but in a socially unsustainable way. This epic is the darkest of the three treated here, as it reflects on the consequences of the *absence* of a socially sanctioned sacrality. The *res gestis* cannot rise to History.

Conclusion

Epics of revolt do come to an end, of course. In *Renaut de Montauban* Charlemagne is finally brought to his senses only when Roland and all the peers of the court abandon him (ll. 354–55). Significantly, Roland calls to the barons "alons nos en, por Dieu omnipotent / Et si laisson Kallon" [Let us depart, for the sake of all-powerful God, / and leave Charles behind] (vv. 12850–51). This is simply the culmination of a number of points in this and the preceding *laisses*, where it becomes clear that Charlemagne will be left in a completely desacralized position if he continues to pursue his vendetta: inappropriate invocation of the sacred (by Charlemagne), the text seems to suggest, is the one way for him to lose his own sacrality. From this turning point late in the

---

[15] For an extended version of the reading I offer here, see my *The Medieval Warrior Aristocracy*, pp. 115–33.

text, we follow the rebel Renaut as he pursues a pilgrimage to Jerusalem and ultimately earns sanctification.

In *Girart de Roussillon* it is the Pope who finally successfully intervenes (ll. 636–67), rebuking Charles and enforcing sacred gifts and foundations of monasteries on the part of Girart and his family. This can only happen, however, once Charles's own men have killed his horse and almost killed him (l. 626). Again, Charles is placed at risk of desacralization owing to his previous misappropriation of the sacred *nomos* for his private feud with Girart.

The conclusions of these two texts offer an answer to the question I posed in my introduction – that is, whether the terms "gift" and "violence" are still theoretically useful in a situation where it is reciprocity and nonreciprocity that seem more crucial. Indeed, in the everyday world of *res gestis*, the two terms do seem to be of little analytic utility. But when one seeks to (re)gain legitimate access to the sacred, it turns out that this can be done either through violence directed against a socially external, nonsacral Other (Roland and William) or a gift directed to the socially internal sacred (Renaut's pilgrimage to Jerusalem, Girard's gifts to monasteries). Another way of saying this is that a socially sanctioned "sacred" encounter with the Other must directly engage (and destroy) the body of that Other, while the same encounter with one's own cultural sacred must always be an indirect exchange (via gift and service) with the *nomos*. Levi-Strauss's original claims about the gift (socially internal) and violence (socially external) turn out to be true, but only in the context of direct engagement with the sacred. This engagement constitutes the limit case, wherein the reasons for the social and linguistic distinction between "gift" and "violence" in the society of the medieval warrior aristocracy become visible.

Raoul de Cambrai, on the other hand, fails to ever truly end, simply stumbling to a close long after Raoul's death. There as well, the text attempts a form of sacred closure, as Bernier, the hero of the second half, goes on a pilgrimage to Santiago de Compostela (ll. 335–36). But he is abortively killed by his archenemy, Raoul's relative Guerri (l. 338), and the cycle of honor continues as the text concludes. The one thing that can be said, however, is that the deontological rebellion of Raoul against the king, the Church, and the sacred "kept" of the Vermandois family in quest of absolute integrity has by the end of the text degenerated into a series of mere battles for honor – there seems little impetus on the part of any character to misappropriate, lay claim to, or assault the *nomos*, the sacred itself, so in a way it is fitting that the text simply fizzles out.

Thus, in two of the three epics we have discussed we can see a concluding reintegration of the narrative into a sacred discourse. But the simple question that must be posed is why it takes so long (in terms of years, in the texts, or verses, for the audience) to get to this point. In fact, the texts merely end in exhaustion once this point is reached rather than reaching a clear narrative conclusion. None of the events *in* the texts can be seen as part of sacrally unfolding History: only their conclusions partake of this discourse. These conclusions are less the *culmination* of the momentum of the text (as in *The Song of Roland*, for example) than the foreclosure and *negation* of the antisacral, antireciprocal momentum that drives the narratives internally. *Raoul de Cambrai* is in a sense the most honest of the texts in revealing the impossibility of integrating the *res gestis* into any sacral History.

All of these texts can be understood as expressing underlying claims for the careful management of the relation of the secular world to the sacred: they decry attempts to invoke the sacred where this is inappropriate (even by kings), as well as attempts to lay claims to access to the sacred by those ineligible to do so. They argue implicitly for carefully controlled access to the sacred and the repression of desires to control or manipulate the social *nomos* on the part of individuals. They present the sacred as an anchoring element for (violent) reciprocity and (violent) performance, but unless violence is to be directed against an Other outside the realm of the group and its socially shared understanding of the sacred, that violence must be desacralized and excluded from the discourse of the sacred. Violence of this latter type is simply historical, not a part of History.

At the same time, the texts implicitly recognize the legitimacy of interventions in the world on behalf of the sacred – ironically, in order to desacralize violence when it threatens to escape the realm of reciprocity. In this light, the texts themselves can be understood as attempted sacred interventions, acts of containment that seek to reinsert their own *textual* gestures and performances into the discourse of History – in particular through their conclusions. Such an attempt itself is not unusual, as Luke Sunderland shows in his examination of the William of Orange cycle, where fidelity to discourse is a key moral act of narrative (*Old French Narrative Cycles*, p. 62). But, from a modern perspective, it is perhaps the "ethnographic" character of the representation of violence in the body of the texts that draws our attention more than their concluding gestures of containment. In their depiction of histories that always threaten to escape the attempt to understand and recount History, the texts offer a nearly unique variety of medieval historiography. These texts struggle to confront forms of violence that escape or occur outside the normal discursive modes employed in medieval society for theorizing both violence and history.

3

Rhetoric, Providence, and Violence in Villehardouin's *La conquête de Constantinople*

Noah D. Guynn

> Quid ... sunt Dei mirabilia, nisi quae hominibus sunt impossibilia?
> [What are God's miracles if not that which is impossible for humans?]
> *Sermo de Annuntiatione Dominica* 3 (attrib. Augustine)

From military commanders to petty knights, ecclesiastical leaders to monastic historians, observers of, and participants in, the Fourth Crusade understood providential rhetoric as an available if contentious strategy for justifying violent conflict. Anyone familiar with the Crusade's trajectory will know that these were events in sore need of justification. The host not only failed to retake Jerusalem from the "enemies of the Cross," as it pledged to do; it also vanquished two Christian cities, first helping the Venetians assert dominion over Zara and then establishing a Latin Empire in Constantinople. Given how unexpected and morally dubious these actions were, it makes sense that a divine master plan should be invoked to justify them and that claims to know God's actions and intentions should in turn strain belief and elicit further doubts.

We can see the tension between belief and doubt at work in three representative sources. On the day of his coronation as Latin emperor, Baldwin I wrote to Pope Innocent III to proclaim that there had been no "viable human plan" that could have led to this "wondrous turn of events"; there could therefore be "no doubt, even among the unbelievers [*infidelibus*], but that the hand of the Lord guided all of these events."[1] Later that year, Innocent echoed Baldwin's claims and added an eschatological gloss: not only was the transfer of empire effected "by the right hand of the Most High" in order to "exalt the most holy Roman Church," but it also stood as a *figura* of Christ's triumph

---

[1] Innocent Reg. 7.152, in Alfred J. Andrea, ed. and trans., *Contemporary Sources for the Fourth Crusade* (Leiden: Brill, 2000), p. 100.

at the end times.² By contrast, Arnold of Lübeck, chronicling the Crusade from the cloister, cast doubt upon providential readings of the conquest of Constantinople and argued that "a worthy ending has not yet made manifest" whether these were "deeds of God or men." Was the conquest hallowed by divine operation? Or did God merely permit it to occur in order to achieve an ulterior goal, just as he had allowed Satan to afflict Job in order to teach endurance?³ If Arnold is suggesting that the crusaders' actions may have been ungodly, he is not alone: the *Eracles* author and Seigneur de Berzé say so explicitly.⁴ Ultimately, though, he avoids absolute judgments, insisting that the significance of the Crusade has not yet been revealed.

Taken together, these three claims manifest the complex relationships in providential rhetoric between human events and theological truths, violence and religion, belief and doubt. Baldwin and Innocent seek to justify violence against Christians on moral and eschatological grounds, but in order to conclude that God was the efficient cause of the conquest, they must first acknowledge – if only to emphatically dismiss – the possibility of more secular explanations (a "viable human plan"). The claim that even Muslims must see the Latin victory as evidence of divine favor is a particularly strained argument – one that demonstrates the extent to which rhetoric aims, in Martianus Capella's words, to produce "credence in a matter of doubt" but fails to eliminate doubt altogether.⁵ When the Latins achieved a conquest that appeared to signal abiding dominion over Byzantium, Baldwin and Innocent sought to ease scruples about attacking fellow Christians.⁶ They did so by invoking a providential rhetoric made famous by Orosius: God's intentional

---

[2] Innocent Reg. 7.154, in Andrea, *Contemporary Sources*, p. 117. The confidence of Innocent's assertion is all the more remarkable given his skepticism about miracles and miracle workers generally: just as Satan "disguises himself as an angel of light" (2 Cor. 11:14), so heretics may disguise themselves as pious agents of the Lord. See Innocent Reg. 1.528, 2.132, in PL 214:483, 695. On Innocent's providential readings of the Fourth Crusade, see Brett Edward Whalen, *Dominion of God: Christendom and Apocalypse in the Middle Ages* (Cambridge, MA: Harvard University Press, 2009), pp. 133–43.

[3] Arnold of Lübeck, *Chronica Slavorum*, Monumenta Germaniae Historica, Scriptores 14 (Hanover: Hahn, 1868), p. 240.

[4] *Eracles* asserts that the crusaders girded themselves with "the Lord God's shield" in order to take Constantinople but threw it down once they were inside, girding themselves instead with "the Devil's shield" and pillaging churches and abbeys (*Recueil des historiens des croisades: Historiens occidentaux*, 5 vols [Paris: Imprimerie Impériale, 1859], 2:275). La "*Bible*" du Seigneur de Berzé, ed. Félix Lecoy (Paris: Droz, 1938), which is the work of a crusader, argues that the Latin forces gave in to greed and lust during the sack and forgot God entirely. God in turn forgot them. See vv. 416–536.

[5] *Martianus Capella and the Seven Liberal Arts, Volume 2: The Marriage of Mercury and Philology*, trans. William Harris Stahl and E. L. Burge (New York: Columbia University Press, 1977), p. 178.

[6] By contrast, there seems to have been little room in medieval society for doubting the legitimacy of waging war against Islam. See Elizabeth Siberry, *Criticism of Crusading, 1095–1274* (Oxford: Clarendon, 1985), pp. 16–20.

design is observable in the world, and earthly victories and defeats are figural signs of divine judgments. At the same time, they were doubtless aware of Augustine's very different theory of history, which Arnold echoes: God gives earthly rewards to the good and the bad in accordance with an order of things that human beings cannot fully grasp and that will reveal itself only in the fullness of time.[7]

Once the differences between these analyses of the Crusade are acknowledged, however, we can begin to see that they are not as distant as they initially appear. Arnold doesn't dismiss providential claims altogether but instead asserts that the true nature of the Crusade cannot yet be known. Likewise, Baldwin and Innocent don't claim to fully comprehend God's actions and intentions but rather articulate their belief in his justification of the conquest – a belief that does not eliminate doubt but responds to it with tremendous force. As Steven Justice has argued, the medieval "formulary of belief" is imbued with such tensions and depends both on skepticism and on the repeated exertions of the will that strive to overcome it. Belief is "not that which goes without saying, the plush carpet of presupposition, but that which has to be said, and then said again, because saying it provokes reactive intellectual energy."[8] By extension, providential histories do not exhibit unreflective certainty about the facts of history or their moral and religious meaning. Instead they attest to a struggle to comprehend and control historical meaning despite awareness that human actions, like the Divine Mind that foresees them, are resistant to totalization. If they didn't strain belief, they wouldn't be a source of wonder. They command belief not by precluding doubts but by repeatedly discrediting them. In the process, they work to bolster a rhetorically constructed, ideologically laden, but internally questioning truth.

In this chapter I will use Justice's "formulary of belief" to critically interrogate providential rhetoric in Geoffroy de Villehardouin's eyewitness prose history of the Fourth Crusade and Latin Empire, *La conquête de Constantinople* (ca. 1212).[9] In their tireless quest for facts, modern historians have often overlooked Villehardouin's use of rhetorical, compositional, and narrative techniques. Indeed, they have generally preferred the *Conquête* to other sources, precisely because they have deemed it to be relatively free of rhetorical or ideological maneuvering. As John Ward argues, however, vital

---

[7] For a useful overview of history and Providence in Orosius and Augustine, see Robert W. Hanning, *The Vision of History in Early Britain: From Gildas to Geoffrey of Monmouth* (New York: Columbia University Press, 1966), pp. 20–43.

[8] Steven Justice, "Did the Middle Ages Believe in Their Miracles?" *Representations* 103 (2008): 13 [1–29].

[9] Parenthetical citations will refer to paragraph numbers in Geoffroy de Villehardouin, *La conquête de Constantinople*, ed. Edmond Faral (Paris: Belles Lettres, 1973), followed by page numbers in *Memoirs of the Crusades by Villehardouin and De Joinville*, trans. Frank T. Marzials (London: Dutton, 1908). I have frequently, and silently, modified Marzials's translation.

historical knowledge is lost when scholars neglect the rhetorical dimension of medieval narrative histories. Like the Latin histories of the First Crusade that interest Ward, the *Conquête* does not seek to produce "a critically ordered and communicated sequence of more or less verified facts," as some scholars have assumed; instead it is a "language-construction" that works "to close out doubt and encourage and create certainty."[10] We should not suppose that the verifiable data it contains is somehow separable from the mysteries, miracles, and metaphors it uses to enjoin belief in a particular emplotment of history. Nor indeed should those mysteries, miracles, and metaphors be taken as signs of unshakable or unquestioning belief. Rather, they are rhetorical strategies that promote "credence in a matter of doubt," even as they generate the "reactive intellectual energy" that is inextricable from medieval practices of belief.

Fulk de Neuilly

Villehardouin's fascination with eloquence and miracles is obvious from the opening paragraphs of his history, which are devoted to the moral reformer Fulk de Neuilly. A humble curate from a rural parish near Paris, Fulk rose to prominence as an itinerant preacher who delivered rousing sermons against the vices of his time, notably usury, prostitution, and clerical concubinage.[11] Villehardouin describes him as a "saint home" [holy man] (2; 1) for whom "Nostre Sires fist maintes miracles" [our Lord wrought many miracles] (1; 1). Indeed, these miracles, primarily cures performed through the laying on of hands, are attested in numerous sources, as are Fulk's moral rigor and zeal.[12] Villehardouin tells us that when news of the firebrand's reputation reached Innocent III, the pontiff sent a legate to authorize him to preach a crusade indulgence with apostolic authority: those who served in the host for a full year would be absolved of all confessed sins. Lured by so generous an indulgence proclaimed by so passionate an orator, "s'en esmurent mult li cuer des gens, et mult s'encroisierent" [the hearts of men were much moved, and many took the cross] (2; 2).

The actual, enduring effects of Fulk's crusade sermons remain debatable, however, and the factors leading to the formation of a host were certainly more diverse and mundane than Villehardouin allows.[13] Fulk's reform mission

---

[10] John O. Ward, "Some Principles of Rhetorical Historiography in the Twelfth Century," in *Classical Rhetoric and Medieval Historiography*, ed. Ernst Breisach (Kalamazoo, MI: Medieval Institute Publications, 1985), pp. 106, 148 [103–65].

[11] See John O'Brien, "Fulk of Neuilly," *Proceedings of the Leeds Philosophical and Literary Society: Literary and Historical Section* 13.4 (1969): 115–20 [105–48].

[12] See O'Brien, "Fulk of Neuilly," 122.

[13] See Penny J. Cole, *The Preaching of the Crusades to the Holy Land, 1095–1270* (Cambridge, MA: Medieval Academy of America, 1991), pp. 87–92.

was addressed primarily, if not exclusively, to the common folk, and there is little evidence to suggest that he directly inspired the French and Flemish noblemen who assembled and led the host. Unlike Peter the Hermit (a key figure in the preaching of the First Crusade), he didn't manage to assemble a popular army; and unlike Bernard of Clairvaux he lacked the prestige that might have allowed him a role in strategic planning for the host itself.[14] The claim that Fulk interrupted the joust at a tournament at Écry in 1199 to shame the knights into joining "the tourney of God" appears to be a specious legend invented by the Romantics. Indeed, several sources suggest, with varying degrees of candor, that these knights took the cross "por doute dou roi de France que il ne les grevast et por ce qu'il avoient esté contre le roi" [for fear of the King of France, lest he should do them harm for having been against him].[15] Villehardouin makes no mention of such fears, nor does he describe any of the secular causes leading to the rise of the Crusade, leaving us to imagine that the movement developed as an emotional response to Fulk's inspired, rousing oratory.

I am not suggesting that Villehardouin was somehow ignorant of, or unconcerned with, the power struggles and tactical calculations surrounding the formation of a battle-ready host. On the contrary, he was a highly experienced military commander who had served with distinction in the Third Crusade and was therefore cognizant of the intricate and delicate negotiations involved in raising an army. Moreover, as marshal of Champagne he would have been intimately acquainted with the aristocracy's fears of the monarchy, which was moving swiftly to consolidate its power by denying the baronage its traditional prerogatives. Rather, I am remarking on the fact that Villehardouin, despite his reputation for sincerity, detachment, and objectivity, has chosen to gloss over a pivotal series of events and causes, with apparent disregard for how relevant they are to an understanding of the Crusade. Here he is focused almost single-mindedly on eloquent speech, supernatural wonders, and the awe and bellicosity they are capable of awakening, and this can hardly be an arbitrary choice. Indeed, throughout the history that ensues, he narrates events in such a way as to demonstrate rhetoric's miraculous capacity to *make history*: to bind men together into a unified host, often against tremendous odds, and to motivate the host to achieve goals that exceed mere human agency. Though he largely eschews florid tropes and set pieces and is unusually accurate and detailed in his reporting of events, he regularly uses literary and rhetorical devices in an attempt to shape the audience's perception of events. As we shall see, he draws heavily on the

---

[14] See O'Brien, "Fulk of Neuilly," 127.
[15] See Edgar H. McNeal, "Fulk of Neuilly and the Tournament of Écry," *Speculum* 28.2 (1953): 374 [371–75], citing *Eracles*, 27.21.

chansons de geste,[16] which share with the *Conquête* an interest in stabilizing a culturally, politically, and religiously unified "imagined community" ("la douce France," God's elect, and so on) in the face of internal and external, real and perceived threats.[17]

A Franco-Venetian Accord

The historical effects of rhetoric and the rhetorical inflection of historiography are especially apparent in Villehardouin's account of the formation of an alliance between the French and Flemish leaders of the Crusade and the doge of Venice, Enrico Dandolo. When the diplomatic corps, which includes Villehardouin himself, travels to Venice in 1201 to ask Dandolo to build a fleet of ships, they make their plea with one voice:

> Sire, nos somes a toi venu de par les hals barons de France qui ont pris le sine de la crois por la honte Jesu Crist vengier et por Jerusalem conquerre, se Diex le vuelt soffrir. Et por ce que il sevent que nulle genz n'ont si grant pooir con vos et la vostre gent, vos prient por Dieu que vos aiez pitié de la terre d'oltremer et de la honte Jesu Crist, coment il puissent avoir navie et estoire. (18; 5)

> [Sire, we have come to you on the part of the high barons of France who have taken the sign of the cross to avenge the shame done to Jesus Christ and to conquer Jerusalem, if God wishes to suffer it. And because they know that no people have such great power as you and your people, they pray you by God that you take pity on the land overseas and on the shame of Christ, and use diligence that our lords should have a navy and a fleet.]

Dandolo responds that he must consult with his various councils before finally appealing to "le conmun de la terre" [the commons of the land] (20; 6). Villehardouin therefore repeats his entreaty several times and eventually appears before an assembly of ten thousand souls in Saint Mark's Basilica. He implores the commoners' aid and then kneels in tears along with the other envoys, declaring they will not rise again until Venice agrees to take pity on Outremer. The response of the throng is immediate, impassioned, and unisonous:

---

[16] On the influence of the *chansons de geste* on the *Conquête*, see Jeanette M. A. Beer, *Villehardouin: Epic Historian* (Geneva: Droz, 1968).

[17] On imagined communities in crusade histories and the *Chanson de Roland*, see Sharon Kinoshita, *Medieval Boundaries: Rethinking Difference in Old French Literature* (Philadelphia: University of Pennsylvania Press, 2006), pp. 15–45.

> Li dux et tuit li autre s'escrierent tuit a une voiz, et tendent lor mains en halt, et distrent: "Nos l'otrions! Nos l'otrions!" Enki ot si grant bruit et si grant noise que il sembla que terre fondist. (28; 8)

> [The doge and all the others cried all together with one voice, and lifted up their hands, and said: "We grant it, we grant it!" Then there was so great a noise and so great a tumult that it seemed as if the earth were falling to pieces.]

Though it is unlikely Villehardouin simply invented this scene, as one scholar has argued,[18] his rhetorical shaping of events is overt. The trembling of the earth is a *figura* derived from Old Testament episodes in which earthquakes symbolize a warrior God leading his host into battle (Judg. 5.4–5; Ps. 68.8; Joel 2.10). Jeanette Beer argues that the phrase "was in such general use ... that its original source was probably forgotten" (*Villehardouin*, p. 25), leaving only a rhetorical cliché understood to evoke God and nature resounding in triumphant accord with the elect. Perhaps more crucially, the scene demonstrates the power of a skilled orator to unite an enormous, diverse group through language and gesture. Villehardouin (the historian) is interested here not only in unanimity but also in univocality: collective consciousness yields a collective discourse that emblematizes the joining of Venetians in common cause with the crusaders, Outremer, and Christ himself.

Collective discourse returns frequently in the *Conquête*, principally at moments of crisis or conflict, and has been understood by scholars as a distinctive feature of Villehardouin's style. Jean Frappier acknowledges that it is a literary borrowing but (taking a page from Émile Durkheim and Jules Romains) insists that it reflects an underlying social reality, the "unanimist" consciousness characteristic of traditional societies.[19] This claim has little merit given what Villehardouin will soon reveal about the fractious nature of the crusading host. Beer, by contrast, describes collective discourse as an "anti-realistic device" (*Villehardouin*, p. 86) that casts doubt upon the claim that Villehardouin is providing verbatim transcriptions of actual speeches. I agree with Beer and would add that it can be understood as a simultaneously constative and performative utterance. On the one hand, it claims to describe a historical reality, even though such a claim places strain on Villehardouin's assertion that he has not lied in his history "de mot a son escient" [by one

---

[18] See Giorgio Cracco, "Dandolo, Enrico," in *Dizionario biografico degli Italiani* (Rome: Istituto della Enciclopedia Italiana, 1986), pp. 454–55 [450–58]. Donald E. Queller and Thomas F. Madden convincingly dispute this assertion in *The Fourth Crusade: The Conquest of Constantinople*, 2nd edn. (Philadelphia: University of Pennsylvania Press, 1997), p. 61.

[19] Jean Frappier, *Histoire, mythes et symboles: Études de littérature française* (Geneva: Droz, 1976), p. 66. For a subtler analysis, see Gérard Jacquin, *Le style historique dans les récits français et latins de la Quatrième Croisade* (Geneva: Slatkine, 1986), pp. 119–57.

word to his knowledge] (120; 29–30). On the other hand, it performs the need to retroactively construct ideological unity on behalf of a Crusade that rather conspicuously lacked it and on behalf of Villehardouin's readers, who had to struggle to reconcile the Crusade's sacred mission with its actual trajectory. The historian does not simply ask us to believe in an unbelievable reality, ten thousand people who spontaneously speak as one. He also uses collective discourse to enjoin his audience to have faith in the political unity, religious coherence, and divine sponsorship of the Crusade, even – or perhaps *especially* – when those claims fly in the face of the realities he describes.

Crisis in Venice

I say "especially," because as Villehardouin seeks to produce "credence in a matter of doubt" he plainly understands that he cannot eliminate doubt altogether, nor does he really try. Instead he repeatedly draws our attention to the conflictive nature of the host and the intensity of its moral and religious qualms, and he renders factional disputes as rhetorical arguments conducted in direct, indirect, and collective discourses. In order to compensate for, and respond to, the factionalism he describes, he also demonstrates the capacity of oratory and providential rhetoric to bind the host together in moments of seemingly insurmountable strife.

Both tendencies are in evidence during the first major crisis of the Crusade: the failure of the host to assemble adequate forces in Venice (as Villehardouin repeatedly reminds his readers, many crusaders traveled "from other ports") and the host's inability to pay for its fleet of ships. The initial acknowledgment of the crisis and the request that the crusaders relinquish private wealth to help pay down the debt take the form of a collective discourse (59; 15), as does an ensuing debate:

> La ot grant descorde de la graindre partie des barons et de l'autre gent, et distrent: "Nos avons paié nos passages. S'il nos en volent mener, nos en iromes volentiers; et se il ne vuelent, nos nos porchacerons et irons a altres passages." Por ce le disoient que il volsissent que li ost se departist. Et l'autre partie dist: "Mielx voluns nos tot nostre avoir metre et aler povre en l'ost que ce que elle se departist ne faillist: quar Diex le nos rendra bien quant lui plaira." (60; 15)

> [Great was then the dissension emanating from the main part of the barons and the other folk, and they said: "We have paid for our passages. If they will take us, we shall go willingly; and if they do not wish to do so, we shall provide for ourselves and will take other means of passage." They spoke thus because they wished that the host should disband. But the other party said, "Much rather would we give all that we have and go penniless with the host, than that the host should disband or break apart; for God will indeed repay us when it so pleases him."]

When the Crusade leaders are unable to collect the sum required, those who withheld funds rejoice, believing they have fragmented the host. However, Villehardouin, foreshadowing a new accord with Venice that he will soon reveal to his readers, adds, "Diex, qui les desconsiliez conseille, ne le vost mie ensi soffrir" [God, who advises those who have been ill-advised, would in no way suffer it] (61; 16). On the one hand, there is apparent neutrality in the historian's willingness to give equal time to the voice of dissent and in his acknowledgment that that voice represents a unified majority. On the other hand, he is at pains to associate the minority with God and allegiance, the majority with Mammon and division. He also uses the device of anticipation, which would have been familiar to his readers from the *chansons de geste*, to suggest the validity of the minority's providential claim: the outcome of the crisis will indeed allow the host to avoid fragmentation and will therefore demonstrate that God favors the new Franco-Venetian accord, which indeed leads to earthly rewards (a Latin Empire), and the minority that defends it.[20]

The new accord forgives the crusaders their debt and requires them to assist the Venetians in reclaiming Zara, which repeatedly rebelled against their political, economic, and ecclesiastical control before placing itself under the protection of Emeric I, King of Hungary.[21] Since Emeric officially joined the Crusade (though apparently without seriously intending to leave home), Zara was also under the direct protection of the Holy See. Despite these complications, Villehardouin reports that the accord was solemnized in Saint Mark's with pious rituals, culminating in the sentimental consecration of a new leader: Dandolo himself. Though he was in his nineties and blind – "n'en veoit gote" [he couldn't see a thing] (67; 17) – the doge announces that he will join the Crusade, kneels to have a cross sewn onto his hat, and then exhibits it to the crowd "porce que il voloit que la gent la veïssent" [because he wanted the people to see it] (68; 17). This calculated display has several effects. Most immediately, it inspires pity and piety among the crowd, thereby swelling the host with new recruits and bolstering its collective faith: "Nostre pelerin orent mult grant joie et mult grant pitié de cele croiz por le sens et por la proesce que il avoit en lui" [Our pilgrims had very great joy and very great faith in this cross because of the wisdom and the valor that were in him] (68; 17). It also evinces the causal relationship between symbolic actions and heightened emotions, exemplary conduct and mass mobilization. Finally, as Beer argues, it endows Dandolo with the qualities of an epic hero, indeed one modeled closely on Charlemagne, to the point that Dandolo is assigned an epic tag ("et gote ne veoit") that distinctly recalls the Frankish king's hoary beard.[22] Parallels such as these would not only have signaled to

---

[20] See Beer, *Villehardouin*, pp. 33–37.
[21] See Thomas F. Madden, *Enrico Dandolo and the Rise of Venice* (Baltimore: Johns Hopkins University Press, 2003), pp. 111–13, 128–29.
[22] See Beer, *Villehardouin*, pp. 48–49, 55–56.

readers that the doge was a leader doughty enough to defend the Christian faith but would also have reminded them of the providential rhetoric that pervades the *chansons de geste* and is associated in particular with Charlemagne, whose prayers are answered by miracles.

Zara: Conquest and Crisis

These epic allusions bear fruit in the next episode of the *Conquête*, in which the host, at Dandolo's behest, achieves a victory at Zara that is so unbelievable it can only be accounted an act of God. Not surprisingly, Villehardouin's account of this incongruous triumph is densely rhetorical. When the host arrives at Zara, the crusaders ask in a single collective voice, "Coment porroit estre prise tel ville par force, se Diex meïsmes nel fait?" [How could such a city be taken by force, if God does not do it himself?] (77; 19). Despite a heated debate (in direct discourse) between Dandolo and the Abbot of Vaux about the legitimacy of attacking Christians; despite an attempt on the part of those "qui voloit l'ost depecier" [who wished to disperse the host] (81; 20) to undermine (in collective discourse) negotiations with the Zarans; and despite the resistance of a heavily fortified city whose walls are draped with images of the cross to signal that they are Christians,[23] Zara is indeed conquered. Dandolo then announces, as if in answer to the question the host posed earlier, "Seingnor, nos avons ceste ville conquise par la Dieu grace et par la vostre" [Lords, we have taken this city by the grace of God, and your own] (86; 21). These words suggest that history itself – the improbable conquering of an unconquerable city – can be taken as evidence of providential teleology: far from having been interrupted or diverted by Venice's economic and political ambitions, the Crusade has been reoriented in accordance with holy wisdom. Moral and religious opposition to the attack and doubts about its feasibility are evoked, but only in order to dampen them through a miraculous occurrence that sets the seal upon the host's sacred mission. In other words, the unification of the host and justification of diversion are achieved through the depiction and repudiation of internal dissent and the use of physical force against an opponent who is in reality an ally.

The Crusade leaders cannot silence opposition to diversion for long, however, and doubts and dissent resurge with each new turn of events. Soon after Zara surrenders, messengers arrive from Philip of Swabia, the German emperor. Speaking with a single voice, they hail the Crusade leaders and

---

[23] This detail is reported by Innocent in a letter addressed to the host. The Zarans, he writes, "hung images of the Cross around the walls. But you attacked the city and the citizens to the not insubstantial injury of the Crucified One, and what is more, by violent skill you compelled them to surrender" (Reg. 5.160 in Andrea, *Contemporary Sources*, p. 43).

deliver Philip's message: he entrusts his brother-in-law Alexius, son of the deposed emperor of Constantinople, into their care; urges them as warriors of God to right the wrongs committed against him and his father by the usurper Alexius III; and offers them generous incentives to do so, including the reunification of the Byzantine Church with Rome and financial and military support for the Crusade (91–94; 22–23). This message precipitates the second major crisis of the Crusade and leads to a series of heated debates, conducted, once again, in direct, indirect, and collective discourses. The Abbot of Vaux and those who (we are reminded) wish to disperse the host speak in collective indirect discourse, declaring "qu'il ne s'i accorderoient mie, que ce ere sor crestïens, et il n'estoient mie por ce meü, ainz voloient aler en Surie" [that they would never consent to it, that this meant falling on Christians, and they had not left home for this reason; on the contrary they wished to go to Syria] (95; 23). Their opponents reply in collective direct discourse, proclaiming that nothing can be achieved by defecting and that the host can only rescue Outremer by diverting to Constantinople. The Abbot of Loos, a "sainz hom et prodom" [holy man and a worthy man], and other clergy "preçoient et crioient merci alla jent que il por Dieu tenissent l'ost ensamble et que il seüssent ceste convenance" [preached and cried mercy to the people, that they keep the host together for God's sake, and that they adhere to the proposed convention] (97; 24). However, the Abbot of Vaux "et cil qui a lui se tenoient repreechoient mult sovent et disoient que tot c'ere mals" [and those who held with him preached quite often, and declared that all this was evil] (97; 24).

In the end, only twelve of the Crusade leaders (including Villehardouin himself) are willing to swear on the accord, and many crusaders choose to defect. Obviously, ethical and religious doubts about the diversion massively outweigh support for it. The covenant with Alexius is sworn nevertheless, and the crusaders set sail for Constantinople. Villehardouin doesn't explain how or why the host changes course. Instead, he uses the recurrence of doubts about the morality of the diversion as an opportunity to remind his audience of the enormity of the obstacles the host has overcome, to instill in them scorn for the defectors, and to urge them to believe in God's championship of the beleaguered but righteous host: "Or poez savoir, seignor, que, se Diex ne amast ceste ost, qu'ele ne peüst mie tenir ensemble, a ce que tant de gent li queroient mal" [Now be it known to you, lords, that if God had not loved the host, it could never have held together, seeing how many people wished evil to it] (104; 25). Villehardouin here uses doubt about historical events (which, he claims, could not have been achieved through human effort alone) in order to depict those events as evidence of a providential miracle. He likewise adopts a form of collective address prevalent in the *chansons de geste* to ask his audience to believe in the unity of a host that he has repeatedly shown to be rife with discord and doubts. At the same time, he does not marshal evidence other than discord and doubts to substantiate his assertion that God "loved the host" and intervened to hold it together. Indeed, he uses historical impossibilities as evidence for substantiating providential claims, and in turn uses these claims to guarantee the validity of the historical knowledge he purveys. From the point of view of historiographical method, the theological rhetoric of Divine Providence precedes, determines, and verifies the narration of events and justifies the violence of the Crusade.

The Conquest of Constantinople

As is to be expected, Villehardouin's commitment to providential rhetoric is nowhere more pronounced than in the series of impassioned speeches that precede the two sacks of Constantinople and the miraculous and violent actions that make them possible. He repeatedly asks his readers to bear witness to the events leading to the first capitulation of the Greeks – an event that led in turn to the coronation of Alexius IV:

> Et sachiez que onques Diex ne traist de plus grant peril nulle gent con il fist cels de l'ost cel jor. Et sachiez qu'il n'i ot si hardi qui n'aüst grant joie. (181; 44)

> [And be it known to you that never did God save any people from such peril as he saved the host that day; and be it known to you further that there was none in the host so hardened who did not experience great joy.]

> Or oiez les miracles Nostre Seignor, com eles sont beles tot par tot la ou li plaist. (182; 45)

> [Now listen to the miracles of our Lord – how beautiful they are wherever it pleases him to perform them.]

Here and elsewhere the devout contemplation of the host's victories and God's miracles is paired with forms of epic address that are endowed with considerable illocutionary force in that they recall the rhetoric of collective memorialization and the ideology of French unity in the *chansons de geste*. Villehardouin calls upon his readers not only to bear witness to historical events but also to share in the fellow feeling ("grant joie") and aesthetico-religious musings that miraculous victories have awakened ("come eles sont beles") and to believe in the reality of God's intervention on behalf of the host. Alexius himself echoes this rhetoric in a speech addressed to the Crusade leadership: "Seignor, je sui emperere par Dieu et par vos" [Lords, I am emperor by God's grace and yours] (194; 48).

The second sack of Constantinople is likewise legitimated by a narrative of secular causes (first, Alexius reneges on the terms of his covenant, and then he is murdered by a usurper named Mourzuphles) and by a providential teleology leading to the reunification of the Byzantine and Roman churches. When Alexius's murder is revealed, the Crusade leaders hold a parliament at which "tous li clergiez" [all the clergy], including those who had "le conmandement de l'apostoille" [powers from the Pope], agree that a murderer must not be allowed to rule and that the Greeks must be compelled to obey Rome:

> "Por quoi nos vos disons," fait li clergiez, "que la bataille est droite et juste. Et se vos avez droite entention de conquerre la terre et metre a la obedience de Rome, vos arez le perdon tel cum l'apostoille le vos a otroié, tuit cil qui confés i morront." Sachiez que ceste chose fu granz confors as barons et as pelerins. (225; 56)

> ["Wherefore we tell you," said the clergy, "that this war is lawful and just. And if you have a right intention in conquering this land and in bringing it into obedience with Rome, all those who die after confession shall have part in the indulgence granted by the Pope." And you must know that the barons and pilgrims were greatly comforted by this.]

Here Villehardouin plainly evokes the tenets of just war theory: the clergy proclaim that the attack is warranted because it is declared by legitimate, indeed apostolic, authority and is waged with righteous intentions – that is, the avenging of regicide and the reunification of Christendom.[24] Villehardouin calls his readers to witness the clergy's unisonous voice, the crusaders' feelings of relief and common purpose at receiving their message, and the healing of wounds of division that results from the decision to sack Constantinople. At the same time, he signals to his readers that the Crusade has encountered yet another crisis of faith: moral and religious doubts have permeated the host, and the crusaders' belief in the righteousness of their cause and the validity of the indulgence has faltered. They are persuaded to fight only after being reassured by the concerted voices of their clergy, who proclaim unequivocally that God will justify the shedding of Christian blood.

Once consensus is achieved, Villehardouin swiftly steps in to proffer evidence that the course of action chosen by the crusaders was indeed divinely authorized. "A l'aïe de Dieu" [With God's help] (228; 57), a nocturnal ambush by Mourzuphles on Latin troops sent to obtain provisions fails; and when the troops counterattack, the usurper loses twenty of his best knights, his imperial banner, and an icon of the Virgin that the Greeks used as a battle talisman. In a subsequent amphibious assault on Constantinople, the enemy is temporarily able to repel the crusaders on account of "noz pechiez" [our sins] (238; 60), and the host incurs substantial losses. The crusaders redouble their efforts, however, and "Nostre Sires lor fist lever un vent que on apelle boire" [our Lord raised a wind called Boreas for them] (242; 61), allowing two ships (*La Pelerine* and *Li Parvis*, *Pilgrim* and *Paradise*) to draw alongside the city

---

[24] See Raymond H. Schmandt, "The Fourth Crusade and the Just-War Theory," *Catholic Historical Review* 61.2 (1975): 191–221.

walls and raise ladders to the top of a fortified tower. The crusaders enter the city through the tower and soon occupy it. After seizing untold booty and garrisoning their troops in lavish homes, they celebrate Palm Sunday and Easter, reveling in "la joie de l'onor et de la victoire que Diex lor ot donné: que cil qui avoient esté en poverté estoient en richece et en delit" [the joy and honor that God had bestowed upon them: for those who before had been poor were now in wealth and luxury] (251; 65). The holy victories marked by these feasts and the Christological inversion *poverté-richece* suggest that righteousness has been fulfilled through conquest and that the crusaders have achieved victory on behalf of and alongside Christ himself. To complete the picture, Villehardouin endorses their jubilation and proclaims that the crusaders' victory could only have been achieved by God's invisible hand:

> Et bien en durent Nostre Seignor loer: que il n'avoient mie plus de .xx. mil hommes armés entre uns et altres, et par l'aïe de Dieu si avoient pris .cccc. mil homes ou plus, et, en la plu fort ville qui fust en tot le monde, qui grant ville fust, et la mielz fermee. (251; 65)

> [And well might they praise our Lord, since in all the host there were no more than twenty thousand armed men, one with another, and with the help of God they had conquered four hundred thousand men or more, and in the strongest city in all the world, which was a great city, and very well fortified.]

Once again, Villehardouin speaks here both as a dutiful historian who scrupulously documents statistical and tactical realities and as a rhetorician who construes unbelievable historical evidence as a reason to believe that God himself was the author of the conquest of Constantinople.

The Latin Empire

At this point, however, the *Conquête* is only at its midpoint. In the second half, Villehardouin's faith will be repeatedly tested as he narrates the election of Baldwin as emperor and Baldwin's attempts to impose Latin rule on Byzantium despite opposition from Nicaeans, Bulgarians, unreconstructed Greeks, and his own allies. The historian's tone shifts perceptibly as he recounts these events: less colorful and animated, his narrative now tends toward dry, undramatic reporting and contains fewer passages of direct discourse. These stylistic shifts have not gone unnoticed and have been interpreted by modern critics as evidence of Villehardouin's loss of faith in the Crusade, which not only failed to reclaim Jerusalem but also found itself mired in protracted struggles with an array of enemies, nearly all of whom were Christian.[25] And

---

[25] See especially Beer, *Villehardouin*, pp. 29–30, 55–56.

yet throughout the remainder of the *Conquête*, Villehardouin offers repeated reminders of God's providential care over the Empire. With God's help and Villehardouin serving as mediator, a feudal conflict between Baldwin and Boniface is resolved, thereby discomfiting the Greeks (who hoped that the Latins would be weakened by internecine strife) and saving Christendom itself (283–89; 78–79). When Theodore Lascaris, a Greek nobleman who fled to Nicaea after the sack of Constantinople, mounts an attack on the Latins at Poemaninon, they defeat him by God's "grace" and "will," despite being vastly outnumbered (319–20; 83). Similar defeats are achieved, again with divine succor, at Adramittium (323; 84), Modon (329; 86), and Arcadiopolis (338; 89).

Even Baldwin's capture by Bulgarian forces and the Latins' humiliating retreat from Adrianople in April 1205 offer him opportunities to recommit to his faith in providential care:

> L'emperere, qui mult ere chargiez endroit lui, rapeloit sa gent, si lor disoit que il ne fuiroit ja et qu'il ne le laissent mie; et bien tesmoignent cil qui la furent que onques mes cors de chevaliers mielz ne se defendi de lui. Ensi dura cil estors longuement. Telx i ot qui bien le fisent, et telx i ot qui le guerpirent. A la perfin, si cum Diex sueffre les mesaventures, si furent desconfit. Iqui remest el champ l'empereres Baudoins, qui onques ne volt fuir. (360; 94)

> [The emperor, who was in great straits on his side, recalled his people, and he told them that he would not fly, and that they must not leave him; and those who were there indeed attest that never did a knight defend himself better with his hands. This combat lasted a long time. Some were there who did well, and some were there who fled. In the end, for so God suffers misadventures, they were discomfited. There on the field remained the Emperor Baldwin, who never would fly.]

The *Conquête*'s epic tone is not muted by the army's rout and the loss of its commander but is, on the contrary, stoked by it: Baldwin's refusal to retreat with the rest of the host and his boldness in the face of certain defeat distinctly recall Roland on the battlefield at Roncevaux – an episode that is replete with invocations of sacred duty and oaths sworn in God's name and on the honor of "la douce France." Villehardouin gives no sign that the host has lost its sense of moral and sacred purpose or that its defeats somehow reveal the lack of an overall plan. On the contrary, he merely nods to an Augustinian conception of history, acknowledging that God sometimes allows misadventures to befall the elect and averring that the full significance of those misadventures will not always be obvious to those who must endure them. He then immediately reiterates his belief that the obstacles are temporary with respect to providential design and that evidence of that design is detectable in the events to which he bears witness, even – or perhaps especially – catastrophic defeats.[26] Faced with the prospect of an indefinite suspension of the Crusade's original goal and a future devoted to pacifying a massive territory threatened from within and on all sides, Villehardouin renews his commitment to providential rhetoric: whether through victories that unify and enrich the host against all odds or through a series of military campaigns that put the crusaders on their mettle, the *Conquête* depicts armed conflict as evidence of, and sanctified by, God's master plan.

Crusade Histories, Medieval and Modern

What do these recurring tests of, and testaments to, faith tell us about the violent history of the Fourth Crusade and Latin Empire and its depiction in contemporary francophone sources? This question cannot be answered without first acknowledging the yawning chasm separating medieval historiography from its modern counterpart. The truth that Villehardouin asks his readers to believe is not just a factual, evenemential reality, but also, and more importantly, a providential teleology that justifies the Crusade and sanctifies armed conflict with fellow Christians. The former truth is a constative enunciation of things that occurred and were recorded, the latter a performative enunciation by which the historian commands the mind to accept on faith what the intellect might otherwise abjure. To quote Justice, faith "is by definition distinct from knowledge and lacks its assurance" ("Middle Ages," 12); it is "that which has to be said, and then said again because saying it provokes reactive intellectual energy" (13). Though modern historians have viewed the *Conquête* as a trustworthy source of verifiable data (and indeed have often cited passages of direct discourse as if they were words actually spoken),[27] it is important for us to acknowledge the extent to which modern and medieval conceptions of historical truth are only partly compatible, and are particularly divergent where facticity is concerned. Medieval readers and writers regularly privilege metaphysical truth and the struggle to achieve conformity of belief through rhetorical means over that which is true merely by dint of having occurred. Put another way, the truths of faith – including faith in the ideology of crusading – require willful exertion, verbal repetition, and belief in the power of rhetoric (sermons, battle orations, historical narratives) to make history, to change its course, or to shape its meaning after the fact.

---

[26] Other eyewitness sources, notably crusading poems by the troubadour Raimbaut de Vaqueiras and Henri de Valenciennes's *Histoire de l'empereur Henri de Constantinople*, suggest that Villehardouin was far from alone in this belief.

[27] See, for instance, Queller and Madden, *The Fourth Crusade*; Madden, *Enrico Dandolo*; and Jonathan Phillips, *The Fourth Crusade and the Sack of Constantinople* (New York: Viking Penguin, 2004).

An analysis of Villehardouin's providential and historiographical rhetoric reveals not only strategies for justifying the Crusade's diversion and its violent assaults on Christian strongholds, but also a continuous rearticulation of doubts about the morality of these actions, doubts that are an inescapable by-product of, as well as a condition for the production of, faith in the Crusade as a just war. This is not to say that Villehardouin is somehow neutral in his attitude toward the events he narrates or that he strives to give equal attention to both sides of a moral debate. On the contrary, such a claim has little relevance in the domain of medieval rhetorical historiography, which, as Ward reminds us, presents "a forceful case for a certain reading of past action" and thereby legitimates and perpetuates the power of a ruling elite.[28] I am arguing something quite different: that the nature of medieval belief systems is such that a dominant ideology does not seek to eliminate doubts or conceal them from view, but instead gives voice to them in order to perform the historian's power to "close out doubt and encourage and create certainty" (Ward, "Some Principles," p. 148) using rhetorical techniques. The function of nearly all Crusade histories is to bind an audience together and recommit them to believing in the ideology of crusading. In the case of the *Conquête*, the moral problems attached to diversion and doubts about God's justification of violence against Christians are themselves a tool of ideology used to confirm faith in the Crusade but also to motivate the violence that sustains it. Attacks on Christian strongholds are preceded by moral qualms, heated debates, and exaggerated rhetoric; but the greater the doubts are, the greater the violence that ensues, and the greater the victory, with the second sack of Constantinople standing as the most dubious but also the most astounding and acclaimed victory of the Crusade.

This, in the end, is the truth that Villehardouin reveals most forcefully. It is not a truth that forecloses or eliminates doubt but one that is, on the contrary, inseparable from it. The *Conquête*'s providential rhetoric – perhaps *all* providential rhetoric – internalizes doubt within belief itself. In doing so, it suggests that belief can never come to rest but must instead struggle to sustain itself by constantly and willfully purging doubt and by striving to manage and contain that which cannot be purged altogether.

---

[28] John O. Ward, "Classical Rhetoric and the Writing of History in Medieval and Renaissance Culture," in *European History and Its Historians*, ed. Frank McGregor and Nicholas Wright (Adelaide: Adelaide University Union Press, 1977), p. 2 [1–10].

PART II
INSTITUTIONS AND SUBVERSIONS

4

Vice, Tyranny, Violence, and the Usurpation of Flanders (1071) in Flemish Historiography from 1093 to 1294

JEFF RIDER

The earliest sources of the history of medieval Flanders do not agree on the origins of the counts. The earliest source, the so-called "Genealogy of Arnold [I]," credibly traces the counts' origin to Baldwin I "Iron Arm," who eloped with and then married Judith, the daughter of Charles the Bald, around 863, while other sources push their origin back three generations and about seventy years to the shadowy "forester" Lideric.[1] The sources do agree, however, that once the line got started the succession proceeded with biblical regularity from father to son until the death of Count Baldwin VII in 1119. "Count Lideric of Harelbeke begat Enguerrand," writes the author of the "Bertinian" genealogy of the counts of Flanders, "Enguerrand begat Audacer. Audacer begat Baldwin Iron Arm ... Baldwin Iron Arm begat Baldwin the Bald ... Baldwin the Bald begat Arnold the Great ... Arnold the Great begat Baldwin ... He begat Arnold," and so on.[2]

This succession from father to son for almost three hundred years was interrupted only once. In 1070, Count Baldwin VI of Flanders – who was also Count Baldwin I of Hainaut by virtue of his marriage to the Countess Richilda of Hainaut, widow of the previous count of Hainaut, Herman – died and left both counties to his older son, the adolescent Arnold III. Less than a year later Baldwin VI's brother, Robert the Frisian – who was count of Holland by virtue of his marriage to Gertrude of Saxony, the widow of the previous count

---

[1] See Jean-Marie Moeglin, "Une première histoire nationale flamande: *L'Ancienne chronique de Flandre* (XIIe–XIIIe siècles)," in *Liber largitorius: Études d'histoire médiévale offertes à Pierre Toubert par ses élèves*, ed. Dominique Barthélemy and Jean-Marie Martin (Geneva: Droz, 2003), pp. 455–76; and Moeglin, "La mémoire d'un héros-fondateur: Lidéric forestier et comte de Flandre," in *La mémoire du temps au Moyen Âge*, ed. Agostino Paravicini Bagliani (Florence: Sismel, 2005), pp. 87–116.

[2] *Genealogia comitum Flandriae Bertiniana*, ed. L. C. Bethmann, Monumenta Germaniae Historica, Scriptores 9 (Hanover: Hahn, 1851), pp. 305–6. All translations are my own unless otherwise noted.

of Holland, Floris I – invaded Flanders and defeated his nephew at the Battle of Cassel on 22 February 1071. Arnold was killed in the battle and Robert became count. This violent transition of power, the first in the history of the county, was a significant moment for the medieval historians who wrote about it, and the ways they framed and explained it tell us something about their attitudes toward the commemoration of violence in the political sphere and how they thought it could be used to teach moral lessons.

The Early Accounts of the Usurpation of 1071

The first historian to write about this violent usurpation of the county was the author of the above-mentioned "Bertinian" genealogy of the counts of Flanders, which was also the first important "node," so to speak, in the medieval Flemish historiographical tradition. Despite this genealogy's name, it was probably composed at the Abbey of Saint Peter in Ghent. The three surviving versions of the text are essentially identical up to the begetting of Baldwin VI and his brother Robert I, but they part ways in their accounts of events in the generation of Baldwin VI and Robert I, a fact that suggests that the violent transition of 1070–71 was a critical moment about which there were different ideas. What one might term the "common" version of the genealogy, which was copied after 1093 and is perhaps the oldest continuation of a lost first version of the text, is found in three manuscripts and describes Robert's usurpation in remarkably veiled fashion: "Baldwin [VI] received two sons from Richilda, the widow of Count Hermann of Mons, Arnold [III] and Baldwin [II, count of Hainaut]. When one of them had been killed and the other driven out by force, Robert [I], who had received the similarly named Robert [II] and his brother Philip from Gertrude, the widow of Count Floris of Frisia, acquired everything and was made heir of the realm" (*Genealogia ... Bertiniana*, p. 306). Arnold's death and Baldwin II's expulsion are not attributed to Robert here: he simply became count after the one had died and the other had been driven from the county. If this version was completed shortly after Robert I's death, as it may well have been, one can understand its author's reluctance to sully the memory, and to offend the friends and dependents, of the recently deceased count, whose son then ruled the county. But it may also be that Robert I's violence was so shocking and troubling that the copyist of this version thought it should not be remembered in writing. No good lesson could be drawn from it.

A second version of the genealogy, which survived in only one manuscript, now lost, and may have been written about ten years later, is rather harder on Robert. After relating the births of Arnold III and Baldwin II of Hainaut, it continues:

Their uncle, Robert, married Gertrude, the daughter of Count Bernard of Saxony and the widow of Count Floris the Frisian, and ruled her realm with her. After he had received a great deal of money from his father, he swore an oath renouncing any claim to Flanders, which he conceded to his brother Baldwin [VI] and his successors by hereditary right. Robert kept quiet as long as his brother was alive, but after his death he killed his nephew Arnold, the count of Flanders, at Cassel with the help of traitors, and acquired his realm through treachery. With the aforementioned widow Gertrude, he begat Philip and Count Robert [II].

(Genealogia ... Bertiniana, p. 306)

The author of this version paints a distinctly different picture of Robert, who is portrayed as an example of princely and worldly vice: greedy and an oath breaker without reverence for custom, he is also something of a coward, has no respect for kinship, consorts with traitors, and is himself treacherous. It is perhaps significant that this version of the genealogy was found in a manuscript from the Abbey of Saint Vaast in Arras, in the southern part of Flanders nearest France, since the principal supporters of Arnold III appear to have come from this part of the county, whereas the principal supporters of Robert appear to have come from the northern part of the county (where the first, "common" version of the "Bertinian" genealogy, discussed above, was probably composed). It may also be significant that this version was composed at least twelve years after the death of Robert I, when it might have been easier to criticize his actions (although his son, Robert II, was probably still the count of Flanders when this later version was written).[3] The differences between the two versions suggest that the usurpation was a fraught moment for early Flemish historians, a moment over which historiographical contests might be fought.

The next historian to write about Robert's usurpation was Lambert, a member of the chapter of the church of Saint-Omer, who included both a verse and a prose genealogy of the counts of Flanders in his *Liber Floridus*, completed in 1120. For the beginning of his prose genealogy, down to Robert I's usurpation, Lambert simply copies the "Bertinian" genealogy, into which he interpolates a substantial passage drawn from the annals of Hincmar of Reims (also known as the annals of Saint Bertin). Intriguingly, Lambert uses the anti-Robert version of the "Bertinian" genealogy that we know through a lost manuscript from Saint Vaast rather than the "common" version of the genealogy (of which a copy was to be found in Saint-Omer, at the Abbey of Saint Bertin, at least in the thirteenth century), even though there is some reason to believe that he knew the "common" version.[4]

---

[3] The third version of the genealogy was probably composed in the thirteenth century and is thus not significant for the present discussion.

[4] In his prose genealogy Lambert includes a clause – "and he drove [*expulit*] Baldwin, the brother of Arnold, from the realm" – that is not found in the second, anti-

Lambert follows the earlier genealogy almost to its end, to the point where it states that Robert "killed his nephew Arnold, the count of Flanders, at Cassel with the help of traitors, and acquired his realm through treachery" (*Genealogia ... Bertiniana*, p. 306). He changes this sentence to read: Robert "killed his nephew Arnold, the count of Flanders, at Cassel with the help of traitors, and drove Baldwin, the brother of Arnold, from the realm and acquired it" (*Lamberti genealogia*, p. 310). He then adds a long passage about Robert's oppression and dispossession of the clergy of Flanders, who, Lambert tells us, complained about Robert, whom Lambert calls a "tyrant," to Pope Urban, who sent a letter of admonishment to Robert in 1091. When Robert ignored the letter the "sad and anxious Flemish clergy" brought their case before a council convened by Archbishop Reginald of Rheims, who dispatched the provosts of Saint-Omer and Watten and the abbots of Saint Bertin and Ham to reason with the tyrant Robert and to threaten to excommunicate him and lay his land under an interdict if he did not mend his ways before the coming Palm Sunday. "Fearing which, he made amends, and having declared that he would henceforward be obedient, he sought and received forgiveness, and thus undid everything he had done, so that none of his successors would dare restore this evil practice" (*Lamberti genealogia*, pp. 310–11). Lambert then copies the final lines of the "Bertinian" genealogy before adding a brief description of the reigns of the subsequent counts up to 1119.

Lambert thus lengthens the portion of the genealogy devoted to Robert substantially – it takes up about 58 percent of his prose genealogy – and portrays Robert as a thoroughly bad man. We get the sense that Robert's reign was a significant moment for Lambert and that what was particularly significant about it was Robert's tyranny and its eventual correction by clerical intervention and his eventual submission to clerical authority. In fact, in Lambert's genealogy Robert's oppression of the clergy seems a greater fault than his attack on his nephew and his usurpation of the county. One gets the sense, however, that both of these actions spring from the same source, that both are the outward signs of an inner flaw, of what Abelard, writing a few years later, called a "vice":

> For instance, being hot-tempered – that is, disposed or easily given to the turmoil that is anger – is a vice. It inclines the mind to doing something impulsively and irrationally that isn't fit to be done at all. Now this vice is

---

Robert version of the "Bertinian" genealogy used by Lambert but was perhaps inspired by the first, "common" version of the genealogy, which states that Baldwin II was "driven out [*expulso*] by force." The *expulso* of the "common" version is echoed in Lambert's *expulit*, and the echo suggests that he may have known this version as well as the anti-Robert one. See Lambert of Saint-Omer, *Lamberti genealogia comitum Flandriae*, ed. L. C. Bethmann, Monumenta Germaniae Historica, Scriptores 9 (Hanover: Hahn, 1851), pp. 310, 306.

in the soul in such a way that the soul is easily given to getting angry even when it isn't being moved to anger. ... So it is vice that makes us disposed to sin – that is, we are inclined to consent to what is inappropriate.[5]

Robert's particular vice is what medieval political theory termed "tyranny," an abuse of power for selfish reasons, and, in his commentary on Romans 13, Abelard noted that a tyrant acts specifically "by means of violence."[6] Lambert's portrayal of Robert I is thus an amplification of his portrayal in the second, anti-Robert, version of the "Bertinian" genealogy, and the overarching "mode," so to speak, of both versions is a clerical condemnation of the vices of secular rulers, of tyrants. Both the author of the second, anti-Robert, version of the "Bertinian" genealogy and Lambert seem to have thought, that is, that Robert's violent usurpation of the county deserved commemoration because it offered historians a "teachable moment" in the history of the counts of Flanders, a moment from which they could draw a moral lesson for their public.

The *Flandria Generosa*

Lambert's genealogy of the counts of Flanders was in turn the starting point for the next major text in the central Flemish historiographical tradition, the *Flandria Generosa*. This is a short Latin chronicle tracing the history of the counts of Flanders from 792 to 1164. It was probably composed at the Abbey of Saint Bertin in Saint-Omer sometime between 1134 and shortly after 1164. The author of the *Flandria Generosa* follows Lambert's text closely down to the reign of Baldwin V. At this point, while respecting Lambert's genealogical framework and incorporating his succinct genealogical information, the author of the *Flandria Generosa* replaces Lambert's critical account of Robert I's reign with a different account based on unknown sources before returning to Lambert's text for his account of the reigns of Robert's son, Robert II, and grandson, Baldwin VII. Robert I's reign thus remains the focal point of the *Flandria Generosa*, just as it had been the focal point of Lambert's prose genealogy, but the author of the *Flandria Generosa* makes the usurpation the key moment of Robert's reign and the most important moment of his chronicle. He replaces Lambert's account of Robert's reign with his own, devoting 32 percent of his entire chronicle to it, and consecrates 97 percent of this account of Robert's reign to an account of his usur-

---

[5] Peter Abelard, *Ethics* 1:4, 7, in *Ethical Writings*, trans. Paul Vincent Spade (Indianapolis: Hackett, 1995), pp. 1–2.
[6] *Commentaria in Epistolam Pauli ad Romanos* 4 [13, u. 2], in *Petri Abaelardi opera theologica*, vol. 1, ed. E. M. Buytaert, Corpus Christianorum, Continuatio Medieualis 11 (Turnholt: Brepols, 1969), p. 286.

pation of the county. In short, 31 percent of the entire chronicle is given over to a description of the usurpation.

The story that the author of the *Flandria Generosa* relates about Robert's usurpation of the county is diametrically opposed to the critical account one finds in the second, anti-Robert version of the "Bertinian" genealogy and Lambert's prose genealogy. It begins with a short passage about the recently widowed, "venerable" Richilda, wife of Baldwin VI, who spent her days in assiduous fasts and prayers and ministering to paupers and lepers, smearing herself with the pus of their lesions and bathing herself in the same water in which she had just bathed them. She despised the world until she died – "but first," adds the author of the *Flandria Generosa*, before she turned to God, "she suffered more than a few troubles."[7] He goes on to recount,

> Once her husband [Baldwin VI] had died, the paradise of Flanders began to lose its peaceful delights through her womanly insolence and the imprudence of her barely fifteen-year-old son Arnold and subsequently to lament bitterly to itself and to God, and [to long for][8] the well-known manliness of Robert, the brother of the recently deceased count. Perceiving this, the quarrelsome and crafty woman fled for protection to King Philip [I] of France. Not ashamed to commit trigamy, she also tried to marry some proud viscount of Normandy named William, thus further alienating some of the leading men and people of Flanders.
>
> The aforesaid Robert, less dear to his father than his mother, and estranged from Flanders by his brother, married Gertrude, daughter of Duke Bernard of Saxony and widow of Count Floris of Frisia ... and she bore him two sons, Robert and Philip, and three daughters. (*Flandria Generosa*, p. 321)

Having informed us of the fate of these daughters, the author tells us that when Robert, who was "residing in Frisia, learned of his brother's death and Richilda's tyranny, he returned to Flanders and arrived in Ghent. He asked the aforesaid woman to meet him there and suggested to her that she hand his father's realm over to him. Stirred up with a woman's rage, she refused and insulted him" (*Flandria Generosa*, p. 321).

"Deeply affected by the woman's pride," Robert ran off to his cousin, King Philip I of France, who initially was scandalized by the insults Robert had had to endure but whose mood was subsequently softened by the four thousand pounds of gold Richilda gave him shortly thereafter. The frustrated Robert returned to Frisia to spend the winter. While he was there, a number of the leading men of Flanders, "deeply troubled by the great cruelty that the woman displayed toward the clergy and the people and profoundly moved

---

[7] *Flandria Generosa (Genealogia Flandrensium comitum)*, ed. L. C. Bethmann, Monumenta Germaniae Historica, Scriptores 9 (Hanover: Hahn, 1851), p. 321.

[8] As Bethmann notes, a verb such as "to long for" seems to be missing here: *Flandria Generosa*, p. 321.

with overwhelming grief by the way she had plundered the churches," sent messengers to him to let him know how they felt about her. Encouraged by their message, Robert returned again to Flanders and holed up in the castle of Cassel, where he was joined by those who favored his cause. Richilda and her young son Arnold gathered an army, were joined by King Philip I and a strong force of French, and besieged Robert. The author of the *Flandria Generosa* tells us that the army Robert led against them was less numerous but more experienced, and his men were "defended by faith as well as covered by iron." The royal army was cut to pieces, Richilda captured, and Arnold "laid low" (*Flandria Generosa*, pp. 321–22).

This tale is remarkable in several ways. First, there is an obvious effort to provoke sympathy for poor Robert through the recitation of his consistent mistreatment and betrayal by those closest to him. The author also makes a clear attempt to assure the reader that Robert is not a tyrant: he tried to negotiate and reason with Richilda and returned to Flanders the second time not on his own initiative but in response to the pleas of the leading men of Flanders. He was, moreover, not the aggressor at Cassel, where he was besieged by a vastly superior force and simply defended himself when attacked. He is portrayed as the pious savior of his "father's realm," whom God favored at the battle of Cassel, providing further evidence of his humility and righteousness.

The portrait of Richilda is as remarkable as that of Robert. After a brief but graphic account of her later piety, which seems utterly out of tune with the author's overall purpose, she becomes the embodiment of "womanly" vices: she is insolent, quarrelsome, crafty, lustful, angry, sharp-tongued, and proud. In this account, remarkably, it is she rather than Robert who oppresses the clergy (and the people) and plunders the churches. The vices that Lambert attributed to Robert are transferred to Richilda: she is the tyrant, violent, oppressive, and greedy. The lack of a known written source for the story and its folktale-like structure – the poor younger son, loved by his mother but driven into exile by his father, returns to claim his heritage, despite manifold trials, from the wicked-stepmother-ish Richilda – suggest that it had a popular, oral origin, while its distribution of vices and virtues along gender lines can perhaps be attributed to its monastic, as opposed to simply clerical, origin. It seems likely, in fact, that the radical shift in the author's attitude toward Robert can be attributed largely to his being a monk at the Abbey of Saint Bertin in the middle of the twelfth century: by this time the abbey was the burial place of at least four of the first thirteen counts of Flanders and had become the quasi-official guardian of the counts' memory, just as the Abbey of Saint Denis was the quasi-official guardian of the kings' memory in France. The overarching mode of this episode, moreover, seems to have shifted from a clerical condemnation of princely vices to a monastic condemnation of women. Like the author of the second version of the "Bertinian" genealogy and Lambert, the author of the *Flandria Generosa* seems to have thought that Robert's usurpation of the county should be commemorated because it offered historians a "teachable moment," but the moral lesson he saw in it and wished to use it to teach was not about secular vices and rulers but about womanly vices and women rulers. Richilda replaces Robert as the violent tyrant and he becomes the innocent and sympathetic foil. The author is thus able to offer a historical example of, and condemn, womanly vice and excuse the violent usurpation of 1071, which here becomes a restoration rather than a rupture: Richilda is, at least from an emotional point of view, the usurper and Robert the rightful heir.

The *Ancient Chronicle of Flanders*

The *Flandria Generosa* forms the starting point of the *Flandria Generosa B*, or, as Moeglin has recently proposed to call it, the *Ancient Chronicle of Flanders* ("Première histoire," p. 458). It was likely composed sometime between 1164 and 1194, perhaps also at the Abbey of Saint Bertin. Moeglin has plausibly suggested that it may have been composed for the court of Count Philip of Alsace (reigned 1157–91; see "Première histoire," pp. 461, 471). Like the *Flandria Generosa*, the *Ancient Chronicle* is a history of the counts of Flanders from 792 to 1164 and it has perhaps generally been perceived as a reworking or expansion of the *Flandria Generosa*. The *Flandria Generosa* does provide the general framework for the *Ancient Chronicle*, but it contributes less than half of its content. The *Ancient Chronicle* might be more accurately described as a compilation of the *Flandria Generosa*, Walter of Thérouanne's *Life of Count Charles*, and large portions of Herman of Tournai's *Restoration of the Monastery of Saint Martin of Tournai*, to which short passages have been added from other works, or by the compiler, to create a more comprehensive, more coherent, more entertaining history of the counts of Flanders from 792 to 1164.[9]

The compiler of the *Ancient Chronicle* followed the *Flandria Generosa* closely up to the reign of Baldwin V, at which point the additions become frequent and copious. The compiler reworks the *Flandria Generosa*'s account of Robert I's usurpation in small but significant ways, and replaces its brief description of the reign of Baldwin VII (1111–19) with the longer account he found in Herman's work, and its brief description of the reign of Charles the Good (1119–27) with almost all of Walter's *Life of Count Charles*. He

---

[9] Walter of Thérouanne, *Walteri archidiaconi Teruanensis vitae: "Vita Karoli comitis Flandrię" et "Vita domni Ioannis Morinensis episcopi" quibus subiunguntur poemata aliqua de morte comitis Karoli conscripta et quaestio de eadem facta*, ed. Jeff Rider, Corpus Christianorum, continuatio medieualis 217 (Turnhout: Brepols, 2006); Herman of Tournai, *The Restoration of the Monastery of Saint Martin of Tournai*, trans. Lynn H. Nelson (Washington, DC: Catholic University of America Press, 1996).

then goes back to Herman for his account of the reign of William Clito (1127–28) before returning in the final passages of his work to the *Flandria Generosa*. On the whole, the compiler of the *Ancient Chronicle* followed his sources faithfully. His most important contribution to the future of Flemish historiography was the artistic combination of them in an effort to tell as complete a story as possible of the counts of Flanders. The ultimate effect of this combination is to shift the weight of the *Chronicle* away from the distant past and to a more recent past, especially the reigns of Baldwin VII, Charles, and William Clito.

Given the *Ancient Chronicle*'s "modern" focus, Robert's usurpation of the county plays a less prominent role in it than it does in the *Flandria Generosa*. Its role as *the* historical exemplum, the teachable historical moment of vice, violence, and tyranny, is largely taken over by the assassination of Charles the Good in 1127 – the second moment of violent transition in the history of the county – to which the compiler of the *Ancient Chronicle* hints Robert's usurpation of the county is in some way linked. The compiler of the *Ancient Chronicle* does include and revise the *Flandria Generosa*'s description of Robert's usurpation of the county, however; and his revision suggests that he had a significantly more sophisticated understanding of this violent transition than the original author and thought it should be remembered in a distinctly different way.

The compiler of the *Ancient Chronicle* makes, for example, a number of important changes to the beginning of what one might call the tale of Richilda and Robert, changes that modify its whole tone. As was noted above, this tale begins in the *Flandria Generosa* with a brief passage about the "venerable" Richilda's later ministry to paupers and lepers and then launches without transition into a long description of the tyrannical Richilda's struggle with Robert. This is not chronological, and it produces a story line that may be admonitory but is hardly edifying. The compiler of the *Ancient Chronicle* obviously felt that this passage was out of place, and the first change he makes to the story of Richilda and Robert is to move the portrait of the venerable Richilda to the end of the story, after Robert has successfully usurped the county, where it makes better chronological, narrative, and moral sense, and to expand it substantially.[10] And whereas the author of the *Flandria Generosa* ends the account by noting only that "she commended her body to the ground at Hasnon, her soul to the mercy of Jesus Christ" (*Flandria Generosa*, p. 321), the compiler of the *Ancient Chronicle* adds that "her soul deserved to be

---

[10] Some passages of the *Ancient Chronicle*, taken from a fourteenth-century manuscript, were printed in the notes to Bethmann's edition of the *Flandria Generosa*, but the entire text has never been published. I have thus used the text in the oldest manuscript of the *Ancient Chronicle*, MS Munich, Clm 23583, which dates from the third quarter of the thirteenth century (see Moeglin, "Première histoire," p. 459). The passage concerning Richilda's piety is found there on fol. 12rb–12va.

cloaked in the robe of immortality and to enjoy the delight of paradise" (fol. 12va). Her piety, asceticism, and ministry to paupers and lepers here atone for her previous faults, for her tyranny and violence, and she makes a good end. The compiler of the *Ancient Chronicle* thus emphasizes her devotion and good works and creates a clear narrative progression from worldly tyranny to otherworldly piety. She becomes a positive example of women's virtues and the good that can be accomplished by a pious noblewoman as well as, earlier in the chronicle, a negative example of women's vices and the perils of a female ruler. The author of the *Ancient Chronicle* makes her an example, at different times, of both a bad woman and a good one and is as interested in her redemption as he is in condemning her.

Having moved the description of Richilda's piety to a more appropriate place, the compiler of the *Ancient Chronicle* begins his story of Richilda and Robert directly with Richilda's "troubles." The author of the *Flandria Generosa* began the long section of his chronicle devoted to Richilda's troubles by mentioning Flanders's loss of its peaceful delights through Richilda's insolence and her son's imprudence, a loss that leads to Flanders's lament "to itself and to God and [to long for] the well-known manliness of Robert, the brother of the recently deceased count." The *Flandria Generosa* then tells how Richilda, perceiving this growing discontent, took two measures to strengthen her position: she "fled" to King Philip of France for protection and "tried to marry some proud viscount of Normandy named William." These measures, however, only served to further alienate the leading men and people of Flanders. The *Flandria Generosa* breaks off the main narrative at this point to give the reader some background on Robert – "The aforesaid Robert, less dear to his father than his mother, and estranged from Flanders by his brother, married Gertrude, daughter of Duke Bernard of Saxony and widow of Count Floris of Frisia" – before returning to the main plot by noting that when Robert, "residing in Frisia, learned of his brother's death and Richilda's tyranny," he returned to Flanders to meet with Richilda and suggest that she hand his father's realm over to him (*Flandria Generosa*, p. 321).

The compiler of the *Ancient Chronicle* revises this material substantially. First, he rewrites the clause "the paradise of Flanders began to lose its peaceful delights … and subsequently to lament bitterly to itself and to God, and [to long for] the well-known manliness of Robert, the brother of the recently deceased count" (*Flandria Generosa*, p. 321) to read "the paradise of Flanders began to lose its peaceful delights. … For this reason, it began to lament bitterly to itself and to God and to Robert the Frisian, the brother of the recently deceased count" (fol. 10rab), suggesting that this lament was made directly *to* Robert rather than simply indicating a longing for his return. The compiler of the *Ancient Chronicle* then evidently decided that the reader would like to know where Robert was and why he had not inherited the county after his brother's death since the people and leading men of Flanders seemed to prefer him to Richilda and her son. He thus inserts at this point a slightly modified version of the next section of the *Flandria Generosa*, the section giving the reader some background on Robert, and adds a key clause to introduce a passage he borrows from Herman's *Restoration* and expands in order to explain the consequences of Robert's being less dear to his father and how he was estranged from Flanders to the benefit of his brother. In the *Ancient Chronicle*, this interpolated insertion begins as follows (the compiler's additions are underlined in the following citation; the passage from Herman is in italics):

> This same Robert [to whom the paradise of Flanders has just lamented its lost delights] had been less dear to his father than his mother. For this reason, his father, Count Baldwin [V], *fearing lest dissension should arise after his death between his sons, Baldwin [VI] and Robert, gave all of his land during his lifetime to Baldwin, and he had* forced *his* vassals and nobles to *pledge homage and fidelity to him,* and had betrothed him to the aforesaid Richeldis, and, furthermore, had forced the aforesaid Robert to pledge fidelity to Baldwin *so that at Audenarde, publicly in the presence of the father and brother and many princes, this same Robert swore upon the relics of the saints that he would not harm either Baldwin himself or his heirs in the county of Flanders in any* way. *When he had completed his oath, he left Flanders and withdrew into Frisia.* And there he received the daughter of Duke Bernard of Saxony and widow of Count Floris of Frisia, named Gertrude.[11]

The compiler copies the rest of the information about Robert's sons and daughters from the section of the *Flandria Generosa* devoted to Robert's background. He then adds a sentence, evidently of his own invention: "And then certain Flemings complained about Richilda to this Robert the Frisian and sent him letters about reclaiming his paternal inheritance." The compiler then returns to the main plot as found in the *Flandria Generosa*: it is at this point, the compiler tells us, that (in response to the letters sent to Robert from Flanders urging him to reclaim his paternal heritage) Richilda fled to King Philip of France for protection and "tried to marry some proud viscount of Normandy named William," and at this same point that Robert, "residing in Frisia, learned of his brother's death and Richilda's tyranny" (through the letters sent to him by unhappy Flemings) and returned to Flanders to meet with Richilda and suggest that she hand his father's realm over to him (fol. 10vab).

This revision of the beginning of the story of Richilda and Robert indicates the differences between the interests and attitudes of the author of *Flandria Generosa* and those of the compiler of the *Ancient Chronicle*. It indicates as well the latter's different ideas about the origins of Robert's

---

[11] *Ancient Chronicle*, fol. 10rb; cf. Herman, *Restoration*, p. 28. I have followed Nelson's translation for the passage from Herman.

violence toward his nephew. The changes he makes – his rewriting of the first sentence to read "the paradise of Flanders began to lose its peaceful delights. ... For this reason, it began to lament bitterly to itself and to God and to Robert the Frisian, the brother of the recently deceased count"; his reordering of the material (moving the description of Richilda's piety to the end of the story, moving up the explanation of Robert's fraught exclusion from Flanders); and his additions ("For this reason, his father, Count Baldwin [V]"; "and had betrothed him [Baldwin VI] to the aforesaid Richeldis, and, furthermore, had forced the aforesaid Robert to pledge fealty to Baldwin"; "And then certain Flemings complained about Richilda to this Robert the Frisian and sent him letters about reclaiming his paternal inheritance") – all create a significantly clearer, better motivated, and more emotionally and psychologically complex narrative. In light of the direct lament to Robert and the letters sent to him urging him to return to Flanders that were added to the *Ancient Chronicle*'s version of these events, Richilda's efforts to strengthen her position – her flight to King Philip and her efforts to marry a Norman nobleman – seem better motivated and more justified, and she seems less impulsive and less insecure. This direct lament and the letters, these repeated strong appeals to Robert, also make his return to Flanders and efforts to claim his father's realm seem even less selfish and tyrannical than they appeared in the *Flandria Generosa*. Richilda's fear thus becomes more reasonable, and Robert is made to look like an even more reluctant savior, a sort of Flemish Cincinnatus.

The compiler's addition of the short phrase "for this reason, his father, Count Baldwin [V]," and his transformation of Herman's "he [Baldwin V] had his nobles pledge homage and fidelity to him" into "*he had* forced *his* vassals and *nobles* to *pledge homage and fidelity to him*, and had betrothed him to the aforesaid Richeldis, and, furthermore, had forced the aforesaid Robert to pledge fidelity to Baldwin" also makes the psychological portrait of Robert more dramatic and greatly increases the intensity of the entire tale. The addition of the single word "unde" (for this reason), in particular, suggests that all the strife and violence that followed had their source in developmental conflicts in this particular family, both evoking Oedipal tensions and recalling the story of Jacob and Esau. The compiler of the *Ancient Chronicle* then emphasizes Robert's father's distrust of, and alienation from, his younger son through the passage he interpolated from Herman's *Restoration* and expanded in significant ways. The compiler of the *Ancient Chronicle* suggests that Baldwin V *greatly* feared dissension between his sons and thus shored up his favorite, Baldwin, in every way he could think of: he made him co-ruler while he was still alive; he "forced" his vassals and nobles to pledge homage and fidelity to him;[12] he married Baldwin to

---

[12] The compiler of the *Ancient Chronicle* changes, significantly, Herman's "he *had*

Richilda (an addition by the compiler); he "forced" Robert to pledge fealty to Baldwin (another addition); and he had Robert swear not to harm Baldwin or his descendants as well. The father's precautions are an indication of his sense of his son's degree of resentment and animosity, as are the fact that he "forces" his vassals and barons to swear homage and fidelity to Baldwin VI and "forces" Robert to pledge fidelity to his brother. The father further demonstrates his lack of care for his younger son by doing nothing for him once he has provided so thoroughly for his brother. The way that Herman and the compiler of the *Ancient Chronicle* tell it, Robert simply goes away to Frisia, where he happens to marry the countess (we know from other sources that this marriage was in fact arranged by his father).

Given the way that the compiler of the *Ancient Chronicle* establishes this conflict, one might conclude that Robert was both identifying with his father and punishing him by killing and displacing his nephew: the violence of one generation passes to the next. The *Ancient Chronicle*'s account of this multigenerational conflict in the house of Flanders is, in any case, significantly more detailed, more coherent, more dramatic, more pathetic, and more suggestive than any previous account, and it better motivates Robert's subsequent actions. It also complicates Robert's character, restoring to him the tyrannical character attributed to him by the author of the first version of the "Bertinian" genealogies and Lambert of Saint-Omer, although this vice is no longer simply "in" him but results from his relationship with his father.

The *Ancient Chronicle* is based on the *Flandria Generosa* and seems, like it, to have been compiled at Saint Bertin. As the foregoing discussion shows, however, the *Ancient Chronicle* is animated by a rather different spirit. Its compiler is far more concerned with motivation and causality, with narrative coherence, drama, psychology, and emotions, than were any of the previous historians who wrote about this violent political transition. His Richilda may still be a tyrant, but he better motivates her fear of Robert, a fear that seems reasonable since it was shared by Robert's father. Moreover, she fully redeems herself in the end through suffering and pious works. His Robert is less innocent and his Richilda is therefore less guilty. What is perhaps most significant here is Richilda's good end. Saint Bertin may be the common place of origin of the two chronicles, but their intended audiences seem quite different. The lessons of the *Ancient Chronicle* are still clerical ones, but they appear to be addressed to a lay audience of both women and men, and both women and men are portrayed in dynamic, morally complex ways. Moeglin's suggestion that the *Ancient Chronicle* was composed for the court of Philip of Alsace thus seems altogether reasonable. It is high history, thoughtful entertainment, for a sophisticated public; and in this more sophisticated setting, the vice

---

[*fecit*] his nobles pledge homage and fidelity to him" (Herman, *Restoration*, p. 28) to "he *had forced* [*coegerat*] his vassals and nobles to pledge homage and fidelity to him" (fol. 10rb).

and tyrannical violence that were first attributed to Robert and then to Richilda in earlier accounts are both more fully and more subtly analyzed and redistributed more equally between them. The vice and violence portrayed in the *Ancient Chronicle*, that is, are less an exemplum, less the occasion for a bald moral lesson, and are more realistic, more an occasion for reflection and evaluation. The description of the events of 1171 by the compiler of the *Ancient Chronicle* suggests that he, like his predecessors, thought that these events held a lesson. But it also suggests that he wrote for a sophisticated lay audience that would turn away from rude clerical lessons and preferred to be presented with more complicated and realistic psychological and moral situations – an audience, in short, that was invited to think for itself. It was, for him, less a moment he could use to teach his audience a moral lesson than a moment from which they might themselves learn.

Les cronikes des contes de Flandres

The *Ancient Chronicle* was in turn translated into French, approximately between 1164 and 1294, and this translation was included in a manuscript (BNF fr. 12203) that was almost certainly commissioned around 1294 by Gui of Dampierre, count of Flanders from 1278 to 1305, or someone in his entourage.[13] This manuscript also contains copies of the *Estoires d'Outremer et de la naissance Salehadin* (a Crusade chronicle covering the period 1099–1230), Geoffroy de Villehardouin's *La conquête de Constantinople*, Henri de Valenciennes's *L'histoire de l'empereur Henri de Constantinople*, and Anonymous of Béthune's *L'histoire des ducs de Normandie et des rois d'Angleterre*. It seems likely that whoever commissioned the manuscript asked that it be copied from an earlier codex containing these four chronicles, and that this person also asked that the French translation of the *Ancient Chronicle* be included in the new copy, where it is entitled *Les cronikes des contes de Flandres*. Gui may even have provided the exemplar of the *Cronikes* from which the copy in BNF fr. 12203 was made. Whoever commissioned the manuscript thus appears to have thought that the *Cronikes* belonged in a volume with these other works, even though it had probably been composed some twenty to thirty years before them and had not, like the other four works in the volume, originally been composed in French.

One might expect that this Latin chronicle of monastic origin would have had to undergo substantial modification, in addition to being translated into French, in order for it to fit into BNF fr. 12203 alongside the four other, more recent, French chronicles, but, surprisingly, the translation of the *Ancient*

---

[13] The text of this translation is printed relatively accurately as *Les chronikes des contes de Flandres*, ed. J. M. B. C. Kervyn de Lettenhove (Bruges: Vandecasteele-Werbrouck, 1849).

Chronicle is really no more than that. The only differences between the Latin and French texts are small ones such as normally occur in the course of translation. The translator translates, for example, the *Ancient Chronicle*'s "This same Robert had been less dear to his father than his mother" (fol. 10rb) as "This Robert was much loved by his mother but very little loved by his father" (*Cronikes*, p. 13). The translation of "dear" [*carus*] by "loved" [*amé*] and the addition of the adverb "much/very" [*moult*] are typical of the kind of amplification one expects in translation, although they also indicate an even greater interest in the emotional dimension of this story.[14] From the point of view of the presentation of the Flemish past, however, nothing changes. This is remarkable. I doubt very much that anyone would have imagined including the *Flandria Generosa* and its tale of Richilda's womanly vice, violence, and tyranny in a collection of French chronicles like BNF fr. 12203. It was a highly monastic chronicle, and even if it had been translated into French, it would not have fit in with the other chronicles in BNF fr. 12203 since it would have been altogether out of keeping in style, language, and length with the other chronicles in this collection, and since it was written according to a different idea of the nature and purpose of historical writing and preaches very different moral lessons.

The inclusion of the *Ancient Chronicle* in BNF fr. 12203 was thus made possible not by its being translated into French, or at least not simply by its being translated into French. It was the transformation of the *Flandria Generosa* into the *Ancient Chronicle* that made this material appropriate for inclusion in BNF fr. 12203, not its translation into French. The work of what we might term cultural adaptation or laicization that made the material of the monastic *Flandria Generosa* available and interesting to a courtly audience was done, probably at the end of the twelfth century, by the compiler of the *Ancient Chronicle*, who shifted its focus toward the immediate past, more than doubled its length by adding immense amounts of contemporary, eyewitness testimony drawn from other sources to the monastic chronicle, and strengthened its narrative qualities: "romancing" it, laicizing it, perhaps for the court of Count Philip of Alsace. One might in fact suggest that the translation of the *Ancient Chronicle* into French and its eventual inclusion in BNF fr. 12203 was largely due to the *Ancient Chronicle*'s ready "translatability" thanks to its having already been "romanced": cultural translation, the

---

[14] The translator evidently did not grasp the subtle implications of the beginning of the next sentence, "*For this reason his* father, Count Baldwin [V], while still living, fearing lest dissension should arise after his death between his sons ..." (emphasis added). He left the "for this reason" out of his translation and changed the "his" to "their," effacing the relationship between Robert and his father as the origin of the subsequent conflict: "And their father Count Baldwin, who greatly feared lest discord break out between his two sons after his death ..." (*Cronikes*, p. 13). The translator thus diminishes the psychological and emotional complexity of the story rather than increasing it and shows us that medieval people were not always the best or most sensitive readers of their own stories.

laicization of the material, seems to have preceded and prepared the way for linguistic translation. Even Latin historiography, that is, appears to have been caught up in what one might term the "Romantic movement" of the second half of the twelfth century, and this is why we find the French translation of a late twelfth-century Latin history of the counts of Flanders alongside four more recent French chronicles in a late thirteenth-century manuscript made for the court of Flanders. The shift from Latin to French was less important than this earlier shift in sentiment that translated a century-old Latin monastic historical tradition, and its exemplary tale of violence, into a tale that could be included alongside more recent works in a manuscript made for the late thirteenth-century Flemish court.

5

Marvelous Feats: Humor, Trickery, and Violence in the *History of the Counts of Guines and Lords of Ardres* of Lambert of Ardres

Leah Shopkow

Lambert of Ardres in his *History of the Counts of Guines and Lords of Ardres* (ca. 1206) tells of an incident at the wedding of Arnold II "the Old" of Ardres and Gertrude of Aalst:

> Now, among the many folk coming together from many regions to attend the nuptials, there was a certain rogue, a beer-drinker – as the custom of that time was. When he dined in the house with the other feasters, he proclaimed and boasted amongst them that he was such a great drinker that if the lord bridegroom would give him some sort of nag or horse, he would drink up a great keg, completely full of beer, that Arnold [the bridegroom] had in his cellar. When the bung had been pulled, he would place his mouth at the opening and not remove it until the keg was empty. And he would void his waste at the same time, as he had just prepared and arranged a place where he might pour out or release the urine from his manly rod. When the bridegroom took the bet, the rogue matched his deeds to the words and emptied the keg – Oh, the gluttony of drinkers! Oh, the indiscreet prodigality of princes! – just as he had predicted and accepted in the bet: he drained, chugged, drank, and, at the same time, urinated.
>
> When it was empty, the wretch jumped amongst them and placed the bung of the keg in his mouth as a sign of jocularity, or rather of gluttony. He began boldly and repeatedly to demand in a clamorous and victorious voice the horse that he won in the agreement and by drinking. But the bridegroom looked at him with burning eyes and ordered that the horse be saddled for him and given to him as quickly as possible according to the agreement. But Arnold's cronies had cut trees into a gibbet, as they were well-informed of the intention of their lord; they jumped up at once and hanged the rogue from the gibbet.[1]

---

[1] Lambert of Ardres, *History of the Counts of Guines and Lords of Ardres*, trans. Leah Shopkow (Philadelphia: University of Pennsylvania Press, 2001), pp. 156–57; *Lamberti*

At the outset, the story may seem a familiar one to a modern audience. A bunch of drunken people make a silly bar-room wager and illustrate the proposition so well known to drinkers that beer is never purchased, only rented. We can imagine (although Lambert does not tell us about this) that the audience offers encouragement, laughter, and jeers as the toper inhales the beer. The laughter continues as the successful wagerer dances around having made himself into the new keg, complete with bung in opening. But then the comic story takes a violent turn, on a pun untranslatable into English but probably originally conceived in French. In the Latin, the drinker asks for a *ronchinum uel equum* (nag or horse) – that is, a horse of a low quality. He is hanged on an *equuleo* (gibbet), which alludes to the Latin *equis* or its diminutive, *equulus*. (In Old French, the word *cheval* does for both gibbet and horse, and so the pun works more neatly.)[2] Thus the foolish bettor comes to a violent end at a wedding feast, presumably entertaining the guests in two ways.

What are we to make of this story, with its slightly grotesque and certainly ambiguous combination of comedy and violence, its seeming lack of pity for the poor fool whose offense is apparently only unseemly vulgarity? Lambert tells us the story under the heading of a "memorable feat" [*hoc memorabile*] or a marvelous one [*mirabile*] performed by Arnold, but why is this a "memorable feat" for Arnold to have performed? And when Lambert uses the word *mirabile*, does he mean that one should marvel at something because it is wonderful or because it is weird? Ambiguous language – language that taken literally can produce the opposite of what the speaker intended – is crucial to his humor. The victim of this story (and the others like it) is a peasant, a man limited to a single language. However, those actually being mocked by the comedy are the elite, who misuse their power over their people. Thus Lambert also treats the violent ends of lords who rely on their coercive power comedically. In Lambert's writing, therefore, comedy is a response to the violence of power.

Before I begin my exploration of Lambert's inclusion of comic elements in some of his violent stories, it would probably be helpful for the reader to know a little more about the text. Lambert began writing his history sometime around 1194 in the small county of Guines, under Counts Baldwin II (1169–1206) and Arnold II (1206–20), and completed it some time after Baldwin's death in 1206. Guines was a very small territory in the south of the plain of Flanders, with a small resource base. It had few grainlands and no port, and the terrain consisted largely of forest, scrub, meadow, and fresh- and saltwater marsh; its people lived primarily by raising animals and

---

Ardensis historia comitum Ghisnensium, ed. Johann Heller, Monumenta Germaniae Historica, Scriptores 16 (Hanover: Hahn, 1859), p. 622. All further citations for this work will appear in parentheses and will give the chapter number common to the Latin edition and the translation, followed by the page number in the translation.

[2] Flemish was also spoken in the area, but the joke doesn't work in Flemish.

farming fish (ch. 15; p. 64). Despite the sparse material circumstances of the county, however, it produced a remarkable writer in Lambert, a university-trained man well-read in the classical school texts, the great Latin histories (for example, Prologue, pp. 43–46; ch. 9, p. 60; ch. 91, p. 124), and local works such as *Flandria Generosa* (ch. 1–2, pp. 54–55).

Lambert's history is something of an anomaly, therefore, as it was produced in a region that would not seem to have the resources, cultural or economic, to produce a history of this complexity. But Guines lay at the crossroads between France and Flanders and between France and England. It was not cut off from the larger world. The local lords and merchants spoke French as well as Flemish, to which its clergy added Latin. The rich monastic library of Saint Bertin lay about thirty kilometers away from Ardres. Lambert's text also occupies a linguistic crossroads between the vernacular and Latin. On the one hand, it was written in Latin and uses complex and convoluted language: it is studded with redundancies like legal boilerplate gone mad, includes many plays on words, and has a thoroughly "planned" quality.[3] On the other hand, it plays with and draws on the vernacular. The work contains a second narrative nested inside the first, the outer narrative told in Lambert's voice in Latin, while the internal narrative purports to be told by Walter of Le Clud in the vernacular (even though it is also in Latin). Furthermore, Lambert adopts the convention of courtly narratives for this part. He sets Walter's narrative in motion in a classic "courtly" way; the young men of the court have been stuck indoors for days by rain, and the old men are keeping them from tearing the place apart by telling them stories, among them the matters of Rome, Britain, and France, as well as romances and vernacular crusade narratives (ch. 97; p. 130). When they run out of this material, Walter stands up to tell the history of the lords of Ardres.

It is in this soup of broad twelfth-century influences, both vernacular and Latin, that Lambert's treatment of violence has to be situated. It was a particular moment in time, when the lines between the two linguistic registers were not so strongly drawn, and when material passed easily either way – when Stephen of Fougères could write a Latin version of a vernacular life of Vitalis of Savigny, and when first Geoffrey Gaimar and then Wace could translate Geoffrey of Monmouth's ironic Latin *History of Britain* into unironic French. It was also a period of experimentation with form and style and mixed genres. But this moment passed, at least on the Latin end of things, and Latin historians seem to have become less likely to experiment with literary form or to draw on vernacular and oral materials.

---

[3] Although the ending of the work has been lost, the table of contents shows that it was in fact completed (see *Historia comitum Guisnensis*, p. 54).

Comedy in a Violent World

Guines was a violent place at the time that Lambert was writing, for it was the turf over which the counts of Flanders and kings of France fought directly between 1180 and 1214. Before that the King of France had intervened whenever there was a Flemish succession crisis, of which there were many. The counts of Guines were drawn into these wars to various degrees, although at the end they were necessarily in the thick of things. However, the violent events that most interested Lambert were relatively local ones, which he might describe with considerable detail. Actual battles are all described without comic flourishes, and with sensitivity to the losses involved on all sides. For instance, when Lambert describes a battle during the succession crisis in Guines (1137–ca. 1142), he treats all sides seriously, albeit in epic style with alternating passages of prose and poetry. His description of the wounding of Baldwin of Ardres is solemn and formal (ch. 58; p. 99).

This is very much in contrast to Lambert's treatment of the wounding and death of one of the early semilegendary counts of Guines, Ralph, a horrible and avaricious man, "so pervaded by the trait of prodigious prodigality, that what he possessed could not suffice him." One day, when Ralph was going to one of those "execrable festivals they call tournaments," he runs into some shepherds and, wanting to see what they really think of him, disguises himself and asks them. This is a bad move, for they have nothing good to say and reply:

> While he strives to equal Hercules, Hector and Achilles, he rampages among his followers, scourging and torturing and beating them. And although he is not ignorant of how *to wage war against the proud*, he little *knows to spare* his wretched subjects. How can this little piece of land satisfy a man whom the whole world could not sate? ... Would that he would drown in the depths of the Seine or the Loire before he returns, or that his eyes would be struck out by an ambush or arrow, so that he cannot come back to punish us further. Or may his guts be run through by the spear of some Romulus, so that his noxious blood will be shed and flow into the depths of Hell!

Lambert then portrays the shepherds as a sort of Greek chorus, cursing the count: "With one voice the companions all cry out; / And say, 'Heed, Nemesis! Bring this about!'" (ch. 18; pp. 65–67). As the reader subsequently finds out, Nemesis obliges.

The comedy in this anecdote works on several levels. These are, after all, some mightily well-educated people for a group of bumpkins: they know the names of the classical heroes, they quote Virgil, and they call upon Nemesis. So part of the fun is the incongruity between the class of the speakers and the high-flown language they use, including a final speech rendered in poetry by the author. But the joke also lies in the uncanny ability of Nemesis to kill the count in all three ways mentioned in the shepherds' curse at once. At the tournament, he is run through the navel with a spear, then shot in the eye with an arrow as his men try to remove him from the field. His men then drop him and run, and the other side despoils him and throws him in the Seine.

Arnold III of Ardres is another lord whose violent end is related in comic terms. Arnold is at fault for the hostility that led to his death, as he was guilty of "harsh monstrosity" (ch. 135; p. 170). His subjects consequently conspired to murder him; they couldn't take him to court because he had already been excommunicated by the bishop for nonappearance. In an initial comic touch, Lambert describes Arnold leaving Ardres so that the priest could say Mass, and sneaking back so he can hear it covertly. That this is the Feast of the Holy Innocents is particularly ironic, since Arnold is anything but innocent. While he is standing outside the church, Arnold is enticed away by one of the conspirators, who tells him that a peasant was cutting down the tallest oak in the forest:

> Now as that man [Arnold] was avaricious and grasping with regard to land and harsh and tyrannical toward his subjects, as I have already said, he hoped and thought with respect to this countryman, that he might get a lot of money from this rustic (who nevertheless didn't exist). So he went alone into Fulbert's Wood with only the betrayer, so that he would not, perchance, be discovered by the countryman. But as he hurried by himself with this man alone along the very narrow path toward the sound made by the traitors, who were hammering on an oak to imitate the sound of a peasant's axe cutting down the oak, the traitor and hireling followed him. Taking out a club ... he struck down (alas!) the lord (alas!) the warlike knight or rather the glory of knighthood (alas!), the man *more beautiful in body than the sons of* Flanders [Ps. 45:2].... And the other accomplices to this betrayal and those who were privy to the plot hastened and laid hands on him; they took out swords or rather most unmerciful daggers and slit his throat without mercy. (ch. 135; p. 170)

The humor here would seem to lie partially in the description of Arnold as "harsh and tyrannical" combined with his assimilation to a type of Christ, betrayed by Judas, and also assimilation to the king, more beautiful than the sons of men in Psalm 44 (in the Vulgate), who reigns with justice and truth (neither of which are Arnold's long suits). It also lies partially in the vivid description of the conspirators hammering on a tree to imitate the sound of the axe falling (since they were not *actually* cutting down a tree, they may have hoped for deniability in the event that Arnold escaped, for there would be no evidence), and partly in wordplay, because a short dagger was called a *misericordia*, a "mercy," because it delivered the "mercy stroke" that dispatched the fatally wounded quickly, but there was no mercy in their use here. (This pun also works nicely in French, where the shared term is *misericorde*.) Finally, all of the parenthetical ejaculations are so hyperbolic as to appear comical.

Lambert's humor takes on a bitter flavor when he describes coercive violence used against the powerless. Gertrude of Aalst, the wife of Arnold II of Ardres, plays a trick on a peasant woman much like the one perpetrated by her husband on the peasant buffoon from the opening anecdote. When her men are collecting sheep for her farm, they demand sheep from a woman who has none but whose children are weeping with hunger. The woman tells them that she will gladly send one of her children in lieu of the sheep (perhaps she envisioned the child becoming a household servant). The servants report this to the lady, who demands the child and then treats the little girl as a piece of property, enserfing her (ch. 129; pp. 162–63). Here, as in the story of Gertrude's husband, the trick involves taking someone at his or her literal word. As the mother had not specified her intentions, Gertrude was left free to embrace the interpretation of the woman's words that were least advantageous to the speaker. But the incident also shows that Gertrude and Arnold were a fitting pair in their savagery.

Lambert employs a similar ironic tone when he describes the improvements Arnold II of Guines made to Ardres in 1196 or 1197, a period of famine. Lambert begins by presenting the work as a pleasurable distraction for the poor and a "marvelous [*mirificum*] spectacle" for the rich, who idled there. This already gently mocking language becomes increasingly ironic, as Lambert suggests that the spectacle is so powerful that only those barely clinging to life would not enjoy it: "Who, indeed, unless he were lazy or nearly dead of old age and care, would not have delighted to see the ever so learned Simon the builder, the master of the geometrical work, proceed hither and yon with his stick in a magisterial way?" Finally Lambert unleashes his most bitter humor, asking who would not enjoy watching Simon tear up "houses and granges and cut down flowering orchards and fruit-bearing trees" and dig up "gardens full of vegetables and flax ... although some people raged and groaned and cursed him in silence?" (ch. 152; p. 190). As in the first anecdote, the story begins lightly and ends in pain, with the words shifting in meaning as the paragraph progresses. We may imagine the reader nodding in assent, becoming uneasy, and then, like those who watched their gardens destroyed, succumbing to dismay.

But Is This Supposed to Be Funny?

But how are we to know that this humor is intentional? And if it is, how it is intended to be received and by whom? Humor has always been seen as an innate human capacity, and there has been general agreement since the eighteenth century that it arises from incongruity.[4] However, as outsiders, our

---

[4] Peter L. Berger, *Redeeming Laughter: The Comic Dimension of Human Experience* (New York: Walter de Gruyter, 1997), esp. chapter 1, "The Comic Intrusion."

sense of what is incongruous is not trustworthy.⁵ We see the juxtaposition of urinating and lactating fountains and sacred subjects as weird and therefore funny, but those who lived in the fifteenth century did not necessarily see them in this way.⁶ Humor is always culturally contextual.

And even if we know that a joke is being told, how are we to know what it is? In Dudo of Saint-Quentin's famous account of the Norman Hrolf doing homage to Charles the Straightforward in 911, Hrolf refuses to kiss the king's foot, instead delegating that responsibility to one of his henchmen. The henchman, refusing to stoop, brings the king's foot to his mouth, toppling the king over backward, whereupon the assembled crowd all laugh.⁷ But what is the joke? Is it the pratfall (in almost all cultures good for a laugh)? Is it that the Normans turn the tables on the king, who hoped to humiliate them by demanding that his foot be kissed (not a part of homage)? Is it that this action foreshadows the Norman role in toppling the last Carolingians (Dudo was writing from the vantage point of a century in the future, around 1015), in which case it may not be a "joke" at all?

One approach to the problem is to look for cues that jokes are being told, such as the laughter of the Normans or the use of words indicative of humor. In a general study of "emotion words," Barbara Rosenwein provides several lists as a starting point for a fuller investigation. Only two of these words, however, relate to humor or comedy, *hilaritas* and *risus*.⁸ To these one might add others: *ludibrium*, *cachinnum*, *facetus*, *ludus*, and *hilarior*.⁹ But Lambert

---

[5] See the still-relevant comments of Clifford Geertz, "'From the Native's Point of View': On the Nature of Anthropological Understanding," *Bulletin of the American Academy of Arts and Sciences* 28.1 (1974): 26–45, about the difficulty of grasping "experience-near" feelings from outside that context, which is precisely the position historians find themselves in vis-à-vis the past.

[6] Catherine Emerson, "Are You Taking the Piss(e)? Early Appearances of the Urinating Boy in the Low Countries and Northern France," in *Grant Risee? The Medieval Comic Presence/La présence comique médiévale: Essays in Memory of Brian J. Levy*, ed. Adrian P. Tudor and A. Hindley (Turnhout, Belgium: Brepols, 2006), pp. 31–47. In their introductory essay in the same volume ("The Medieval Comic Presence," pp. 1–16), Tudor and Hindley also point out that "the kind of laughter which may seem out of place today need not always be considered disrespectful" (p. 9).

[7] Dudo of Saint-Quentin, *De moribus et actis primorum Normanniae ducum auctore Dudone Sancti Quintini decano*, ed. Jules Lair (Caen: Le Blanc-Hardel, 1865), pp. 168–69. Emily H. Albu in "Dudo of Saint-Quentin: The Heroic Past Imagined," *Haskins Society Journal* 6 (1994): 111–18, and *The Normans in Their Histories: Propaganda, Myth and Subversion* (Woodbridge, UK: Boydell, 2001), pp. 40–44, has noted the parodic and satiric elements in this text.

[8] Barbara H. Rosenwein, "Emotion Words," in *Le sujet des émotions au Moyen Âge*, ed. Piroska Nagy and Damien Boquet (Paris: Beauchesne, 2008), pp. 101, 103 [93–106].

[9] Ross Balzaretti, "Liutprand of Cremona's Sense of Humor," in *Humor, History, and Politics in Late Antiquity and the Early Middle Ages*, ed. Guy Halsall (Cambridge: Cambridge University Press, 2002), p. 117 [114–28].

gives few signals as to his intentions apart from his use of the word *mirabile* and its variants.

In the absence of such verbal cues, it may be helpful to situate Lambert's writing in the comic context of both vernacular and Latin contemporary writing, particularly since Lambert lived his day-to-day life in the vernacular world. The late twelfth century was rife with works that combined comedy and violence. Humor and violence were frequently mixed in the vernacular epic, including some of those that Lambert mentions. The first surviving fabliaux were written in this period in northeastern France, in Arras, around two days' journey from Guines. Violence was common in the fabliaux: Yves Roguet has reckoned that someone is killed in 4 percent of the surviving fabliaux, while someone is struck in 37 percent and threatened in 54 percent.[10] Still, it is clear that people were intended to laugh at least at some of these stories.[11]

Many of the fabliaux feature love triangles in which one of the parties is humiliated, if not injured or killed. Traps and ruses were staples of these stories. One of Lambert's comic stories contains just such a situation, as it contains a mixture of mutual deception, greed, lust, and violence. When Lambert's patron, Arnold II of Guines, catches the eye of Ida, the twice-widowed Countess of Boulogne, at a tournament, the two begin a torrid affair. Ida burns with the kind of lust later associated with the "merry" widow in vernacular texts:

> And hence she enticed Arnold of Guines as much as she could and loved him with a sexual passion, or at least, she pretended she did out of feminine frivolity and deception. Thus, as messengers and secret signs went back and forth between them carrying tokens of true love, Arnold loved her with a similarly loving return – or pretended to love her out of manly prudence and caution. But he did aspire to the land and dignity of the county of Boulogne once he had won the favor of this countess through this exhibition of real – or feigned – love. (ch. 93; p. 126)

Ida, however, has another suitor, Renaud of Dammartin. She wavers back and forth between Arnold and Renaud (whom she eventually marries), lusting after the one most likely to be attainable at any given moment. In the end, Renaud carries her off, at which point she lures Arnold in to "rescue" her. The story ends with Arnold captured and fleeced for ransom, returning home humiliated but perhaps wiser (ch. 94–95; pp. 126–29). The existence of fabliaux about the fall of the unwary, the greedy, the hypocritical, and the headstrong would have primed the audience to see the humor in this story,

---

[10] Yves Roguet, "La violence comique des fabliaux," in *La violence dans le monde médiéval*, Senefiance 36 (Aix-en-Provence: Centre Universitaire d'Études et de Recherches Médiévales d'Aix, 1994), p. 457 [457–68].

[11] Berger, *Redeeming Laughter*, p. 52, points out that we may well laugh at a joke even if we find it offensive because the joke breaks through our proprieties.

despite its violent implications, and also to accept Ida's responsibility, since the women in these stories were frequently duplicitous.

A humorous approach to violence also appears in Latin satire. Although satire was written before the twelfth century, the twelfth century, if it did not rediscover satire, certainly produced it in a quantity that had not been equaled since antiquity.[12] It is simply impossible to list all the authors of the period who either wrote satires or dipped in the satiric well, although satire had a stronger presence among Latin writers than in the vernacular in the twelfth century. Historians of this period, even those writing from monastic environments, could and did draw on satire for their work and were more likely to do so the more seriously they took their role as moral instructors, for twelfth-century readers of satire saw it as a mode of reproving vice.[13]

Satire was certainly part of his education, but Lambert may also have met some of the satirists of his day. William aux Blanches Mains, the brother-in-law of Louis VII and the brother of Henry the Liberal of Champagne, who first served as bishop-elect of Chartres, then as archbishop of Sens and then of Reims, was a notable literary patron.[14] (William's brother Henry and his sister-in-law Marie of Champagne were patrons of both Latin and vernacular works.) Walter of Châtillon, the author of satiric poetry, dedicated his verse epic the *Alexandreis* to William, and John of Salisbury was probably appointed bishop of Chartres at William's direction.[15] William came to Guines at least once (ch. 87; pp. 120–21), so Lambert would have met him and others in his entourage. Who knows what sorts of literary exchanges (or violent jokes) there may have been?

Putting Comedy and Violence to Work

No matter where comedy crops up, however, it does social work. The fabliaux, at least in some cases, seem to have represented a sort of revenge humor, in which resented people get their comeuppance and the hearers can

---

[12] On the place of satire in twelfth-century literature, see Rodney M. Thomson, "The Origins of Latin Satire in Twelfth-Century Europe," *Mittellateinisches Jahrbuch* 13 (1978): 73–83. See also Ronald E. Pepin, *Literature of Satire in the Twelfth Century: A Neglected Mediaeval Genre* (Lewiston, NY: Edwin Mellen Press, 1988).

[13] Estrella Pérez Rodríguez, "Reading Juvenal in the Twelfth Century," *Journal of Medieval Latin* 17 (2007): 239–41 [238–52], notes that a discussion of this point was part of the normal *accessus* to the satires of Juvenal.

[14] Thomas Haye, "*Nemo Mecenas, nemo modo Cesar*: Die Idee der Literaturförderung in der lateinischen Dichtung des hohen Mittelalters," *Classica et mediaevalia: Revue danoise de philologie et d'histoire* 55 (2004): 214n28 [203–27].

[15] See Ludwig Falkenstein, "Guillaume aux Blanches Mains, archevêque de Reims et légat du siège apostolique," *Revue d'histoire de l'Église de France* 91 (2005): 10 [5–25].

identify with the winners.[16] The combination of comedy and violence in the epics played a different role for the most part. In most of the epics, the audience was encouraged to laugh "with" the heroes of the tale (who generally survived) and to have sympathy for their plight, thus reinforcing noble values.[17] In satire, however, the comically violent story was a weapon of social critique. Most Latin satire was written to be enjoyed by an in-group.[18] Lambert's scope wasn't as narrow, however, nor was his work solely influenced by Latin satire, although the burden of his stories was always moral. In the case of the murders of Ralph of Guines and Arnold III of Ardres, avarice and cruelty render the victims odious, and in both cases the avarice arose from overspending in other areas; the court satirists often connected avarice with its opposite, prodigality.[19] For Lambert, Ralph's excessive avarice was connected to his prodigality, because the more he gave to his retinue, the more revenue he needed to support this giving (ch. 18; p. 65). Similarly, Arnold III was gracious to his knights but harsh to his subjects. Lambert does not accuse his patron, Arnold II of Guines, directly of avarice, but he does accuse him of extraordinary prodigality, as he gives away everything he has (and some things that belong to others) when he is knighted (ch. 91; p. 124). Lambert attributes Arnold's humiliation at Ida's hands to his having levied a tithe to go on crusade and then spending the money in riotous living (ch. 95; p. 128). However, the realities of power remain: the powerful are only sometimes punished for their actions, and those who punish them suffer dearly for it if they are not themselves powerful. The only remedy against such people may be the punishment in the court of opinion that Lambert offers. After all, what else can it mean to say that Arnold II's summary execution of a pathetic drunk is a "marvelous feat" if it is not an invitation to laugh at a man who had provided enough drink at his own wedding for it to resemble the "triennial feast of Bacchus" (ch. 123; p. 156). What else could Arnold have expected?

---

[16] Giovanna Angeli, "Du récit à la scène: Rire grinçant et sadisme ludique de la farce," in *Quant l'ung amy pour l'autre veille: Mélanges de moyen français offert à Claude Thiry*, ed. M Colombo Timelli and T. Van Hemelryck (Turnhout, Belgium: Brepols, 2008), pp. 355–56 [349–59].

[17] See Manuel Braun, "Mitlachen oder Verlachen? Zum Verhältnis non Komik und Gewalt in der Heldenepik," in *Gewalt im Mittelalter: Realitäten-Imaginationen*, ed. Manuel Braun and Cornelia Herberichs (Munich: Wilhelm Fink Verlag, 2005), pp. 381–410, esp. pp. 395–400.

[18] Thomson, "Origins of Latin Satire," 76, comments about satire, "It is not a product of folk-literature, but of higher education." For similar thoughts, see Berger, *Redeeming Laughter*, p. 69, who sees most sorts of humor as rooted in the real world, except for the humor of "esoteric esthetic elites who cultivate an idiosyncratic sense of humor that deliberately eschews what other people find amusing."

[19] See John of Salisbury, *Entheticus maior*, in John of Salisbury, *Entheticus maior et minor*, ed. and trans. Jan van Laarhoven, 3 vols (Leiden: Brill, 1987), vol. 1, 3.86–87, ll. 1301–24, pp. 190–93; John of Hauville, *Architrennius*, ed. and trans. Winthrop Wetherbee (Cambridge: Cambridge University Press, 1994), 5.9–6.10, pp. 128–61.

Lambert's approach to violence reflects contemporary discussions of violence and dissolute conduct in a period when both clerics, through "learned moralizing," and the most important secular rulers, through "accountability," were attempting to bring "coercive power" under control.[20] In this case the learned moralizing was in Latin, but Stephen of Fougères was addressing the same issues in his vernacular *Livre des manières* in the previous generation, albeit without the comedy.[21] Ideas about appropriate conduct for the powerful passed back and forth between Latin and French discourses, ultimately culminating in vernacular treatises on chivalry and the chivalric deeds of heroes rescuing the abused from their abusers.

These observations lead to a final question. If at least part of the function of Lambert's history was to offer a critique of a violent lordship uninformed by the restraints of law and custom, and if the means by which Lambert carried out this critique is to ridicule those who engage in this kind of violence, and if the figures he ridiculed were ancestors of his patrons, for whom could he really have intended the work? One cannot imagine that Baldwin II of Guines would have been pleased with the way he was depicted, as a short, touchy man who couldn't keep his drawers on and would rather go hunting than go to Mass (ch. 87–89; pp. 120–23). Although Lambert praises Baldwin's interest in learning – he was a restlessly curious man, deeply interested in books, which he had translated for his use and kept in his library, which had its own librarian – his comment that Baldwin dared to argue with the clergy contains a quiet rebuke (ch. 80–81; pp. 113–15). Lambert does say he began the work to regain Baldwin's favor, but he seems to have waited until after Baldwin's death to publish it.

Arnold II of Guines was probably a safer patron. It is possible that Lambert was confident that Arnold would never read the work, as he was unlikely to have known Latin.[22] Arnold also seems to have been more even-tempered than his father, an impression confirmed by Lambert's contemporary William of Andres.[23] So Lambert may have felt it safe to give Arnold a book in which

---

[20] On this subject see Thomas N. Bisson, *The Crisis of the Twelfth Century: Power, Lordship, and the Origins of European Government* (Princeton, NJ: Princeton University Press, 2009). Although Bisson deals with these issues throughout his book, see esp. pp. 322–28 (on accountability) and pp. 445–56 (on learned moralizing). For the culture of "learned moralizing" about power in the twelfth century, see also Richard W. Kaeuper, *Chivalry and Violence in Medieval Europe* (Oxford: Oxford University Press, 1999), pp. 12–19.

[21] Étienne de Fougères, *Le livre des manières*, ed. R. Anthony Lodge (Geneva: Droz, 1979).

[22] See the "Introduction" in my translation of the *History of the Counts of Guines*, p. 8 [1–40].

[23] Shopkow, "The Narrative Constructions of the Famous (or Infamous) and Fearful Virago, Beatrice of Bourbourg," *Historical Reflections: Réflexions historiques* 30 (2004): 64–65 [55–71].

Arnold came in for some personal criticism softened by humor, while also receiving some praise for his undoubted merits, and his father, who sometimes disapproved of his heir (see ch. 92; p. 124), and his more remote forebears came in for rather more mockery. It was a book of advice in the guise of a history, but it was designed to be palatable to the man who paid the bills. Lambert may even have taken it upon himself to interpret his work for his lord. The work *was* for Arnold's glory, if he grasped the "morality," for he would then be a good and successful lord. It is impossible to say whether Lambert spelled out this purpose at the end of his book, for that end is now lost, but this program can be discerned hovering in the text itself. And a bit of comedy, authorized for lay hearers by fabliaux and epics, might have helped the satiric lessons go down more smoothly.

In writing this work, Lambert took his place beside the other satirical writers of the second half of the twelfth century, who would have recognized its strategies and its moral framework. Perhaps he hoped for "over-readers" – that is, readers to whom the text was not explicitly addressed. John of Salisbury clearly expected readers for the *Entheticus maior* from among the learned denizens of the courts he frequented.[24] For patrons of this kind of work and the writers who wrote for them had to share a language,[25] not just the Latin language in this case, but a moral language. All involved had to be able to look at violence in a sufficiently distanced way to appreciate a little mockery that would reveal the illusions of vainglory by which the world often deceived knights (ch. 33; p. 80).

The impulses that drove Lambert, however, were turned in other directions in the following generations. The twelfth century was the high-water mark for Latinity in Western Europe[26] and perhaps for literary experimentation also. It was certainly not the last time that comedy and violence were mixed together in the same stew, but Latin histories turned in a different and more sober direction, as increasingly their audience was clerical. It was left to vernacular works more clearly directed at lay audiences – sermons, fabliaux, epics, and satires – to mix laughter with tears and teach against violence through the "marvelous feats" of comedy.

---

[24] Jonathan M. Newman, "Satire between School and Court: The Ethical Interpretation of the *Artes* in John of Salisbury's *Entheticus in dogmata philosophorum*," *Journal of Medieval Latin* 17 (2007): 125 [125–42].

[25] Haye, "*Nemo Mecenas*," 212–14, 225.

[26] Michael Richter, "A Socio-Linguistic Approach to the Latin Middle Ages," in *The Materials, Sources and Methods of Ecclesiastical History*, ed. Derek Baker (Oxford: Blackwell, 1975), pp. 69–82.

6

Dismembered Borders and Treasonous Bodies in Anglo-Norman Historiography

MATTHEW FISHER

From 1272 to 1307, Edward I wielded the power of the English monarchy and a formidable bureaucracy against a seemingly endless list of enemies domestic, foreign, and merely adjacent. The innovations in legal theory and practice that took place during his reign were numerous, but concurrent with the processes of legal systemization and standardization there were rampant abuses and glaring exceptions. One of those exceptions was treason, an act of war punished as a capital crime and manufactured as a series of spectacles anticipating its legal definition.[1] Those judged guilty of treason were subjected to extreme punishments applied in new combinations and sequences: they were dragged on the ground to the place of execution before being subjected to ritual punishments, including hanging, dismemberment, and various combinations of beheading, disembowelment, castration, and burning. Among other aims, such elaborate executions were staged to be interpreted. That is, execution represented an attempt by the monarchy to shape the context and reception of the dismembered and disseminated body, particularly those of Welsh and Scottish insurgents who rebelled against English rule. Confronted by the dismembered quarters of treasonous bodies, some contemporary chroniclers described those partial bodies as texts to be read exegetically, corroborating the moralizing, tropological narrative shaped by king and court, a narrative in which punishment responds to crime. Beyond these causal and explanatory narratives, however, there remained a contest over how to embed the readings of dismembered bodies in larger historiographical narratives. The spectacle of the scaffold did not resolve the

---

[1] Reading public execution as spectacle is, of course, indebted to Michel Foucault, *Discipline and Punish: The Birth of the Prison*, trans. A. Sheridan (1977; New York: Vintage, 1995). Note the important reconsideration of Foucault in Lorna Hutson, "Rethinking the 'Spectacle of the Scaffold': Juridical Epistemologies and English Revenge Tragedy," *Representations* 89 (2005): 30–58. See also Katherine Royer, "The Body in Parts: Reading the Execution Ritual in Late Medieval England," *Historical Reflections* 29 (2003): 319–39.

ambiguities of the dismembered body, which at once witnessed the ritualized humiliation of the king's enemies and recalled the relics of saints' bodies.[2]

The political and military conflicts between the English and their Welsh and Scottish neighbors occupied much of Edward I's reign. His successful conquest of the Welsh in 1284 erased what had been a border between the two countries, however unstable it had been. The 1284 Statute of Rhuddlan incorporated Wales into England and imposed upon it England's laws and its bureaucracy, bringing Edward's rule over the island of Britain closer to the unity under the legendary Brutus imagined by Geoffrey of Monmouth in the *Historia regum Brittaniae*.[3] Scotland proved more intractable, and despite its crisis of succession in the last decade of the thirteenth century, Edward never ruled over the whole island. The border between the two countries was marked by continuous and fluid violence flowing in both directions. Against this backdrop, Edward I and his lawyers developed what would come to be known as the "royal thesis of treason."[4] Articulated not against domestic (English) enemies, but very specifically against the rebellions of the Welsh and Scottish, war against the king became a judicial crime rather than a military proposition. This effectively transformed the narrativization of antiroyal conflict from what was the moralization of a military contest, assessed as right and wrong, into a judicial frame of crime and punishment. Slippage between the two narrative frames is, of course, always possible, and medieval texts staged a contest over narrating the same events and shaping their interpretation.

Torture as the core of the process of execution is essentially public. As Foucault describes for a later period, "The tortured body is first inscribed in the legal ceremonial that must produce, open for all to see, the truth of the crime" (*Discipline and Punish*, p. 35). The ceremony marks the power of the sovereign for his subjects, but it also points to the precarious nature of that power: executing the traitor simultaneously registers the threat posed by the traitor to the king as authentic. In a similar fashion, the tortured body anticipates the tortures of the damned soul, offering its audience the continuous narrative of condemnation authorized by the crown. Again, though, such a reading is precarious in the medieval world, where suffering and humiliation can mark heavenly favor and even blessedness rather than certain damnation. It is this doubled set of interpretations of political opposition and bloody

---

[2] See Caroline Walker Bynum, *Resurrection of the Body in Western Christianity, 200–1336* (New York: Columbia University Press, 1995).

[3] See, broadly, Rees Davies, *The First English Empire* (Oxford: Oxford University Press, 2000) and *The Age of Conquest: Wales 1063–1415* (Oxford: Oxford University Press, 1987); and David Carpenter, *The Struggle for Mastery: Britain 1066–1284* (Oxford: Oxford University Press, 2003).

[4] See J. G. Bellamy, *The Law of Treason in England in the Later Middle Ages* (Cambridge: Cambridge University Press, 1970), p. 39.

public execution that trouble Edward I's executions of his Welsh and Scottish enemies. The dismembered body of the traitor recalls too closely the dismembered body of the saint, something made more problematic still by Thomas Becket's canonized, legitimate opposition to the king.

Dismembering the Rebel, Uniting the Kingdom

In the wars Edward I conducted against both of England's immediate neighbors, the Welshman Dafydd ap Gruffydd seems to have been the first prominent victim of Edward's judicially structured torture. In 1283, the Welsh annals *Brenhinedd y Saesson* note, Dafydd "was put to a dire death."[5] Dafydd, the brother of the Welsh prince Llywelyn ap Gruffydd, was a party to the incredibly complex political strife between the English and the Welsh throughout the second half of the thirteenth century. Dafydd's relationship with Edward extended back to 1263, when Dafydd had sworn loyalty to him as part of a rebellion against Dafydd's brother Llywelyn, who was by then the "undoubted master of native Wales from early 1258 until his death almost twenty-five years later."[6] Dafydd was the first to experience Edward's performatively orchestrated and judicially justified execution process.[7] Writing soon after Dafydd's execution in 1283, the Oseney annalist remarks that it was "morti retroactis temporibus inauditae" [a type of death hitherto unheard of].[8] Since the Oseney annalist, who was located some 125 miles away from the event itself in Shrewsbury, heard of the execution and wrote about it for his monastic brethren and wider audiences, such torture and

---

[5] Quoted in *Brut y Tywysogyon or The Chronicle of the Princes: Peniarth MS 20 Version*, trans. T. Jones (Aberystwyth: University of Wales Press, 1952): "Ac yno nos Nodolic y llas ef o angav gorthrwm" [And there (Shrewsbury) on Christmas Eve he was put to a dire death] (p. 217). Continuations to the text of the *Brut y Tywysogyon* in Peniarth MS 20 extend to 1332, and the manuscript can be dated to the fourteenth century.

[6] Davies, *Conquest*, p. 317. See also Danielle Westerhof, "Deconstructing Identities on the Scaffold: The Execution of Hugh Despenser the Younger, 1326," *Journal of Medieval History* 33 (2007): 87–106. Westerhof notes, "Only five underwent the full range of capital punishments … [Dafydd ap Gruffydd], William Wallace (1305), Gilbert Middleton (1318) … Andrew Harclay (1323) … [and Hugh Despenser the Younger (1326)]" (101).

[7] See Bellamy, *The Law of Treason*, p. 23n2. Bellamy notes, "In the process at Shrewsbury against David ap Gruffydd in 1282 the English state trial had its origins and the *quasi* treason of levying war against the king took on a new status and importance" (p. 24). See also Robert Bartlett, *The Hanged Man: A Story of Miracle, Memory, and Colonialism in the Middle Ages* (Princeton, NJ: Princeton University Press, 2006), pp. 47–48.

[8] Printed as *Annales Monasteria de Oseneia* in *Annales monastici*, ed. Henry Richards Luard, 4 vols (London: Longmans, Green, Reader, and Dyer, 1864–69), 4:294 [3–352].

execution ceased to be "unheard of." Edward I's execution practices were emphatically made visible to all, both in England and across the border in Wales, and the exceptional was instead used to set precedent. The distribution of Dafydd's quarters throughout the island crafted a political narrative, a rhetoric of execution that signified complexly across temporal and geographical boundaries, marking the end of Dafydd ap Gruffydd, the end of the Welsh revolt against Edward I, and the end of Welsh sovereignty.[9] Dafydd's dismemberment points to Edward's attempt to reassemble the island into a political, not merely a geographical, whole.

Evincing rather more relish in the gory details than his colleague at Oseney Abbey, the annalist recording the Dunstaple Annals vividly enumerates the punishments Dafydd suffered. More intriguingly, he offers an exegetical commentary teasing out the judicial reimagination of political acts, typologically connecting the punishments to his putative crimes:

> Quia proditor fuit domini regis, qui eum militem fecerat; tractus est equis lento passau ad locum suspendii. Quia homicidium fecerat Fulconis Trigald, et aliorum nobilium Angliae; suspensus est vivus. Quia illud fecit tempore Dominicae Passionis; propter blasphemiam viscera ejus incendio sunt cremata. Quia in pluribus locis Angliae mortem domini regis fuerat machinatus; membratim est partitus, et per climata Angliae ad terrorem malignantium destinatus. Caput autem ejus in Turri Londoniae super palum altissimam est affixum, versus mare.[10]

> [Because he was a traitor to the lord king, for whom he had done military service, he was drawn slowly by a horse to the place of his hanging. Because he had murdered Fulk Trigald and other English noblemen, he was hanged alive. Because he did these deeds during Easter and was thus a blasphemer, he was disemboweled and his viscera burned. Because he had plotted the death of the king in several places in England, his body was divided and sent to the corners of England, to the terror of those inclined to doing evil. His head, however, is at the Tower of London, affixed to the highest stake, facing the sea.]

Seemingly unperturbed by the graphic details, the author of the Dunstaple Annals then relates that in the same year there was a request for aid to support the wars in Wales and also describes how both the abbey's bakery and the brewery underwent significant construction. The jarring juxtaposition of the momentous and the trivial is a classic annalistic gesture, but in the process Dafydd's tortured body no longer has the exceptional status of having endured

---

[9] Davies, *Conquest*, pp. 351–54.

[10] Printed as *Annales de Dunstaplia* in *Annales monastici*, 3:294 [3–408]. The Dunstaple Annals survive in London, British Library MS Cotton Tiberius A.x, which preserves a number of hands following the entry for 1221, but, as the text's editor Luard notes, "none later than the thirteenth century" (*Annales monastici*, 3:ix).

a new type of punishment, previously "unheard of." Instead the Dunstaple Annals present a controlled reading of the execution that makes safe the spectacle of the execution itself by embedding it in a manifestly continuing narrative of English judicial and royal power. The display of the power of the state becomes, in this reading, a measured response to extreme crimes committed, framed by the logic of criminal and religious justice.[11] The interpretive structure of the Annals' reading palliates the violence of the ritual, diminishing the horror of the execution in a rhetoric of legal and legalistic justification. The piecemeal legal explication of Dafydd's multiple crimes renders what was wholly innovative about his execution as a logical consequence of his crimes. His head was sent to London, and his body "to four English cities."[12] Dafydd's partial body, at once foreign and conquered, thus mirrors Edward I's absorption of Wales into England.

The reading of Dafydd ap Gruffydd's execution in the Dunstaple Annals is shaped by the formulations of the legal sentence. The execution offers its audiences a narrative that not only can be understood as the cause and effect of crime and punishment but is also open to the complex and plural responses of multiple audiences, including those present at the various stages of the execution itself, the residents of those towns in which Dafydd's quarters and head were displayed, and the writers and readers of historiographical texts that retold the execution. The narrative of the execution thus extends beyond the killing; the dissemination of the parts of an executed body transforms those parts into texts, a record available to those not present either temporally or spatially that attests to the emphatically past nature of a life once lived. Transferred from the initial spectacle to the dismembered body, the narrative of the execution can be read in accordance with the ideological agendas of the authors of the execution as an injunction against emulation – that is, as a warning not to rebel against the sovereign power of England. In turn, readers of the dismembered text rely upon a doubled imagination, projecting their identity and personal political narratives onto the partial body and simultaneously reading death and dismemberment onto their own bodies. But this imagined "terror" for those "inclined to doing evil," as the Dunstaple annalist describes it, is only one of the possible multiple narratives written by the body parts of the executed. Read teleologically, from treason to inevitable execution, the body offers a narrative framed by the executioner, an argument that the execution was an act of justice rather than of war. Still within that frame, the audience must also read the implicit narrative of the traitor's

---

[11] Thus Foucault writes in *Discipline and Punish*, "It pinned the public torture on the crime itself; it established from one to the other a series of decipherable relations" (p. 44).

[12] J. B. Smith, "Dafydd ap Gruffudd (*d.* 1283)," in *Oxford Dictionary of National Biography*, 60 vols (Oxford: Oxford University Press, 2004), 14:895–97. Dafydd was executed at Shrewsbury, but no source I am aware of specifies the cities to which his body was sent.

life lived before the condemnation and execution as inevitable. The body divided, however, becomes multiple texts and enables audiences to decode or construct multiple potential narratives. Audiences might variously resist the tidy story of crime and punishment that judicial power seeks to tell as authenticating its own process.

Constructing Texts around the Dismembered Body

After the conquest and legal absorption of Wales into the newly expanded English kingdom, a series of events led to the unexpected failure of the Scottish royal line and the protracted debate over Scottish sovereignty known as the Scottish Question.[13] The last decade of the thirteenth century saw Edward engage with the idea of English overlordship over Scotland, a contest that took place first in the courts but later on the battlefield. The cultural legacy of one of Edward I's more successful enemies, the legendary Scottish rebel William Wallace, is nuanced and manifold, given the continued currency of his role in contemporary formations of Scottish identity.[14] Wallace's execution and his divided body attracted competing narratives in the historiographical record. Consider the unique account found in the *Annales Londonienses*, attributed to the Londoner Andrew Horn, chamberlain of the city from 1320 to 1328.[15] The *Annales* describe Wallace's execution in 1305 thus: he was "detrahatur" [dragged] from Westminster to the Tower of London, on to Aldgate, and then to Smithfield, a rather circuitous route of some five miles.[16] Wallace was then "suspendatur et postea devaletur" [hanged and disemboweled], "decapitetur" [decapitated], and "decolletur" [quartered]. Finally, "cor, hepar et pulmo et omnia interiora ... comburentur" [his heart, liver, lungs, and entrails were burned]. Wallace's quarters, as they are technically known, were then to be displayed in Newcastle, Berwick, Stirling, and Perth. His head was to be placed over London Bridge, where those responsible for arranging the grisly trophy needed to take care that it was "conspectu tam per terram quam per aquam transeuntium" [visible to both those crossing by land and those on the river] (*Annales Londoniensis*, p. 142). This last clause is notable: those

---

[13] See R. James Goldstein, *The Matter of Scotland* (Lincoln, NE: University of Nebraska Press, 1993).

[14] See Andrew Fisher, *William Wallace* (Edinburgh: John Donald, 2001).

[15] Printed in *Chronicles of the Reigns of Edward I and Edward II*, ed. W. Stubbs, 2 vols, Rolls Series (London: Longman and Co., 1882–83), 1:3–251. See also Jeremy Catto, "Andrew Horn: Law and History in Fourteenth-Century England," in *The Writing of History in the Middle Ages*, ed. R. H. C. Davis and J. M. Wallace-Hadrill (Oxford: Oxford University Press, 1981), pp. 367–91, and Ralph Hanna, *London Literature, 1300–1380* (Cambridge: Cambridge University Press, 2005).

[16] "Detrahatur a palatio Westmonasterii usque Turrim Londoniarum, et a Turri usque Allegate, et sic per medium civitatis usque Elmes" (*Annales Londonienses*, p. 141).

who sentenced Wallace seemed concerned that the dismembered body of the traitor would be visible, and thus available to be witnessed and to be read by all those passing by. Beyond offering an obvious warning to any would-be Scottish rebels residing in London (surely a very small population), the distribution of Wallace's quarters to four northern and Scottish towns was also a pointedly provocative gesture, one that worked to enlarge the audience of the spectacle of the execution. Not only did Wallace's body parts engage those geographically diverse audiences, forcing them to view Wallace's death as a local experience, but the body also tied the peripheries of the country to the central site of execution, evoking the extent of Edward's power.

In the first quarter of the fourteenth century, and thus within a few years of Wallace's death, the Augustinian canon Piers Langtoft composed his Anglo-Norman *Chronicle*. The unresolved similarities and tensions between romance and history writing were productively deployed throughout the late thirteenth and early fourteenth centuries, though Langtoft's text marks the slow decline of Anglo-Norman's role in that dialogue. Translated into Middle English within a few decades of its composition, Langtoft's *Chronicle* offered learned and literate audiences a popular imagination of the past, with all the contradictions such intersecting and overlapping expectations generate. Langtoft notes of Wallace's body:

> Copé li fust le cors en qatre porciouns;
> Chescun pende par say en memor de ses nouns!
> En lu de sa banere cels sunt ses gunfanouns.[17]
>
> [His body was chopped into four parts;
> Each hangs by itself, in memory of his name!
> Instead of his banner these are his gonfanons.]

In Langtoft's account, Wallace's dismembered body points to the memory of his name. The passage emphasizes the pastness of his existence and the strictly incorporeal memory of him that survives; by transforming Wallace's body into a memory of Wallace, the notoriously anti-Scottish Langtoft moves to preclude reading the parts of Wallace's body as relics, rather than, essentially, memento mori. Moreover, Wallace's body parts become his gonfanons, the flags or pennons bearing his heraldic insignia – his arms have become his arms, as it were. The Anglo-Norman "gunfanun" is more typically found in romance texts, such as Thomas's *Romance of Horn, La destructioun de Rome*,

---

[17] See Jean Claude Thiolier's edition of Piers's *Chronicle: Pierre de Langtoft: Le règne d'Édouard Ier* (Créteil, France: Université de Paris XII, 1989), ll. 2360–62. Note that Thiolier presents the texts of two "redactions" of part of the *Chronicle*. See also *The Chronicle of Pierre de Langtoft in French Verse, from the Earliest Period to the Death of King Edward I*, ed. and trans. Thomas Wright, 2 vols (London: Longmans, Green, Reader, and Dyer, 1866–68).

and Thomas of Kent's *Le roman de toute chevalerie*.[18] The heraldic resonance of the dismembered body is significant, and Langtoft's transference of the term to Wallace is noteworthy. The custom of displaying heraldic banners and shields had spread across England and Scotland in the second half of the twelfth century. Heraldry's increasing social importance can be measured by the first appearance of heralds on the royal payroll under Edward I.[19] The symbolic play of the heraldic, then, was very much a feature of Edward I's reign. Heraldry is also about identity, specifically social identity and genealogy. Arms offer the reader a pictorial narrative of social, and thus political, relations extending back through time. For Langtoft, Wallace's dismembered body becomes an encoded text to be read, prompting an audience to recall the consequences of treason, but also pointing to Wallace's own abortive genealogy, a heraldic testament to his defeat.

Langtoft also writes to resist, and indeed to preclude, the sanctification of Wallace's quarters as relics. In addition to the discourse of pastness constructed through the image of Wallace's quarters as his heraldic banners, Langtoft situates Wallace's execution in the midst of the "songs" for which his *Chronicle* is perhaps most famous.[20] There are nine sets of verses in the last part of the *Chronicle* that are commonly described as songs, as some of them are rhetorically presented as if sung by English or Scottish soldiers.[21] Two of the songs are entirely in Middle English, and four of the nine, including the one following the description of Wallace's execution, are in Anglo-Norman and conclude with a Middle English stanza, a casual multilingualism that the

---

[18] See the *Anglo-Norman Dictionary* entry for "gunfanun," available online at www.anglo-norman.net. The word enters Middle English as "gonfanon" and is found almost exclusively in romances in the Auchinleck Manuscript, as well as in Robert Mannyng's translation of this passage.

[19] See David Simpkin, *The English Aristocracy at War: From the Welsh Wars of Edward I to the Battle of Bannockburn* (Woodbridge, UK: Boydell, 2008): "It was not until the 1270s that rolls of arms began to proliferate. ... This growth in heraldic activity may be attributed, to some extent, to Edward I's predilection for all things chivalric and his employment of heralds at the royal court" (pp. 20–21).

[20] See Thea Summerfield, "The Political Songs in the Chronicles of Pierre de Langtoft and Robert Mannyng," in *The Court and Cultural Diversity*, ed. E. Mullally and J. Thompson (Cambridge: D. S. Brewer, 1997), pp. 139–48, and "The Testimony of Writing: Pierre de Langtoft and the Appeals to History, 1291–1306," in *The Scots and Medieval Arthurian Legend*, ed. R. Purdie and N. Royan (Cambridge: D. S. Brewer, 2005), pp. 25–41.

[21] The verses are two-stress tail-rhymed lines, as opposed to the long-line alexandrines of the *Chronicle*, and scribes resorted to various measures to accommodate the verses on the manuscript page, frequently interrupting the single-column *mise en page* with a temporary quasi-bicolumnar layout. They are presented as tail rhyme in at least seven of the nineteen manuscripts that preserve the *Chronicle*, including London, British Library MSS Cotton Julius A.v; Royal 20.A.ii; Harley 114; Cambridge, Cambridge University Library MS Gg.i.1; Sidney Sussex College MS 43; Oxford, Bodleian Library MS Fairfax 24; and All Souls College MS 39.

scribes of most manuscripts found completely untroubling, save the scribe of London, British Library MS Royal 20.A.xi, who felt the need to note "Engleis" in the margin next to the two Middle English songs in that manuscript.[22] The verses again describe the distribution of Wallace's body, this time with a rather scathing irony:

> Pur finir sa geste,
> A Loundres est sa teste.
> Du cors est fet partye
> En .IIII. bones viles,
> Dount honurer les yles
> Ke sunt en Albanye.
> And tus may you here,
> Ai ladde to lere
> To biggen in pays,
> It falles in his eghe
> [Þ]at hackes over heghe
> Witte at Walays.[23]

[To finish the tale, at London is his head. His body is made into pieces, in four good towns, thereby giving honor to the islands that are in Scotland. And thus you may hear: For a lad to learn to dwell in this land, it falls into his eye who chops too high, consider Wallace.]

The verses explicitly end the "geste" of Wallace, and the *Chronicle* has progressed from stressing the emphatic pastness of the "memor de ses [Wallace's] nouns" to an ironic reading of his quarters as "giving honor" to the islands of Scotland and the "good towns" therein. Wallace indeed aimed too high, and the proverbial wisdom cautioning against overweening ambition cleverly deploys "hackes" to resonate strongly with the current state of Wallace's divided body. Langtoft renders Wallace's failure as proverbial and commonplace, fit for the instruction of a young boy, and firmly contextualized as the stuff of schoolroom jingles, thereby precluding the body from being understood as in any way sacred.

Wallace's execution was staged and constructed to generate a particular and dominant narrative, of rebellion met with execution. It offered a discourse positing unimaginable torture and execution as the fitting response to what should be impossible to imagine – treason against the crown. In contrast to the careful explication of Wallace's death, consider the 1279 execution in London of almost three hundred Jews, all accused of coin clipping. Given the

---

[22] See MS Royal 20.A.xi, fols. 110v and 126r.
[23] Langtoft, *Chronicle*, ll. 2363–74. Thiolier edits the Middle English as "Yat hackes over heghe," but "Yat" is surely an error for "þat."

obvious and conventional anti-Semitic tropes surrounding Jews and money, these deaths occasioned little surprise from contemporary chroniclers and annalists, receiving a bare if specific notice in the *Annales Londoniensis*: "et .ccxciii. Juedaei distracti et suspensi" [and 293 Jews were drawn and hung].[24] The *Annales* do not construct this into a judicial narrative rather than a record of crime and execution: here the workings of justice do not require explication, as the deed was never potentially an act of war rather than a crime.

The exacting specificity of the sequence of Wallace's execution prompted historiographical accounts to expect – and, if those expectations were unmet, to develop – symbolic significance at every level. John Pike, probably working in London at the end of the 1320s, wrote an account of Wallace's execution preserved in London, British Library, MS Arundel 220.[25] Pike, writing in Latin, was part of the growing number of writers composing history outside the confines of a monastery. In addition to deploying the reductively standardizing framework to read and narrate Wallace's crimes (and thus render the punishments as fitting), Pike notes the disposition of Wallace's remains: "Post hoc in quatuor partes divisus ... caputque ejus suspensum est Londoniis super pontem, manus dextra super pontem apud Novum Castrum super Tynam ultra cloacas communes, pes dexter apud Berewyk, manus sinistra apud Strivelyn, et pes sinister apud Perth" [After this, he was divided into four parts ... his head was suspended above London bridge, his right hand above the bridge at Newcastle upon Tyne beyond the common sewers, his right foot at Berwick, his left hand at Stirling, and his left foot at Perth].[26] The specificity about the distribution of Wallace's body in the Arundel 220 text is not, to my knowledge, found in other accounts.[27] In transforming Wallace's quarters, undifferentiated except for their final destinations, back into the specific parts of a body, Pike's text opens up a rhetoric of relics and the accompanying discourse of miracles. Wallace's dismembered quar-

---

[24] Quoted in Robin Mundill, *England's Jewish Solution: Experiment and Expulsion, 1262–1290* (Cambridge: Cambridge University Press, 1998), p. 26.

[25] I am grateful to Emily Runde for examining the manuscript for me at one stage during the writing of this chapter. The text is printed in *Illustrations of Scottish History, from the Twelfth to the Sixteenth Century: Selected from Unpublished Manuscripts in the British Museum and the Tower of London*, ed. Moses Steven (Glasgow, 1834). The manuscript has been refoliated since Steven's edition; quotations here will use the more recent foliation. See Antonia Gransden, *Historical Writing in England, c. 550 to c. 1307* (London: Routledge, 1996), p. 222. Note that Gransden incorrectly conflates a later Thomas Pike with the chronicler.

[26] *Illustrations of Scottish History*, p. 54. MS Arundel 220, fol. 281v.

[27] Rishanger, one of Pike's sources, alludes to Wallace's death but does not narrate it in an entry for 1298: "sed Willelmus Walleys, qui postea fuit Londoniis suspensus." See William Rishanger, *Chronica et Annales*, in *Willelmi Rishanger ... Chronica et Annales, regnantibus Henrico Tertio et Edwardo Primo*, ed. Henry Riley (London: Longman, Green, Longman, Roberts, and Green, 1865), p. 414.

ters deposited first in England and then across the border in Scotland testified to Edward's power over the island, and also to how that power could or should be read. Pike's detailed placement of Wallace's hands and feet renders Wallace's execution potentially resistant to the kind of textual closure that precludes further reading, interpretation, or contestation. Instead of the certainty of death and the punishment of the law, Pike offers the uncertainty of relics and the miraculous.

Narratives are never without their ambiguities, and though the law may discourage further interpretation, texts remain ever susceptible to reinterpretation. The danger that the dismembered body might be appropriated as an object of veneration haunts the violence committed by the English, Scottish, and Welsh. At the Battle of Stirling Bridge in 1297, the Scottish forces under Wallace famously defeated the English. One of the leaders of the English side was Hugh de Cressingham, Edward I's appointed treasurer of Scotland from 1296 onward. The holder of that position was never likely to be popular, but his apparent effectiveness in collecting taxes made him a particular object of Scottish vitriol. A better administrator than a military leader, he was one of the English slain at Stirling Bridge, where, according to one redaction of Langtoft's *Chronicle*, Wallace and his company sought "pur occire les Engleis, toldre lur membre e vie" [to kill the English, to take their limbs and their lives] (l. 1178). Langtoft uses the more conventionally formulaic version of the phrase earlier in his chronicle, when Balliol swears homage to Edward I as his sovereign lord, offering up life and limb in his service, "de vie e de menbre e de terrien honur" [with life and limb and earthly honor].[28] In describing Cressingham, however, Langtoft deploys the phrase rather more resonantly, pointing subtly to a different aspect of Cressingham's death. Cressingham, so profoundly detested by the Scottish, was skinned at Stirling Bridge: "Quem excoriantes Scotti diuiserunt inter se pellem ipsius in modicas partes, non quidem ad reliquias set in contumelias. Erat enim homo pulcher et grassus nimis, uocaueruntque eum non thesaurarium set traiturarium regis" [The Scots stripped him of his skin and divided it amongst themselves in small parts, not indeed for relics but for insults, for he was a handsome and exceedingly fat man, and they called him not the king's treasurer but the king's "treacherer"].[29] The explicit attempt to qualify the implications of

---

[28] Langtoft, *Chronicle*, p. 256. Langtoft also uses the phrase earlier in a similar context: "Si li aidera en fin, durante membre a vie. / Ton homage te rend sus e weive ta seignurie" (ll. 544–45).

[29] Walter Guisborough, *The Chronicle of Walter of Guisborough, Previously Edited as The Chronicle of Walter of Hemingford or Hemingburgh*, ed. H. Rothwell, Camden Third Series (London: The Royal Historical Society, 1957), p. 303. Translation by J. Russell, in *Reportage Scotland: History in the Making*, ed. Louise Yeoman (Edinburgh: Nuath Press, 2000), pp. 33–34. The so-called Norwich Continuation (formerly known as the Wroxham Continuation) to *Le livere de reis de Engletere*, found in Cambridge, Trinity College MS R.14.7, relates only the section headings of Langtoft's *Chronicle* as they survive in

skinning the corpulent Cressingham, "not for relics but for insults," is neatly indicative of the interpretative crises posed by acts of symbolic violence. The body divided or dismembered always threatens to be understood as sacred rather than profane, whether through the ritualized (and, eventually, formalized) processes of judicial execution, or the more impromptu skinning carried out by the Scottish at Stirling Bridge.

Veneration or Damnation: The Dismembered Body as Relic

From a Scottish perspective, Wallace's execution and dismemberment and the distribution of his body offered an opportunity to contest the authorized reading of the partial body, and they argue for a kind of political sanctity. In his fifteenth-century history the Scottish Walter Bower notes of the aftermath of the execution in his *Scotichronicon*: "Et eius membra per diversa loca Anglie et Scocie in opprobrium Scotorum turribus suspenduntur. In hoc iste tirannus putabat famam nobilis Willelmi delere in perpetuum, eo quod visus sit oculis insipiencium tam vili morte terminari" [His limbs were hung up on towers in different places in England and Scotland to dishonor the Scots. By this that tyrant thought to destroy the fame of the noble William forever, since in the eyes of the foolish his life seemed to be ended with such a contemptible death].[30] Bower goes on, however, quoting verses that rewrite the teleologically framed crime and fitting punishment model of Wallace's death. Instead, he attaches virtue to the life lived rather than its end: "Mors justi rapida quam precessit bona vita / non minuit merita si moriatur ita" [The sudden death of a just man after a good life / does not lessen his merits if he dies thus] (*Scotichronicon*, 6:314–15). This is, of course, a profound theological question rather than a political one, but Bower's recontextualization of the execution of Wallace, which approaches becoming the martyrdom of Saint William Wallace, is readily apparent. Emphasizing a contemplative rather than political context, Bower quotes Boethius's *De consolatione Philosophiae* and excoriates those who seek fame, redefining the discourse of treachery and treason by condemning those who exploit short-term notoriety instead of aspiring to being worthy of memory: "Sunt aliqui qui nomen suum scandalose vilificant; cuiusmodi sunt isti proditores et subtiles tergi-

---

London, College of Arms, MS Arundel 14, and notes only Cressingham's death: "Puis coment Willam Waleys fist tuer Sire Hue de Cressingham au pount de Estrivelyn, tantke li roys fust ale en Flaundres." See *Le livere de reis de Brittanie e Le livere de reis de Engleterre*, ed. John Glover (London: Longmans, Green, Reader, and Dyer, 1865), p. 318. Note Ian Short's caveat that Thiolier's localization of MS Arundel 14 to the Welsh Marches or Hereford is "very speculative," in Geffrei Gaimar, *Estoire des Engleis*, ed. and trans. Short (Oxford: Oxford University Press, 2009), p. xviii.

[30] Walter Bower, *Scotichronicon*, ed. D. E. R. Watt, 9 vols (Aberdeen: Aberdeen University Press, 1987–98), 6:312–15.

versatore" [There are some who scandalously make their name cheap; of this kind are those traitors and crafty renegades] (*Scotichronicon*, 6:314–15). In renarrating Wallace's death 150 years later, Bower transforms Wallace's execution into a moral debate rather than a political contest, thus preparing the ground for Wallace's textual sanctification.

The always-imminent threat of political sanctification was a crucially problematic aspect of Edward I's ritualized political executions. Edward had faced such interpretative slippage before he was crowned, in the death of the Earl of Leicester, Simon de Montfort, at the Battle of Evesham in 1265. Though defeated in battle, the Earl of Leicester was, according to some sources, dismembered after death: "Et maintenant tote la gent de value de luy se turnerent, e puis autres le decolerent, et lé mains et les pes lui mutilerent e le corps, de pieça mort, de totes parts plaierent. Et ke de nul turment est oi: les privés membres de nature nettement lui couperent" [And straightaway all the knights of importance turned away from him, and then some others beheaded him, cut off his hands and feet, and riddled his body, long since dead, all over with wounds. And no such torment has ever been heard of: they cut his private parts clean off].[31] Simon's dismemberment was a lynching, and thus wholly extrajudicial. The trope of previously unheard-of torment positions the murder as exceptional, and thus distinct from the narratives of judicial execution authored and authorized by royal power. Still more problematic for Edward I was the formation of a cult around Simon de Montfort's remains. Several accounts remark upon a great storm rising at the moment of his death and a great darkness descending around Evesham, as for example in the Middle English *Chronicle* attributed to Robert of Gloucester:

> Suich was þe morþre of einesham uor bataile non it nas
> & þerwiþ Iesu crist wel vuele ipaied was
> As he ssewede bi tokninge grisliche & gode
> As it vel of him sulue þo he deide on þe rode
> þat þoru al þe middelerd darkhede þer was inou
> Al so þe wule þe godeman at euesham me slou
> As in þe norþwest a dark weder þer aros
> So demiche suart inou þat mani man agros.[32]

[Such was the murder of Evesham, for battle it was not. And Jesus Christ was evilly repaid thereby, as he showed by tokens both grisly and good. As it happened when he died on the Cross, that through all the earth there was a total darkness, so it was when

---

[31] See O. de Laborderie, J. R. Maddicott, and D. A. Carpenter, "The Last Hours of Simon de Montfort: A New Account," *English Historical Review* 115 (2000): 408–11 [378–412].

[32] Robert of Gloucester, *The Metrical Chronicle of Robert of Gloucester*, ed. William Aldis Wright, 2 vols (London: Eyre and Spottiswoode, 1887), 2:765, ll. 11736–43.

> the good man at Evesham was slain. And in the northwest a dark
> storm arose, so suddenly dark that many men were terrified.]

The suggestion that Montfort was not only martyred but also sacrificed in the manner of Christ's crucifixion is surprisingly unsubtle. As the fourteenth-century Benedictine monk William Rishanger notes in his *Chronicle*, "Fama fert, quod Simon, per sui mortem, multis claruit miraculis, quae, propter metum Regum, in publicum non prodierunt" [Report has it that Simon, after his death, was distinguished by many miracles, which, for fear of the king, were not made known in public].[33] The dismembered body offers itself as a text with humiliation and degradation written upon its parts, to be read as a warning and injunction against emulation. At the same time, it threatens to become a relic, made piecemeal precisely because of its sanctity.

Forty years after Simon de Montfort's murder, William Wallace's execution prompted some of the same processes of underground sanctification, and his body parts threatened to become relics. The process that politically and historically, if not religiously, canonized Wallace (as attested by his status in contemporary Scottish culture) finds full articulation by the fifteenth century. As the *Scotichronicon* argues:

> Fuit, inquam, vir almus, quod probatum est post ipsius mortem, cum ipsi plerique Anglici veridice testantur, quod quidem in ipsa Anglia sanctus heremita raptus in spiritu vidit quasi innumeras animas de penis purgatorii liberatas, quasi prestolantes aditum regni celestis, quoadusque per ministerium angelorum maximo cum honore introducta fuit et premissa anima ipsius Willelmi Wales. (*Scotichronicon*, 6:315–17)

> [He was, I say, a kindly man, which was proved after his death, as most of the English testify truthfully, because indeed a holy hermit in England, carried away in spirit, saw practically countless souls freed from the pains of purgatory, who seemed to be awaiting entrance into the Kingdom of Heaven, until with the help of angels there was introduced and sent onward with the greatest honor the soul of this William Wallace.]

Bower thickly overdetermines Wallace's sanctification, doubly authorized by an English holy hermit testifying to Wallace's intervention for souls trapped in purgatory, and "most of the English," who, though presumably naturally disposed to oppose Wallace's sanctity along ethnic lines, instead "veridice testantur" to Wallace's sanctity.[34] In the *Scotichronicon*, Wallace's judicial

---

[33] Rishanger was a monk at St Albans Abbey, and his *Chronicle* exhibits consistently probaronial sentiments. See Rishanger, *Chronica et Annales*, pp. 36–37.

[34] Bower's narrative conjunction loosely recalls the *Vita Haroldi*, the late twelfth-century text that records how King Harold survived the Conquest and the Battle of Hastings and ultimately retired to a quiet hermitage in Chester. See *The Waltham Chronicle*, ed. and trans. Leslie Watkiss and Marjorie Chibnall (Oxford: Oxford University Press, 1994).

execution has become the martyrdom of a saint, and his body parts have become relics. The pieces of his corpse, distributed by Edward I to intimidate and discourage, are instead the means by which the pains of souls in purgatory are ended and salvation can be achieved for both the English and the Scottish.

For all of the sovereign's power as exhibited in the spectacle of the scaffold, that spectacle is also the moment that marks the sovereign's powerlessness over the next life.[35] The potent symbolism of executions involving drawing, quartering, and the distribution of the parts of the body to urban spaces was authored as a way to combat dissent, but heterodoxies could be secular or sacred. Edward I was exceptionally aware of the need for symbolic closure, particularly when facing the insurgency of the Welsh and Scottish. In 1278, while on a visit to Glastonbury, Edward I supposedly ordered the opening of a twelfth-century tomb of King Arthur, and the exhumation and transfer of the bones found in the tomb, said to be those of Arthur and Guinevere.[36] Despite Edward's attempts to quell Arthur's status as a symbolic rallying point of Welsh insurgency, Arthur remained available for those who would rise up against English power.[37] Edward I's reburial of the bones of Arthur and Guinevere evinces his awareness of the need to control the historiography of his realm, particularly when confronted with the prophetic and the miraculous. The same can be said of the spectacular executions of Dafydd ap Gruffydd and William Wallace. Although their dismemberment rendered their bodies ambiguous, both holy relics and political traitors, the distribution of their quarters took place very pointedly across the national boundaries for which both Dafydd and Wallace had died and attempted to (re)inscribe. Dafydd's execution marked the end of the Welsh rebellion and the success of Edward I's conquest of Wales. Wallace's execution did nothing to settle the contest over Scotland. His partial body hung over two countries carved out of a single island, the borders between the two contested and porous, as were the narratives that framed those remains for those who would read them.

---

[35] Foucault writes in "Society Must Be Defended," "Death was the moment when we made the transition from one power – that of the sovereign of this world – to another – that of the sovereign of the next world." Quoted in Michael Meranze, "Michel Foucault, the Death Penalty, and the Crisis of Historical Understanding," *Historical Reflections* 29 (2003): 201 [191–209].

[36] The passage is drawn from Gerald of Wales's *De principis instructione*, translated in Gerald of Wales, *The Journey Through Wales and The Description of Wales*, trans. Lewis Thorpe (Harmondsworth: Penguin, 1978), pp. 281–82.

[37] Thus the letter from 1307 claiming of Robert Bruce that "these preachers have told the people that they have found a prophecy of Merlin, that after the death of 'le Roy Coveytous' the people of Scotland and the Welsh shall band together and have full lordship and live in peace together." Quoted in G. W. S. Barrow, *Robert Bruce and the Community of the Realm of Scotland*, 2nd edn. (Edinburgh: Edinburgh University Press, 2005), p. 223.

7

The Good, the Bad, and the Beautiful: Violence in the *Canso de la Crozada*

KAREN SULLIVAN

The scene of violence described in the *Canso de la Crozada* is a terrible one.[1] Ramon Roger, the Count of Foix, has attacked a group of Germans and Frisians, massacring them and mutilating those he did not kill by gouging out their eyes and cutting off their hands. Confronting the count at the Fourth Lateran Council of 1215, Folquet de Marseille, the Bishop of Toulouse, protests,

> n'a tans mortz e trencatz e brizatz e partitz
> que lo cams de Montjoy ne remas si crostitz.
> ... Laforas a la porta es tals lo dols e·l critz
> dels orbs e dels nafratz e d'aicels meg partitz,
> que negus no pot ir si no lo mena guitz. (145.18–23)

> [He has killed, slashed, broken, and mutilated so many that the field of Montgey remains covered with them.... Out there at the gateway rise the moans and cries of the blind, the wounded, men who have lost their limbs or cannot walk unless a guide leads them.]

Through Folquet's words, we have the impression of gaining access to a historical reality. Other sources from this time confirm that Ramon Roger did, in fact, ambush these men as they were traveling between Revel and

---

[1] The *Canso de la Crozada* was composed between 1210 and 1228 by two authors, Guilhem de Tudela (who contributed *laisses* 1–131) and an anonymous Continuator (who contributed *laisses* 132–214). It can be found in one surviving manuscript, MS FF 25425 in the Bibliothèque Nationale in Paris. Citations of this work will be made parenthetically and will refer to *laisse* and line numbers in *La chanson de la Croisade Albigeoise*, ed. and trans. Eugène Martin-Chabot, 3 vols (Paris: Honoré Champion, 1931–61). I have consulted *The Song of the Cathar Wars: A History of the Albigensian Crusade*, trans. Janet Shirley (Aldershot: Ashgate, 1996), but all translations are my own.

Cuq-Toulza in April of 1211.² In his representation of this incident, Folquet accentuates not only how these Germans and Frisians suffered during their encounter with Ramon Roger's men, but also how they continue to suffer in the aftermath of that encounter, unable to see, unable to walk without assistance, and, presumably, from their position by the gate, unable to sustain themselves without begging. Though these men remain nameless, the specificity with which the bishop describes them and the voice he gives them as they lament their state personalizes their suffering. It is hard to read his words without feeling pity for these massacred or maimed men and anger at the count who brought about their plight.

However terrible this scene of violence may be, it is nevertheless worth remembering that even if we do, to some extent, gain access to a historical reality through Folquet's words, this reality is being selected and framed. The bishop refers to the Germans and Frisians as "peregris, per cui Dieus fo servitz" [pilgrims, by whom God was served] (145.16). As Ramon Roger sees it, however, these Germans and Frisians were not genuine "pilgrims," heading to Rome or some other shrine, but, rather, "raubadors, fals trachors, fe-mentitz / que portavan las crotz, per que eu fos destrusitz" [robbers, false traitors, and oath-breakers, who were wearing crosses, through whom I have been destroyed] (145.54–55). In other words, they were soldiers participating in the Albigensian Crusade of 1209–29 who, under the pretext of zeal for religious orthodoxy, were striving to crush barons like himself.³ Sympathetic toward those German and Frisian "pilgrims" who have been ill-treated by Ramon Roger, Folquet appears in no way sympathetic toward the Occitan lords who, like Ramon Roger, have lost their lands, or toward their subjects,

---

² For accounts of the massacre at Montgey, see the three major chronicles of the Albigensian Crusade: Guilhem de Tudela, *La chanson de la Croisade Albigeoise*, 69–70; Guilhem de Puylaurens, *Chronique, 1145–1275*, ed. and trans. Jean Duvernoy (Paris: CNRS, 1976), §16; and Pierre des Vaux-de-Cernay, *Hystoria albigensis*, ed. Pascal Guébin, 3 vols (Paris: Champion, 1926–39), vol. 1, §218. See also Robert of Auxerre, *Chronicon*, in Monumenta Germaniae Historica, Scriptores 26 (Hanover: Hahn, 1882), p. 276; and Aubri des Trois-Fontaines, *Chronica*, in Monumenta Germaniae Historica, Scriptores 23 (Hanover: Hahn, 1874), p. 892.

³ Etienne Delaruelle argues convincingly, in "L'idée de la croisade dans la chanson de Guillaume de Tudèle," in *Annales de l'Institut d'Études Occitanes: Actes du Colloque de Toulouse (9, 10 et 11 septembre 1963)* (Toulouse: Publication du Conseil d'Études, 1962–63), pp. 49–63, that Guilhem de Tudela, though supportive of the Albigensian Crusade, does not perceive this war as a crusade because Occitania lacks the historical, spiritual, and eschatological resonance of the Holy Lands. Rita Lejeune discusses the *Canso* in the context of Occitan epics of the crusades, including the *Canso d'Antiocha*, which Guilhem de Tudela cites as his model, in "L'esprit de croisade dans l'épopée occitane," in *Paix de Dieu et guerre sainte en Languedoc au XIIIᵉ siècle*, Cahiers de Fanjeaux 4 (Toulouse: Privat, 1969), pp. 143–73. Yves Dossat discusses the poem in the context of the Latin chronicles of the Albigensian Crusade in "La croisade vue par les chroniqueurs," in *Paix de Dieu*, pp. 221–59.

who have often been abused by these crusaders.[4] He makes no mention, for example, of the villagers of Bram, who in 1210 had their eyes gouged out and their ears, noses, and lips cut off by these soldiers.[5] If Folquet's words arouse pity and anger, it is also true that he is using this massacre as an *argumentum ad misericordiam* to support his larger contention that Ramon Roger should be stripped of his lands. "Cel que los a mortz ni brizatz ni cruichitz / ja no deu tenir terra" [He who killed, broke, and tortured (these men) must never hold land again] (145.24–25), he concludes. The point is not that the scene of violence at Montgey can be reduced to Folquet's "propaganda" on behalf of the Crusade, even if the bishop is admittedly the war's most eloquent champion. Rather, the point is that the degree to which such scenes of violence are moving or even intelligible to those who hear of them depends upon the circumstances within which they are understood to occur. As terrible as the plight of the Germans and Frisians may seem to be, it is one thing to lament the sufferings of pilgrims in the service of God, who happened to fall victim to a rapacious lord, and another thing to lament the sufferings of soldiers in the service of the pope, who were invading the lands of the lord who took vengeance upon them.

If the clash between Folquet de Marseille and Ramon Roger de Foix at the Fourth Lateran Council illustrates the way in which the perception of violent events, such as the massacre at Montgey, is always already mediated by rhetoric, the clash between the clerics and crusaders and the Occitan barons throughout the *Canso* can be seen to illustrate this tendency as well. On one level, the poem condemns certain acts of violence. Though Guilhem de Tudela, the author of the first third of the work (*laisses* 1–130), which covers the events from 1204 to 1213, takes the side of the crusaders, and

[4] As is now conventional, I am using "Occitania" as a term of convenience to refer to the Occitan-speaking lands encompassed within the French kingdom since the end of the Albigensian Crusade, though it imputes a unity and cohesion to this region that never existed. As Linda Paterson discusses in *The World of the Troubadours: Medieval Occitan Society, c. 1100–c. 1300* (Cambridge: Cambridge University Press, 1993), pp. 1–4, these territories were united linguistically and culturally in the Middle Ages, but they were fragmented politically, with some of their lords owing fealty to England, some to Aragon, and some to France, and all of them tended to rule with a remarkable independence from their nominal overlords. The authors of the *Canso de la Crozada* refer to the object of the Albigensian Crusade not as a single geographic entity but rather as a series of autonomous fiefdoms, such as the counties of Toulouse, Foix, and Comminges, which were under the rule of separate lords.

[5] An anonymous collection of exempla recounts how Folquet was one day delivering a sermon in which he compared heretics to wolves and Catholics to sheep. A heretic, whose nose had been cut off and eyes gouged out by Simon de Montfort, interrupted him, asking if he had ever seen a sheep bite a wolf in this way. Folquet replied that the heretic had been bitten by a dog that had been sent to protect the sheep. See *Anecdotes historiques, légendes, et apologues tirés du recueil inédit d'Étienne de Bourbon*, ed. A. Lecoy de la Marche (Paris: Librairie Renouard, 1877), pp. 23–24n3.

though his anonymous Continuator, the author of the remaining, far more beautiful, two-thirds of the work (*laisses* 131–214), which covers the events from 1213 to 1219,[6] takes the side of the Occitan barons, both poets nonetheless express compassion for the suffering that was occurring in Occitania during the first part of the thirteenth century. Still, as Susan Sontag points out, an act of violence, no matter how gruesome, registers as an act of violence only if it makes sense within the perceiver's preexisting patterns of thought.[7] The Nazis' gassing of civilians at Auschwitz has resonated in Western culture in a way in which the Allies' bombing of civilians in Dresden has not because the former symbolizes the evils of nationalized racism and anti-Semitism, while the latter represents no equivalent moral pathology. In like manner, only the atrocities of the Occitan barons resonate for the crusaders and only the atrocities of the crusaders resonate for the Occitan barons because only the harsh deeds of one's enemy seem to threaten the structure of the world as one knows it. For both sides of the Albigensian Crusade, it is not physical violence (that is, the killing, the robbing, or the exiling of people) that is most troubling, however strong a visceral reaction these acts may produce in those who see, hear, and read about them. Rather it is the metaphysical violence (that is, the destruction of a social and cultural order) symbolized by these acts that most disturbs.[8]

The Evil of Violence

Both the Catholic clerics and the Occitan barons represented in the *Canso* condemn certain acts of violence. As far back as the tenth century, clerics had opposed what they saw as the warlike tendencies of the barons, whether by attempting to persuade them not to fight during certain sacred times in the Christian calendar, such as Sundays and Lent, or by attempting to persuade them not to harm certain vulnerable sectors of feudal society, such as clerics, pilgrims, peasants, women, and children.[9] Since the Third Lateran Council in 1179, clerics had been speaking out, particularly against the mercenaries who were disrupting the peace in Occitania by pillaging churches and monas-

---

[6] Guida Saverio has recently argued that the Continuator can be identified as Gui de Cavaillon, an ally of Ramon VI, the Count of Toulouse. See "L'autore della seconda parte della *Canso de la crotzada*," *Cultura neolatina* 63 (2003): 255–82.

[7] See Susan Sontag, *Regarding the Pain of Others* (New York: Picador, 2003), pp. 35–36.

[8] See Judith N. Shklar, *Ordinary Vices* (Cambridge, MA: Belknap Press, 1985), pp. 7–44.

[9] See Thomas Head and Richard Landes, eds., *The Peace of God: Social Violence and Religious Response in France Around the Year 1000* (Ithaca, NY: Cornell University Press, 1992); and Delaruelle, "Paix de Dieu et croisade dans la chrétienté du XIIe siècle," in *Paix de Dieu*, pp. 51–71.

teries and abusing defenseless populations; against the heretics who were disrupting the faith in this region by promulgating their false doctrines and thus leading the people astray; and, most of all, against the lords who were protecting both of these groups on their lands by failing to take action against them. When Innocent III ascended the papal throne in 1198, he renewed what was now called the *negotium pacis et fidei* (business of peace and faith),[10] and he sent his legates throughout the region to induce the local lords to swear to maintain these two intertwined principles. As of 1209, however, the Occitan barons opposed what they saw as the destructive tendencies of the crusaders with whom the Catholic clerics were allied, who were disrupting the peace in Occitania by killing, robbing, and expelling its people. Like the clerics represented in the *Canso*, who perceive the Occitan barons as violent not only because they tolerate those who threaten the body but also because they tolerate those who threaten the soul, the barons depicted in this poem perceive the crusaders as violent not only because they exile and impoverish them but also because they debase what was known in Occitan as *Paratge* – that is, "Nobility," in the sense of a nobleman's capacity to reside on his own lands and to display largesse toward others.[11] The clerics and the crusaders in this text understand social order as the vertical relation between God, the Church, the lord, and the people, while the Occitan barons understand it as the more lateral relation between the lord and his vassals or between kinsmen. Both sides, however, view the most offensive violence not as that perpetrated against their lives, their property, or their homes, but as that perpetrated against the social order, as they envision it.

For Guilhem, and indeed for the clerics and crusaders depicted in the *Canso* as a whole, the original act of violence in the Crusade was the murder of the papal legate Peire de Castelnau, who in the early years of the thirteenth century had been demanding that the Occitan barons swear to uphold the *negotium pacis et fidei*. In May of 1207, Peire had excommunicated Ramon VI, the Count of Toulouse and the most important baron in Occitania, for his failure to take this oath. As part of this excommunication, Peire placed Ramon's lands under interdict and authorized his vassals to rise up against him. In January of 1208, Peire met with Ramon at Saint-Gilles to try to resolve this difficult situation. The discussion proved unproductive, however, and the two parties parted on bad terms. As Peire and his attendants were crossing the Rhône, Guilhem relates,

> Us escudiers, qui fo de mal talent
> per so qu'el agues grat del comte an avant,

---

[10] See Marie-Humbert Vicaire, "'L'affaire de paix et de foi' du Midi de la France," in *Paix de Dieu*, pp. 102–27.

[11] On *Paratge*, see C. P. Bagley, "*Paratge* in the Anonymous *Chanson de la Croisade Albigeoise*," *French Studies* 21.2 (1967): 195–204.

> l'aucis en traïcio dereire en trespassant,
> e·l ferit per la esquina am son espeut trencant:
> e pueish si s'en fugit am son caval corant
> a Belcaire, d'on era, on feron sei parant. (4.11–16)
>
> [A squire who was of evil disposition killed him treacherously, passing behind him, so that he might have the count's favor. He struck him through the spine with his cutting sword, and then he fled on his galloping horse to Beaucaire, whence he came and where his kinsmen were.]

With this attack this squire defines himself, not, obviously, through his attachment to God or his clerics, but through his attachment to his lord, for whom he kills the legate who excommunicated him, and through his attachment to his kinsmen, from whom he expects protection from any potential repercussions of this deed. By juxtaposing the agency of the squire, who acts "en traïcio" [treacherously] (4.13) in striking an unarmed cleric from behind, with the passivity of the legate, who submits to his fate and forgives his assailant, Guilhem accentuates the brutality of this attack. With a gesture toward heaven and an address toward God, Peire defines himself by his attachment to his Creator, to whom he turns at the moment of his death: "Sas mas al cel levant / el preguet Domni-Deu, vezent tota la jant / que·lh perdo sos pecatz al cel felo sarjant" [Raising his hands to heaven, he prayed before all his people that the Lord God would pardon the sins of this wicked sergeant] (4.17–19). Though this murder is the act of one squire who was functioning without authorization from above, Guilhem makes clear that it is reflective of Occitan society as a whole. Like the squire, who displays hostility toward the legate, the Occitan population had for years been displaying hostility toward such emissaries, dismissing their efforts to persuade them to abandon their heresy by saying, "Ara roda l'abelha" [There buzzes the bee] (46.9). If this murder is not an isolated act of violence but instead emblematic of this society, Guilhem suggests, it is both because the squire and the society to which he belongs privilege an earthly connection to their lord and kinsmen over a spiritual connection to God and his clerics and because the sword in Peire's back expresses the brutality to which such a preference necessarily leads.

Although for the clerics and the crusaders the original act of violence in the Crusade is the murder of Peire de Castelnau, the final such act of violence would be, they fear, the dispossession of Simon de Montfort, the titular Earl of Leicester and the leader of their campaign. At the Fourth Lateran Council these parties defend Simon against the Occitan lords, who argue that even if Simon's confiscation of Ramon VI's lands were held to be justified because of the count's failure to bend to the Church's will, his refusal to permit Ramon VI's son, *lo coms joves* (the Young Count) and the future Ramon VII, from inheriting these lands cannot be regarded as legitimate. In this poem

Simon is defined not through his attachment to his lord, King Philip Augustus of France, or to his kinsmen, barons of France, England, and Flanders, but through his attachment to the Church. He reminds those around him, "Ez eu fas de la Glieiza los faitz e·ls ditz e·ls mans" [I am doing the deeds of the Church, her words, and her commands] (160.24). He enjoys the right to rule the lands he has acquired, Folquet tells the pope, not because he is the son of their previous lord and thus the rightful heir, but rather because "Lo comte de Montfort ... es vers obediens / e filhs de santa Glieiza ..., / e cassa iretgia, mainaders e sirvens" [The count of Montfort ... is a true, obedient man and son of the Holy Church ..., and he drives out heresy, mercenaries, and men of war] (148.4–8). The true family bond is not that between a father, who is lord of a domain, and a literal son, who inherits that property, but between the Church, which authorizes the Crusade, and a figurative "son," who carries out her order. By the same token, the bishop continues, the true "dezeretamens" [disinheritance] (148.16) would take the form not of Simon's continued possession of the Young Count's lands but of the proposed transfer of these lands to the Young Count. "Co potz dezeretar aisi cubertamens / lo comte de Montfort?" [How can you thus covertly disinherit the Count of Montfort?] (148.4–5), he demands indignantly. This dispossession would be not an act of kindness toward the Young Count but an act of violence toward Simon, Folquet insists, because the Church would be privileging the son of a count of Toulouse who has failed to expel the mercenaries and heretics from his lands over the son of the Church who has succeeded in this endeavor.

In contrast, for the Continuator and the Occitan barons he portrays, the original act of violence in the Crusade is not the murder of Peire de Castelnau but the dispossession of Roger II Trencavel, the young son of the late Ramon Roger Trencavel, Viscount of Béziers and Carcassonne. After Ramon VI saw the French troops assembling to invade his lands, he reconciled himself with the Church and, in doing so, deflected the crusaders' attack to other Occitan lords' lands, including those of the twenty-four-year-old viscount. Under Simon's leadership, the crusaders overthrew Carcassonne and imprisoned the viscount in his own dungeon, where he soon died under mysterious circumstances. Only two years old at the time, Roger found himself expelled from his lands and forced to live the life of a *faidit* (or dispossessed knight), like many noblemen of his time. At the Fourth Lateran Council, Ramon de Roquefeuil, a vassal of the Trencavel family, appeals to Innocent on behalf of the now eight-year-old child:

> Senher dreitz apostolis, merce e pietat
> aias d'un effan orfe, jovenet ichilat,
> filh del onrat vescomte, que an mort li crozat
> e·n Simos de Monfort. ...
> E por an mort lo paire e·l filh dezeretat,
> senher, ret li la terra! (146.32–35, 40–41)

[Right lord pope, have mercy and pity on an orphan child, exiled in his youth, the son of the honored viscount, whom the crusaders and Sir Simon de Montfort put to death.... As the father was put to death and the son disinherited, lord, return to him his land!]

Like the squire who killed Peire, Ramon defines himself not by his attachment to the Church and its clerics but by his attachment to his lord, "the honored viscount," to whom he remains loyal, and by the attachment between kinsmen, which he defends, including the right of a son to inherit his father's property. By juxtaposing the agency of Simon and the other crusaders, who "[l'] onrat vescomte ... an mort" [put the honored viscount to death] and "an ... dezeretat" [disinherited] his son, with the passivity of their victims, young Catholics who did nothing to provoke this behavior, the Continuator accentuates the harshness of their treatment of this father and son. Cast out of his "home" (*repaire*), where he is safe, into the "world" (*mon* or *setgle*), where he is exposed to dangers, the young Roger, like his fellow *faidits*, goes wandering in the world, rootless and bereft. If this dispossession is not an isolated act of violence, undertaken at the very beginning of the Crusade, but rather, as the Continuator suggests, an emblematic act of violence reflecting the crusaders' pervasive mentality, it is because Simon and the crusaders privilege a spurious connection to God (to whom the viscount was no less faithful) over a genuine connection to one's lord and kinsmen.

Although for the Occitan barons the original act of violence in the Crusade was the dispossession of the viscount's son, they feared that the final such act of violence would be the dispossession of the future Ramon VII. The Young Count is defined not by his attachment to the Church but by his attachment to his illustrious family. As the descendant, on his father's side, of Ramon IV of Saint-Gilles, one of the great heroes of the First Crusade, and, on his mother's side, of King Henry II of England and Eleanor of Aquitaine, and thus the nephew of King Richard the Lion-Hearted and the current King John, the Young Count is, Innocent acknowledges, "de la plus auta sanc que sia ni que es" [of the highest blood that can be or is] (149.57). He enjoys the right to rule these lands, his supporters tell the pope, not because he is "vers obediens / e filhs de santa Glieiza" [a true, obedient man and son of the Holy Church] (148.5–6) but because he is the son of the current ruler. Despite Folquet's contention that one's affiliation with the Church and, by extension, the faith should determine one's right to hold land, Simon's own men repeatedly recognize that one's affiliation with one's family is more important in this regard. The Count of Soissons expresses doubt that Simon will ever retake Toulouse now that it has returned to the count's possession, "per so que·l coms Ramons, que es dux e marques, / la clama per linatge, e sabem que vers es, / e sos fils lo com joves, qu'es nebs del rei Engles" [because Count Ramon, who is duke and marquis, claims it through his lineage, and we know that he is right, as well as his son, the Young Count, who is the nephew of the king of the English] (202.77–79). These Frenchmen refer to the Young Count as the "senhor natural" [natural lord] (169.79; 188.88), whose right to his parents' property is self-evident, whatever the Church's canonists may say. The true disinheritance, these counselors make clear, would take the form of Simon's usurpation of the Young Count's holdings. Though the crusaders and the Occitan barons both feel sharply the pain of impending dispossession, they situate this pain differently, depending upon whether they see the son of the Church or the son of the previous lord as the legitimate heir. It is not so much the violence toward a particular individual as the violence toward the perceived social order, symbolized by the violence toward a particular individual, that disturbs them.

The Good of Violence

Both the crusaders and the Occitan barons condemn certain acts of violence while defending others. As far back as the Council of Clermont in 1095, clerics had been attempting to foster peace not just by curbing the barons' aggression but also by directing that aggression overseas, against the Muslim host in the Holy Land. When clerics spoke out against the violence in Occitania in the late twelfth and early thirteenth centuries they echoed the calls to crusade in the East, using the language of peace to advocate war. The authors of the *Canso* likewise distinguish desirable and undesirable uses of force. In a wicked act of violence, Guilhem suggests, the subject, like the squire, is an active and guilty perpetrator, and the object, like Peire, is a passive and innocent victim. Because the ends for which the subject acts, like the defense of his lord, seem so nebulous, the act of violence functions as an end in itself, stark in its brutality. In contrast, in a good act of violence, he indicates, the object, like the Occitan barons, is an active and guilty party who has brought this punishment upon himself, and the subject, like the crusaders, is the instrument through which that party is rightly punished. Because the ends for which the subject acts – in this case, the defense of peace and faith – seem so clear-cut, the act of violence functions as a means toward this goal. As an end in itself, violence is repugnant, but as a means toward an end, it becomes negligible. Like Guilhem, the Continuator distinguishes between wicked violence and good violence; unlike the former, however, the latter regards good violence not as a necessary evil but as a paradoxical good. As Gui de Cavaillon tells the Young Count when they turn toward war in the second section of the poem, "Oimas es la sazos / que a grans obs Paratges que siatz mals e bos" [Now is the season when *Paratge* requires that you be bad and good] (154.7–8). Though these poets can be disturbed by violence, it is only when they see that violence is undermining the social order rather than supporting it.

Troubled by the violence of Peire de Castelnau's murder, Guilhem is nevertheless unmoved by the violence of the Crusade this murder provoked because this violence is merely a means by which sinners must be punished. In the years leading up to the Crusade, Guilhem recalls, the Church had sent preachers into Occitania, urging the people to amend their ways; yet, he relates,

> No·s volon covertir cela gent esbaya,
> qu'en son mant home mort, manta gent peria
> e o seran encara, tro la guerra er fenia
> car als estre non pot. (2.27–30)
>
> [This lost people did not want to convert, for which many men died and many people perished, and they will continue to do so until the war is finished, for it cannot be otherwise.]

The reason for which these people have been dying and will still die, he suggests, is not that crusaders are killing them but that the people are refusing to abandon their false doctrines. In the prologue to the poem, Guilhem similarly announces

> que·l païs er ars e destruzit
> per la fola crezensa qu'avian cosentit
> e que li ric borzes serian enpaubrezit
> de lor grans manentias, don eran eriquit,
> e que li cavalier s'en irian faizit,
> caitiu, en autras terras. (1.8–13)
>
> [that the country would be burned and destroyed through the foolish belief to which (the people) had consented; that rich burghers would be impoverished of their great holdings, from which they had been enriched; and that the knights would depart, dispossessed and wretched, for other lands.]

Again, the reason for which these people have been suffering is not that crusaders are killing, robbing, and expelling them from their lands but that they agreed upon a "fola crezensa" [foolish belief]. Though Guilhem accentuates the agency of the squire who had killed Peire, he does not even name the agent who kills, burns, and destroys in Occitania, let alone represent him as responsible for his deeds. The source of this violence lies not in the person who kills, robs, or exiles but in the person who is killed, robbed, or exiled, as he has brought these sufferings upon himself. Although Guilhem perceives the violence from which the people suffer, he does not perceive the crusaders as causing that suffering because he understands this violence to be the inevitable fate – "als estre non pot" [it cannot be otherwise] – of those who fail to heed God's representatives on earth.

Not only will people who refuse to repent of their errors necessarily be punished, Guilhem indicates, but those who are swept up in these people's sin will also necessarily be swept up in their punishment. He acknowledges that Ramon Roger Trencavel was "pros ... larg ... cortes" [valiant, generous, and courtly] (15.4), as well as "catholicals" (15.6), but he complains that the viscount was not able to control his vassals, who kept heretics in their castles and towers. He writes, "Car era trop joves, avia ab totz amor, / e sels de son païs, de cui era senhor, / no avian de lui ni regart ni temor, / enans jogan am lui co li fos companhor" [Because he was too young, he had love from all, and those of his country, whose lord he was, did not have respect or fear of him. Instead, they joked with him as if he were their companion] (15.8–11). Rather than obeying their lord out of fear, as they should, his subjects treated him as their equal, out of love, and this lateral rather than vertical power structure brought about all of their deaths.[12] Countering rumors that were then circulating, Guilhem denies that the crusaders caused the viscount to die in prison: "So qu'es a venir no pot hom trespassar. / Le mals de menazo le pres adoncs, so·m par, / per que·l covenc morir" [Man cannot change that which is to come. Dysentery took him, so it seems to me, from which he had to die] (40.14–16). The fate of a war, which determines that a young lord should suffer because of the actions of his vassals, is like the fate of an illness, which determines that a young lord should die because of an intestinal inflammation. Guilhem concludes, "El meteis ne morig, a mot granda dolor, / dont fo pecatz e dans" [And he himself died of it, to very great grief, which was a misfortune and a loss] (15.15–16). The destruction of the viscount, like that of other innocents in the Crusade, is a "pecatz" [misfortune], which one might lament, but not a crime, for which one might hold someone responsible.

Troubled by the dispossession of the Occitan lords, the Continuator is unmoved by the violence to which they turn in order to regain their lands because this is merely a means by which they may restore their rights. A council such as the Fourth Lateran Council constitutes a place where opposing parties attempt to work out their differences peaceably, through speech, and not violently, through force, yet the Continuator indicates that

---

[12] On the weakness of Occitan feudalism, see Paterson, *World of the Troubadours*, pp. 10–36. Simone Weil stresses the remarkable unity the Continuator attributes to Occitan society in "L'agonie d'une civilisation vue à travers un poème épique (février 1943)," in *Le génie d'Oc et l'homme méditerranéen*, ed. Joë Bousquet (Marseille: Cahiers de Sud, 1943), pp. 99–107; reprinted in Simone Weil, *Écrits historiques et politiques* (Paris: Gallimard, 1960), pp. 53–59. In contrast to Simon de Montfort, who demands that Toulouse submit to him, Weil writes, Ramon VI "ne lui donne pas d'ordres, il lui demande son appui; cet appui, tous l'accordent, artisans, marchands, chevaliers, avec le même dévouement joyeux et complet" [does not give (the city) orders; he asks it for its support. And all grant this support to him – whether they are artisans, merchants, or knights – with the same joyous and complete devotion] (p. 56). In contrast to the crusaders, who burn heretics, she observes, Occitan Catholics display no resentment toward their Cathar neighbors, who provoked the war against their region.

this seemingly rational exchange of words does not necessarily lead to a more just result than a seemingly irrational exchange of blows. Though the Occitan barons argued well for their lands at this gathering, the poet reports that the numbers of prelates on Simon's side was such that "lai no val als comtes dreitz ni fes ni razos" [neither Right, nor Faith, nor Reason did the counts any good] (143.25). In a meeting with Innocent, the Young Count makes clear his unhappiness with this outcome and his intention to gain through war what he could not gain through discussion: "E, pus ieu vei que torna del tot al esgremir, / senher, re als no·t vulh demandar ne querir, / mas que·m laiches la terra si la posc conquerir" [Since I see that everything comes back to fighting, lord, I want to ask or seek nothing else from you but that you leave me the land, if I can conquer it] (152.57–59). The pope is torn. On the one hand, he inaugurated the Crusade that had dispossessed, at least temporarily, the Occitan barons who had failed to defend the peace and the faith. He is presiding over a council that has just ratified this dispossession on a more permanent basis. On the other hand, he recognizes the worthiness of this youth, the legitimate son of one of those barons, who has himself committed no crime for which he deserves to be disinherited. Innocent had earlier advised the Young Count, "Qui·t dezereta ni·t vol dezenantir, / be·t sapias defendre e ton dreit retenir" [Know well to defend yourself and to retain your right against any who want to disinherit you or cast you down] (152.36–37). Now, faced with the Young Count's stated intention to restart the war, he neither approves nor disapproves of his plan but merely sighs and kisses and blesses him. He recommends, "Tu garda que faras e apren que vulh dir / que tot cant que s'escura a obs a esclarzir" [Take care with what you do, and learn what I want to tell you – that all that becomes dark must, sooner or later, become light] (152.62–63). He leaves it to the Young Count to apply to his situation, as he sees fit, the image of the night sooner or later turning to dawn. Although the pope and, even more, the Continuator know that violence – the rebellion of the Raimondines in Provence and the Toulousain – will be the result of this discussion, they represent this violence not as violence but rather as the restoration of the right of a young man to recover his home when speech has failed to do so.

If the Continuator defends the Occitan lords' turn toward violence it is not only because they are attempting to restore their rights but also because, in doing so, they are attempting to restore *"Dreitz"* [Right] itself. What is at stake, the poet suggests, is not only this or that particular lord's ownership of his fiefdom but a general principle for which the Young Count and all of his supporters are struggling. Gui de Cavaillon informs the Young Count, "E si Pretz e Paratges no·s restaura per vos, / doncs es lo mortz Paratges e totz lo mons en vos" [If Worth and *Paratge* are not restored through you, *Paratge* dies, and all the world in you] (154.14–15). What is at issue here is not only the Young Count's right to inherit his lands but the right to inherit lands itself; *Paratge*, which can be cultivated only if one has inherited those lands; and even "the world," which dies if such *Paratge* dies. In 1183 the troubadour Bertran de Born had similarly represented universal qualities as dependent upon a particular leader for their survival. In the *planh* (or lament) "Mon chan fenis ab dol et ab maltraire," Bertran informs Henry the Young King (the Young Count's uncle) that, now that he has died,

> E jois e amors
> non an que·ls manteingna
> ni qui ja·ls reveigngna.
> Mas lai vos sigran,
> c'ab vos s'en iran
> e tut ric faig benestan.[13]

> [Joy and love have nobody to maintain them or to bring them back. They will follow you; like all mighty, honorable deeds, they will disappear with you].

By attempting to regain his lands, the Young Count is affecting not only his own life and the lives of his subjects but the world as a whole. It is because of the universal implications of a particular act of violence that, for both Guilhem and the Continuator, the act of violence can at times be justified.

The Beauty of Violence

Although both Guilhem and the Continuator affirm the moral value of violence under certain circumstances, the Continuator also affirms the aesthetic value of this practice. On one level, as we have seen, he provides a linear narrative of the events of the Crusade as the Occitan barons leave the Fourth Lateran Council and inspire the men of Provence and Toulouse to rise up against the invading armies. He defends violence here as a means by which the barons can restore their rights and *Dreitz* itself. On another level, however, the Continuator periodically interrupts this linear narrative to provide descriptions of the battles in Provence and the Toulousain – descriptions that, by focusing upon the confrontation of knights, the clash of weapons, and the mutilation of bodies, seem as if they could pertain to any number of medieval wars. The distinction between the crusaders and the Occitan barons, with their different notions of social order, disappears in the blinding experience of combat. Here the poet defends violence not as a means to an end but as an end in itself, in which both sides find satisfaction.

It is because battles entail a purely physical encounter of two clashing

---

[13] Bertran de Born, "Mon chan fenis ab dol et ab maltraire," in *The Poems of the Troubadour Bertran de Born*, ed. William D. Paden Jr., Tilde Sankovitch, and Patricia H. Stäblein (Berkeley: University of California Press, 1986), p. 219 [218–23], vv. 23–28.

forces that the Continuator depicts them not only as bloody but also as beautiful. He admires the sight of knights assembled for battle, with their weapons shining in the sun: "Dels escutz e dels elmes, on es li ors batutz, / i vengon tans ensemble co si fossan plogutz / e d'aubers e d'ensenhas tota la plassa lutz" [So many of them came together that the whole place shone with their shields and helmets (where there was beaten gold), and with their hauberks and blazons, as if it had rained] (184.9–11). He admires the sound of these knights as they approach each other: "E li corn e li graile e las trompas e·l vent / fan brandir la ribeira, l'aiga e l'element" [The horns, the clarions, the trumpets, and the wind make the bank, the water, and the air tremble] (197.70–71). He admires the sensation of weapons of all kinds coming into contact with each other:

> Li dart e las lansas e li espieut brandit
> e las massas furbidas e li destral brunit ...
> d'entramabas partz lai vengo complidament aizit
> que l'ausberc e li elme son brizat e croisit. (193.51–57)

> [Javelins, lances, brandished spears, furbished maces, polished axes ... came there from both sides, at their ease, so that the hauberks and helmets were broken and smashed.]

If a battle is beautiful, he indicates, it is because of the masses of warriors it brings together, the brightness of their arms and armor, and the reverberations of their weapons crashing against each other, seemingly of their own accord. Even when the Continuator describes the corpses of the knights in the aftermath of the combat – with "ubrir mant costat / e manta camba fraita e mant bratz detrencat / e mant peitz escoichendre" [many sides opened up, many legs smashed, many arms sliced off, many chests torn apart] (188.56–58) – he marvels at the many different kinds of bodily transformations that can be witnessed. Flesh and blood are strewn on a field, he relates, "qu'entre blanc e vermelh lo camp an colorat" [so that the field is colored white and red] (188.64). If a battle is beautiful, he suggests, it is because of the fragmentation of a once unified body into parts and the colorfulness of those parts on the grass. He depicts not a good host defeating its evil counterpart, like the Franks who defeat the Saracens in *La chanson de Roland*, but the blur of battle, where the distinction between one army and another, let alone between a good army and an evil one, is lost. With the multitude, the diversity, and the extraordinariness of the elements it brings into play, a battle provides a vivid contrast to the poverty, the uniformity, and the ordinariness of our everyday sensory lives.

Yet the Continuator depicts battles as beautiful, not only insofar as they entail a purely physical encounter of two clashing forces, but also insofar as they symbolize a metaphysical value, namely valor. Whether they are crusaders or Occitan barons, all of the knights willingly risk their lives for something dearer. Outside Toulouse, where he will soon meet his end, Simon declares, "Mais val moiram ensemble o que siam guarit / no que tengam lo seti tant longamen aunit" [It is better that we die together or that we be saved than that we hold this shameful siege for so long] (193.14–15). Bernart de Comminges, an Occitan lord, similarly announces, "Mais val mortz ondrada c'aisi viure aunitz" [An honored death is worth more than a shamed life] (209.75). Like Bertran de Born, who had affirmed,

> Et atressi·m platz de segnor
> qand es primiers a l'envazir
> en caval, armatz, ses temor,
> c'aissi fai los sieus enadir
> ab valen vassalatge,[14]
>
> [It pleases me, too, when a lord is first to the attack on his horse, without fear, for thus he inspires his men with valiant courage,]

the Continuator describes the Young Count as rejecting his men's advice that he not expose himself in battle and instead "denant totz abrivatz / com leos o laupartz, can es descadenatz" [racing on before all of them, like a lion or a leopard, when he is unchained] (211.115–16). Whether they are crusaders or Occitan barons, all of the knights risk their lives in the knowledge that when they die they may go either to heaven or to hell. The crusader Robert de Beaumont predicts that, before Toulouse is taken, "entre colps e coladas e plagas e tensos / saubra Dieus e Diables cals esperitz es bos" [what with blows, grapplings, wounds, and single combats, God and the devil will know which soul is good] (195.28–29). Of the field of Montoulieu outside this town, where many have been slaughtered, the pro-Occitan poet writes, "Novelament i pobla iferns e paradis" [Hell and paradise are there populated anew] (194.81). With its participants' eagerness to throw themselves into the melee despite the dangers it presents to their bodies and souls, a battle provides a gripping contrast to the self-interestedness and self-protectiveness of our everyday existence.

In the *Canso*, the poets seem to deplore physical violence, such as the murder of a cleric or the dispossession of a rightful lord, but what they are actually deploring is a metaphysical violence, such as the destruction of the bonds between God and his believers, between a lord and his vassals, or between one kinsman and another. Insofar as they protest this physical violence, it is only because it symbolizes this metaphysical counterpart. In her chapter in this collection, Rosalind Brown-Grant observes how, in the fifteenth-century *Livre des faits de messire Jacques de Lalaing*, physical violence is repre-

---

[14] Bertran de Born, "Be·m plai lo gais temps de pascor," in *Poems of the Troubadour Bertran de Born*, p. 340 [338–45], vv. 21–25.

sented as a social ritual by which one knight is integrated into a chivalric community. Here, too, physical violence possesses no meaning in and of itself but only acquires meaning within the social and cultural context within which it transpires. Although physical violence is perceived as morally bad when it is perpetrated upon a passive, innocent victim, such as a cleric or a child, it is seen as morally good when it is perpetrated upon an active, guilty malefactor, such as a heretic or a foreign invader, and as morally neutral but aesthetically good when it is undertaken between two equal, eager parties who both value honor more than life, as it is in the Continuator's section of the poem. Throughout the *Canso*, violence is ultimately never about violence, but it is always about an ethos that deserves to be defended. For that reason, it is never condemned as such.

PART III
GENDER AND SEXUALITY

8

Political Violence and Sexual Violation in the Work of Benoît de Sainte-Maure

DAVID ROLLO

Late in his *Chronique des ducs de Normandie* (ca. 1170–80), Benoît de Sainte-Maure makes an analogy:

> Vez, merveilles poez entendre
> Qu'en vos deit mostrer e aprendre:
> Qu'Agamennon e li Grezeis
> Ne bien plus de quatorze reis
> Ne porent Troie en disz anz prendre;
> Unques n'i sorent tant entendre.
> E icist dus od ses Normanz
> E od ses autres buens aidanz
> Conquist un reiaume plenier
> E un grant pople fort e fier,
> Qui fu merveille estrange e grant,
> Sol entre prime e l'anuitant. (39873–84)[1]

> [Now you can hear a marvel that should indeed be brought to your attention. Agamemnon and the Greeks, including more than fourteen kings, could not take Troy in ten years. So much was beyond the scope of their abilities. Yet this duke, with his Normans and other worthy retainers, conquered an entire kingdom and a great, strong, proud people. And, what is truly cause for great marvel, he did so entirely between early morning and nightfall.]

The favorable comparison of the Norman victory at Hastings with the ineffectual Greek siege of Troy may appear unexceptional hyperbole: Benoît was writing under royal commission, and such fulsome praise of the Conqueror could be assessed as a predictable gesture of deference toward his great-

---

[1] Citations refer to line numbers in Benoît de Sainte-Maure, *Chronique des ducs de Normandie par Benoît*, ed. Carin Fahlin, 2 vols (Uppsala, Sweden: Almqvist and Wiksells, 1951–67). All translations are my own.

grandson, Henry II. However, Benoît's relationship with his appointed task was complex. Although not as explicitly impatient with the role of Plantagenet apologist as was Wace, his dismissed predecessor,[2] Benoît took subtle pains to distance himself from his material and his patron: several times in the *Chronique* he pauses to comment on the unrelenting demands of his undertaking, and he questions the integrity of the written past he produces by lauding the inexpressible mysteries of past, present, and future as they are held within the purview of Divine Providence.[3] This same spirit of diffidence, I contend, marks the terms of Benoît's apparently anodyne celebration of the Conqueror's victory. Mention of the siege of Troy not only establishes a troubling series of correspondences between the events leading to 1066 and the classical archetype of military conflict – both involved acts of perjury and wanton violence – but also evokes, as a palimpsest to the written history of the Normans, Benoît's own *Roman de Troie* (ca. 1155–70). The *Chronique* is underwritten by a preexisting narrative that dismantles its claims to historicity and serves to endorse the prerogatives of Benoît himself, the necromancer of the written word who supplements history with the glamorous sorcery of fiction and thereby creates the illusion of lives that have been irrevocably lost.[4]

Writing a generation before Benoît, William of Malmesbury attests to a crisis of historiographic partisanship that was precipitated by the events of 1066: the English and their Norman overlords have written about the Conqueror with vastly differing inflections, their views either excessively critical or excessively flattering, depending on ethnic perspective. Because he was descended from both populations, William, for his part, strives to adopt a position of neutrality.[5] At first glance, nothing could appear farther removed from Benoît's stated affiliations: he glorifies the Normans, who are for him a separate category from not only the English but also the French. As I have demonstrated elsewhere, however, Benoît at the same time shows circumspection in negotiating the oath of fealty that Harold was said to have sworn to the Conqueror, employing ambiguous third-person pronouns in order to make Harold, from one perspective, seem to swear to be faithful to nothing but his own resolve to become King of England and to resist any

---

[2] I discuss Wace's at times uncooperative response to the task of writing the history of the Normans in *Historical Fabrication, Ethnic Fable, and French Romance in Twelfth-Century England* (Lexington, KY: French Forum, 1998), pp. 141–65.

[3] See *Historical Fabrication*, pp. 226–32 and 241–43, respectively.

[4] For Benoît's subversion of the historical truth of Troy, see *Historical Fabrication*, pp. 167–221. For his necromantic control of the past, see my *Glamorous Sorcery: Magic and Literacy in the High Middle Ages* (Minneapolis: University of Minnesota Press, 2000), pp. 90–96.

[5] William of Malmesbury, *Gesta regum Anglorum*, ed. William Stubbs, 2 vols (1887–89; repr. New York: Kraus, 1964), book 3, prologue. Subsequent references refer to book and section numbers. All translations are my own.

other pretense to the crown, including that of William.[6] The effect is twofold: the Norman invasion of England loses its allegedly sanctified justification; and Harold, perjurious and false according to Norman historians, emerges as the champion of his Anglo-Saxon homeland. The circumspection that Benoît brings to bear demands the same on the part of the reader, particularly when interpreting the unnuanced terms in which Benoît proceeds to praise the Conqueror's magnanimity on the field of Hastings and to celebrate his benevolent, pacifying rule over a turbulent and lawless land.

Since the *Chronique* is a work of dynastic glorification, it is predictable that Benoît makes no mention of the initially disastrous results of Norman rule, particularly the decimation of the northern peasantry.[7] Yet omissions such as these not only mark the *Chronique* as a work of censorship through which the less flattering aspects of the Norman invasion and its consequences will be erased from the narrative of history. They do so in the context of a reign that is inaugurated by accusations of perjury and falsehood and described by an author who draws attention to his own equivocal relationship with his material. As I shall now argue, Benoît himself was faced with the prospect of being perjurious and false either to his patron or to his role as historian. He negotiated this delicate balance by gesturing back to that conflict he evokes after Hastings, the Trojan War, and to his own prior treatment of the violence it occasioned.

Although *Troie* cannot be considered historiography, in depicting the fall of Ilion it addresses matters of pressing historical relevance, particularly the discontinuity of empire. By the third quarter of the twelfth century, when Benoît is presumed to have been active, this threat had been a constant in Insular politics for over a hundred years. Most recently, the Norman/Angevin succession had been disrupted by Stephen of Blois's arrogation of the crown and the civil war that had sporadically divided the kingdom between 1135 and 1153. And, more significantly for the francophone public for whom Benoît wrote, in the 1060s the last undisputed Anglo-Saxon king, Edward the Confessor, had died without an heir and England had been invaded by a foreign army led by a foreign duke. Even though Benoît in *Troie* never directly relates these contemporary concerns to the Trojan past as he does in the *Chronique*, cultural context made analogies inevitable. By the mid-1130s Geoffrey of Monmouth's *Historia regum Britanniae* had begun to circulate. Therein the "island beneath the setting sun and beyond the realm of Gaul"

---

[6] See *Historical Fabrication*, pp. 232–38. A very different, unambiguous reading of the oath is given in Penny Eley and Phillip E. Bennett, "The Battle of Hastings according to Gaimar, Wace and Benoît: Rhetoric and Politics," *Nottingham Medieval Studies* 43 (1999): 74 [44–75].

[7] On this aspect of the *Chronique*, see *Historical Fabrication*, pp. 223–47. For an early twelfth-century account of the depopulation of the north of England after the Conquest, see William of Malmesbury, *Gesta regum Anglorum*, 3.249.

is referred to as "another Troy" in which kings will be born of the lineage of Brutus "and all the world will be subject to them."[8] By the time Benoît undertook *Troie*, therefore, Britain – and, by extension, England – had been celebrated as a new Troy for more than thirty years. Accordingly, when, later in the *Chronique*, Benoît alludes to the Trojan War as he assesses the Norman victory at Hastings, he in effect renders explicit an analogy that is already implicit in his earlier work. In the process he also returns to preoccupations that are addressed therein: in *Troie* he exploits the fall of Troy as a context through which to meditate upon the problems of perjury, genealogy, and bastardy that had beset the recent Insular past; and in the *Chronique* he once again engages these issues, not necessarily in conscious dialogue with the ideas laid forth in his first romance, but certainly in response to the same historical circumstances and through a common nexus of images. These involve acts of violence perpetrated upon the bodies of women and the political ramifications those acts were to have upon future genealogies that had come, however spuriously, to be related to the restitution of the Trojan polity.

Foreclosed Bloodlines: The Death of Polyxena

In narrating the fall of Ilion, Benoît is Trojan in his sympathies, attributing the destruction of the city to the treachery of Antenor and Aeneas. Through this anti-Virgilian bias, he undermines the leadership of both dignitaries and mitigates the glory of the Trojan settlements they allegedly went on to establish (a point to which I shall return). At a slightly later stage, he complements these implied but forceful charges of moral disqualification with a direct denial of genealogical legitimacy: members of the Trojan diaspora may indeed have gone on to found dynasties in Italy, Britain, and Dacia, but they were not of the house of Priam, and they arrogated rather than inherited their titles. The context for these dynastic meditations is the death speech that Benoît scripts for Polyxena, the last loyal citizen of Troy to speak at length in the romance and, ultimately, a metonym for the polity into which she was born.

Troy falls. By night twenty thousand Greek troops enter the city. By daybreak, ten thousand Trojans lie dead. The narrative persona makes some reference to the extent and nature of the massacre, yet he does so with little detail and with restrained pathos. It is rather Polyxena who bears witness to the carnage, upbraiding her captors before she too is slaughtered:

> D'ocire e d'espandre cerveles
> E d'estre en sanc e en boëles
> Deüsseiz estre tuit saol,

---

[8] Geoffrey of Monmouth, *Historia regum Britanniae*, ed. Acton Griscom (London: Longmans, 1929), 1.11. Citations refer to book and section number. All translations are my own.

> E aveir en autel refol
> Qu'un meis entier avez esté
> Si cruëlment ensanglenté
> De l'ocise des cors dampnez
> Que c'est merveille quos avez
> De ma mort faim ne desirier.
> Volez vos vos rasaziier
> Ancor de mei? Ço sacheiz bien,
> Que jo ne vueil por nule rien
> Vivre après si faite dolor. (26491–503)

> [You should be entirely sated with killing, spilling brains, and being in blood and bowels. You should by now have had your fill, since for a whole month you have been so cruelly covered in blood from the slaughter of doomed bodies. It is a marvel that you have hunger and desire for my death. Do you really wish to satisfy yourselves even further with me? Know, then, that I for nothing wish to live after pain inflicted in this way.]

The butchery of the Trojans resolves a metaphorical feast on the flesh of the dying, as the Greeks spill brains, blood, and bowels in an effort to feed a hunger and quench a thirst that prove insatiable. Polyxena casts herself as the next offering to these voracious appetites, a body to be consumed by a bloodlust that she comes progressively to describe in sexual terms:

> Je ne verreie mais nul jor
> Chose que me reconfortast
> Ne que leece me donast.
> N'istra de mei fille ne fiz
> Par quei seit vis n'abastardiz
> Li lignages dont jo sui nee.
> Ne refus pas ma destinee:
> O ma virginitee morrai. ...
> Vienge la mort, ne la refus,
> Quar n'ai talent de vivre plus.
> Mon pucelage li otrei:
> Onc si bel n'ot ne cuens ne rei.
> Ne vueil pas que cil l'aient pris,
> Qui mon chier pere m'ont ocis. (26504–11, 26521–26)

> [I shall not a single day more see anything that could comfort me or give me pleasure. No girl or boy shall come out of me by whom the lineage from which I was born would be vilified or bastardized. I do not refuse my destiny: I shall die with my virginity intact.... Let death come, I do not refuse it, for I have no wish any longer to live. I grant it my maidenhead – never did count or king have any so fine. I do not want it taken by those who killed my dear father.]

The Greek hunger and desire for Polyxena's death ("de [sa] mort faim ne desirier" [26491]) resolves into a desire to take the maidenhead from her living body. To prevent her lineage from being vilified and bastardized in this way, Polyxena bequeaths her virginity to death itself before being killed by Neoptolemus at the grave of his father, Achilles, who purportedly died because of his infatuation for her:

> La bele, la pro e la sage
> E de totes la mieuz preisiee
> A Neptolemus detrenchiee
> Sor la sepouture son pere.
> Tot ço vit Ecuba sa mere:
> Del sanc de ses fines beautez
> Fu li tombeaus ensanglentez. (26546–52)

> [The beautiful, the worthy, and the wise, of all women the most respected, Neoptolemus hacked to pieces on the grave of his father. Her mother Hecuba saw it all. The tomb was spattered with the blood of her exquisite beauties.]

Polyxena may escape rape, but the circumstances of her death border on inverted necrophilia. Sacrificed to father by son, she accepts her destiny ("destinee" [26510]) and is cut to pieces ("detrenchiee" [26548]) on top of the space enclosing the prone corpse of the man who in life was never able to defile her body. Her blood bespattering the grave functions, with grotesque hyperbole, as a substitute for the blood that was never shed with the loss of her maidenhead.

The death of Polyxena receives no elaboration in either of the Latin paradigms that served as Benoît's principal sources. In the *De excidio Troiae historia* Dares states that Neoptolemus cut Polyxena's throat at the tomb of his father ("Polyxenam … Agamemnon Neoptolemo tradit, is eam ad tumulum patris iugulat").[9] In the *Ephemeris belli Troiani* Dictys, to even more laconic effect, simply has him kill her there ("Polyxena … per Neoptolemum Achilli [est] inferias missa").[10] Benoît has, therefore, purposefully added the threats of rape and bastardized lineage.[11] On the most obvious level, the slaughter of

---

[9] Dares, *De excidio Troiae historia*, ed. Ferdinand Meister (Leipzig: Teubner, 1873), 43. Citations refer to section number.

[10] Dictys, *Ephemeris belli Troiani*, ed. Werner Eisenhut (Leipzig: Teubner, 1973), 5.13. Citations refer to book and section numbers.

[11] In the former he is perhaps showing the influence of Ovid, who in *Metamorphoses* 13 describes Polyxena, shortly before her death, requesting that no man be permitted to touch her virgin body ("tactuque viriles / virgineo removete manus" [466–67]). Many details differ, however: in the Latin, the Trojan princess makes no reference to future lineages, is sacrificed at the behest not of Ulysses but of the recently revenant ghost of Achilles, and is killed by a nameless high priest rather than Neoptolemus. (She is

Polyxena functions as a political synecdoche for the wider massacre of her fellow Trojans, who, like her, have the destiny ("destinee" [26060, 26113]) of being cut to pieces ("detrenchiez" [26080, 26082, 26092]). Her wish never to give birth, moreover, also finds its lexical analogue in the terms in which Benoît describes the Greek butchery of the Trojan populace:

> Li portal furent bien guardé
> Qu'uns n'en eissist ne eschapast,
> Qu'om n'oceïst e detrenchast.
> Es braz as meres alaitanz
> Ont detrenchiez les beaus enfanz.
> Après font d'eles autretal:
> L'ocise est tote comunal.
> Tote la nuit dura ensi,
> Desci que l'aube resclarci. (26078–86)

> [The city gates were well guarded to prevent any from leaving and escaping without being killed or cut to pieces. They hacked up the beautiful children nursing in the arms of their mothers and then did the same to the mothers themselves. The slaughter was universal. Thus it lasted all night, until the dawn again brightened.]

The Greeks resolve not to allow any Trojan to leave the confines of the city ("li portal furent bien guardé / qu'uns n'en *eissist* ne eschapast" [26078–79; emphasis added]) in order to pursue a near genocidal extermination of the foe who defied them for ten years. Polyxena, on the other hand, resolves not to allow any girl or boy to leave her body ("n'*istra* de mei fille ne fiz" [26507; emphasis added]) in order to prevent the royal bloodline from being vilified by socially inferior and illegitimate offspring. Yet in both cases genealogical rupture is emphasized and a particular Trojan future foreclosed. In the first, complete extermination is never achieved, since several members of the royal household are taken into captivity (Cassandra, Helenus, Andromache, and the sons that she bore Hector), Antenor is permitted to survive in exile, and Aeneas embarks on the journey that will eventually lead him to Italy. The city of Ilion, nonetheless, is never restored, and Aeneas is emphatically not a worthy and magnanimous heir to the royal house of Priam. In the work of Benoît he has no genealogical connection with the bloodline Polyxena protects and can make no pretense to anything that could remotely be associ-

---

considerably more laconic, moreover, speaking for a mere sixteen lines as opposed to the sixty of her vernacular analogue.) The edition cited here is that of Frank Justus Miller, rev. G. P. Goold, 2 vols (Cambridge, MA: Loeb Classical Library, Harvard University Press, 1984).

ated with magnanimity. Hecuba, for example, addresses him as follows after he has stood by and watched the murder of Priam:

> La reine veit Eneas:
> "Coilverz," fait ele, "Satanas,
> Vis e hontos e reneiez
> Sor toz traïtors desleiez." (26163–66)
>
> [The queen saw Aeneas: "Coward, Satan, abject and shameful and false, disloyal above all traitors."]

In *Troie*, Aeneas, "coilverz Satanas," the accomplice of Antenor, "coilverz Judas" (26135), is responsible not for the preservation of Trojan culture but for its destruction.[12]

Discontinued Bloodlines: The Nightmare of Arlette

In contrasting the invasion of England and the siege of Troy, Benoît in the *Chronique* places the Normans in the vanquishing role of the Greeks. Genealogically, however, their affiliations were said to lie elsewhere: part of the Trojan diaspora allegedly settled in Dacia and became the ancestors of the modern Scandinavian populations, including the Vikings from whom Rollo, the first Duke of Normandy, and his followers traced their descent. Early in the *Chronique* Benoît recognizes this Norman pretense to Trojan origins (645–62), yet he does so to implicitly unflattering effect. Since, as Benoît informs us, the founder of the Dacian colony of Trojan refugees was Antenor, the ancestors of the Normans took as their leader the man Benoît himself in *Troie* refers to as the "Judas" of the Trojan people. Indeed, the implication of Antenor in Norman history is extremely unfortunate if considered in the light of the genealogical questions that Benoît raises late in *Troie*: it is Antenor

---

[12] In *Bloodless Genealogies of the French Middle Ages: Translatio, Kinship, and Metaphor* (Gainesville: University Press of Florida, 2005), pp. 16–49, Zrinka Stahuljak analyzes the *Roman d'Enéas* (by consensus considered coeval with *Troie*) as a concerted effort to circumvent precisely the problem of discontinuity inherent in Enéas's implication in Roman history. Not of the lineage of Priam, Enéas makes an apparently superseding claim to descent from the founder of Troy, Dardanus, but this then brings into question the legitimacy of the line of Priam, under whom Troy reached the apogee of its power. If the Troy that is to be restored was the product of rupture from the point of origin, then the object of restoration is the mark of discontinuity itself. In *Enéas* this problem is negotiated through recourse to Virgil's theory of metempsychosis: only the mistakes of the past can be reborn and, through rebirth, rectified; and thus Rome becomes all that the flawed Troy never was. Benoît in *Troie* makes no such gesture to pagan (and, assessed in the Christian context, heretical) theories of reincarnation and never elaborates on the purportedly glorious future that awaits Enéas.

who betrays Polyxena to the Greeks, and he is quite plausibly among the unspecified "Seignor" to whom she explains her resolve to die rather than be raped and polluted by any of those present.[13] The infelicitous convergence of perjury, bastardy, and vilification that is evoked by the first leader of the Nordic Trojans strikingly anticipates a similar nexus of problematic attributes associated with the leader of their Norman descendants who prevailed at Hastings. That, of course, is William the Conqueror, the bastard son of Robert I who, according to Wace, admitted on his deathbed that he was wrong to have invaded England.[14]

William was born out of wedlock to a certain Arlette, "fille d'um borzeis" from Falaise (*Chronique*, 33469). In negotiating this potentially compromising detail, Benoît appears at his most cooperative, celebrating the advent of the Conqueror as an occurrence of nearly unprecedented dynastic majesty.[15] Yet, viewed from particular rhetorical perspectives, this mask of regal scrivener transparently reveals the less cheerful countenance of the author that lies beneath.

Robert first encounters Arlette as she is washing clothes at a stream. Apparently overcome by lust at once, he sends one of his chamberlains to impress upon her father the material advantages that will present themselves if his daughter consents to a night of sex. Lest this arrangement bear any hint of prostitution, Benoît emphasizes the honor Arlette felt and her wish not to enter the duke's lodging covertly on foot, but to ride there in full view of any who should be watching. He concedes that she felt trepidation but claims that it proved unwarranted:

> Si dunc seüst estre devine,
> Moct par eüst sis cuers grant joie,

---

[13] Polyxena begins her death speech "Seignor ... vil concire / avez tenu de mei ocire" [Sirs, vile was your decision to have me put to death] (26475–76).

[14] Wace, *Le roman de Rou*, ed. A. J. Holden, 3 vols (Paris: Picard, 1970–73), 3.9141–48. Citations refer to part and line numbers. All translations are my own.

[15] Penny Eley provides precisely this type of reading in "History and Romance in the *Chronique des ducs de Normandie*," *Medium Aevum* 68 (1999): 82–83 [81–95]. I see no reason to reject Eley's contention that Arlette is initially described in terms reminiscent of biblical paradigms to create something of a Norman Rebekah or Mary. As will become clear, however, I read Arlette's eventual experiences in far less positive terms. If, indeed, as Eley argues, Benoît surrounds Arlette with an aura of secularized sanctity, he does so only to emphasize the brutality with which it is violated. Benoît's treatment of the Conqueror's conception receives an even more celebratory reading from Huguette Legros in "Naissance d'un héros: De la bâtardise à la légende dans la *Chronique de Benoît de Sainte-Maure*," in *Guillaume le Conquérant face aux défis*, ed. Huguette Legros (Orléans: Paradigme, 2008), pp. 135–47. For general admonitions against such complacent grammatical readings of twelfth-century writing, particularly that produced for Henry II, see *Glamorous Sorcery*, pp. ix–xxv, and, with specific regard to the practice of Benoît, pp. 57–96, 108–21.

> Quer des Etor, le proz de Troie,
> Cil qui fu fiz deu rei Priant,
> Ne sui recorz ne remembrant
> Que meudres princes fust puis nez
> Qu'en li fu la nuit engendrez. (33588–94)

> [If she had known how to see into the future, her heart would certainly have been overjoyed, for, since Hector, that worthy of Troy who was the son of Priam, I can neither recall nor remember that a prince was afterward born who was better than the child who was engendered in her at night.]

Though on first sight the mention of Hector flatters William, ultimately it is not to the Conqueror's advantage since it acknowledges that he is not the equal of the Trojan prince. As though to palliate this recognition of inferiority, Benoît proceeds to introduce two other monarchs of irreproachable credentials:

> Buens fu Artur e Charlemaigne,
> Qui a force conquist Espaigne,
> Mais quant l'estoire vos ert dite
> Que de cestui avum escrite,
> Ne direiz pas, au mien espeir,
> Que prince peüst plus valeir. (33595–600)

> [Arthur was good, as was Charlemagne, who conquered Spain by force. But when the story I have written about this other prince will be told you, I am quite certain that you will not say that any could be more worthy.]

The Conqueror, therefore, is more magnificent than Charlemagne and Arthur; and we, the readers and listeners, will be persuaded of as much as we progress through the text. If, however, following Benoît's advice, we indeed bring our judgment to bear and determine that the Conqueror was a prince of unmatched worth, we will do so only if we adjust our expectations of what it may mean to be of princely blood. Immediately after making the act of interpretation an objective concern, Benoît adds:

> Eissi consent Dex maintes feiz
> Choses que l'on tient a desleiz,
> Dum l'on veit granz biens avenir,
> Eissi com ci poreiz oïr.
> Si tot oct pechié eu delit
> Que li dus oct en li la nuit,
> Qui segun lei, com esposee,
> Ne l'a mie despucelee,
> Si fu apert e pareissant.

>   E bien fu a toz connoissant
>   Que Dex enama e maintint
>   L'eir qui des deus nasquié e vint. (33601–12)

> [As you can now hear, God often consents to things that may be taken as dishonorable but from which a great good manifestly comes. If there was anything sinful about the pleasure the duke got from her that night, it was nonetheless open and undisguised. According to the young woman herself, the duke did not take her virginity, since she was married. It was clearly known to all that God loved and watched over the heir who was the offspring born of the two.]

Faithful to official biography, Benoît states that William was the product of this union. Yet, despite his insistence on facts that are well known to all ("si fu apert e pareissant / e bien fu a toz conoissant"), he has just introduced information of considerable magnitude that has so far been passed over in silence: Arlette was in fact married and not a virgin. Under these circumstances, and despite Benoît's confident assertion that Robert was the father of Arlette's child, the reader, called upon to exercise judgment, must pause in order to question the means whereby such confidence can be justified. At a later stage, Benoît returns to this question of paternity, yet he does so in terms that further complicate the issue:

>   Granz fu li biens, ce fu vertez,
>   Quer en ceste danzele Alrez
>   Esteit ja engendrez Guillaeaume
>   Qui d'Engleterre oct le reiaume.
>   A paine ert encor conneüe
>   Sinn a tel avision veüe
>   Qui hautement aveira puis,
>   Qu'aprés orreiz, si cum je truis.
>   Moct a Aurez, la pro, la sage,
>   Bien empleié son pucelage. (33739–48)

> [Great was the good, in truth, because in this young woman, Arlette, was already engendered William, who ruled the kingdom of England. This truth was scarcely already known, perceived only in a vision of lofty import that will later manifest itself (and that you shall soon hear about, just as I find it written). Arlette, the worthy and the wise, put her virginity to extremely good use.]

Arlette loses her maidenhead in the best possible circumstances when William is conceived. Yet Benoît has already stated that she is no longer a virgin when she becomes the duke's concubine, leaving only one conclusion: if William is the result of a loss of maidenhead for which Robert is not responsible, then Arlette is already by this stage pregnant, presumably by her husband.

According to this alternative to the official dynastic truth that Benoît has already told, William was not a bastard at all. He was conceived in wedlock, yet under conditions that vastly differed from those Benoît appears to celebrate: the future King of England (and great-grandfather of the monarch for whom Benoît writes) was the son of a middle-class couple from Falaise. Lineage, in this case, was not vilified and bastardized by illegitimate union with a social inferior. It was ruptured altogether, with wide-ranging political consequences: the Norman invasion of England had no justification, since it was undertaken by a man who bore the ducal title under the most perjurious and false of circumstances and professed to a crown to which his bourgeois blood had no dynastic right.

Although each engages the historically pressing question of genealogical discontinuity, the stories of Polyxena and Arlette could not appear more different. Polyxena, "la belle, la pro e la sage" (*Troie*, 26546), refuses to allow the vilification and bastardization of the royal house of Troy, while Arlette, "la pro, la sage" (*Chronique*, 33747), assures an even more deleterious outcome for the ducal house of Normandy. Also disparate are their responses to sex. Polyxena refuses any man's attentions without compromise, while Arlette assents to those of Duke Robert without complaint. Cast into metaphor, however, her experience proves far more troubling than is grammatically apparent. The duke has his way:

> Mais ainz que parust li matins,
> Se fu la danzele endormie,
> Qui merveille fu esfreïe,
> D'um gré songe qu'ele sonjoct.
> Quant ele plus sofrir neu poct,
> Un plaint jeta e un haut cri:
> Dotosement se resperi
> E tressailli si faitement. (33712–19)

> [Before the appearance of morning, the maiden fell asleep. She was utterly terrified by a nightmare she had. When she could no longer bear it, she screamed and cried aloud. In terror she awoke, trembling at what she had dreamed.]

The previous activities, which Arlette apparently bore with equanimity ("tot li sofre" [33708]), give way to a dream that becomes so unbearable ("plus sofrir neu poct" [33716]) that the young woman wakes up screaming. She describes to the duke what she imagined:

> "Sire," fait eu, "ne sai por quei
> Fors tant, quer celer neu vos dei.
> Or m'ert avis en mun dormant
> C'un arbre eisseit de mei si grant,
> Si lonc, si dreit, si merveillos

> Qu'au cel ateigneit ci sor nos.
> Son ombre, dum sui esfreïe,
> Aümbroct tote Normendie
> E mer e la grant terre engleise." (33723–31)

> ["Sire," she said, "I don't know why I reacted as I did, except for the following, which I tell because I should hide nothing from you. In my sleep I thought that a tree was coming out of me that was so big, so long, so straight, so dreadful that it reached the sky above us.[16] Its shadow, which terrified me, covered all of Normandy, the sea, and the great country of England."]

If what preceded this dream was a night of blissful sex, this is a curious coda. Certainly, the dream almost immediately receives a genealogical gloss, since Benoît soon pauses to congratulate Arlette for having already conceived the Conqueror (33739–48). Thus presaged, it would seem, are the glorious achievements of Arlette's son, who emerges as an offshoot of near celestial magnitude. Yet this celebration of future glory is unsettled by the horrific nature of Arlette's experience. The terror she feels is not only ill-suited to dynastic apologetics; it is also derived from Wace's *Roman de Rou*, the bilious vernacular history that Henry II ostensibly found so unflattering that he commissioned Benoît to write the *Chronique* in its stead. Wace, too, has Arlette scream and shake in fear ("jeta un plaint, si tressaili" [3.2855]), and he, too, glosses her dream in genealogical terms:

> "Sire," dist ele, "je ne sai,
> se n'est pur ceo ke je sunjai
> ke un arbre de mun cors isseit,
> que vers le ciel amunt creisseit;
> de l'umbre ki entur alout
> tute Normendie aümbrout." (3.2859–64)

> ["Sire," she said, "I don't know why I reacted as I did, except in response to what I dreamed. A tree was coming out of my body that grew upward into the sky. With its surrounding shadow it covered all of Normandy."]

In his habitually disobliging manner, Wace limits the legitimacy of the Conqueror's territorial pretensions: the magnificent offspring anticipated here may touch the heavens, but the shadow of his temporal dominion does not extend beyond Normandy. Benoît corrects the omission and reinstates England

---

[16] I have translated "merveillos" as "dreadful" since it often has a negative meaning for Benoît. For examples from early in *Troie*, consider lines 1378 (qualifying "serpenz," rhyming with "hisdos"), 5933 (qualifying "tormente," complemented by "laide" and "oscure," rhyming with "tenebrose"), 6026 (qualifying "mal"), and 9309 (qualifying "venjance," complemented by "pesme," rhyming with "dolerose").

to the Norman imperium. Nonetheless, despite this apparently conciliatory gesture, he follows his predecessor in transforming the happy anticipation of future magnificence into a vision of menacing horror. If anything, in fact, he moves beyond Wace, explicitly stating that what Arlette experienced was a nightmare ("um gré songe" [33715]) and making her scream at the sight of a shadow that loomed terrifyingly above her.

These are disobliging moves from an author who elsewhere sustains the grammatical demeanor of obliging scribe. More apposite to the exigencies of propaganda would have been recourse to the far more benign version of Arlette's dream found in William of Malmesbury's *Gesta regum*, a work that both Wace and Benoît knew: "Cujus magnitudinem futuram matris sompnium portendebat, quo intestina sua per totam Normanniam et Angliam extendi et dilatari viderat" [His future greatness was portended in a dream of his mother's, in which she saw her womb stretch and dilate across all of Normandy and England] (3.229). What the Conqueror's mother sees in the Latin version, although bizarre, does not terrify, and it involves a hyperbolic pregnancy rather than a hyperbolic offspring. Benoît, then, follows Wace in choosing a nightmare over a dream, a nightmare, moreover, in which the product of parturition rather than parturition itself is emphasized.

It is plausible to genealogical concerns that an offspring is rendered as a tree.[17] It is also logically conceivable that a scion of this type be portrayed as sprouting from his mother, perhaps from her stomach or side. Both Wace and Benoît employ the verb "eissir" to designate this process. Wace's usage is vague: the Conqueror simply comes out of his mother's body, with no mention of how or where. Benoît, nonetheless, elsewhere addresses precisely the context of reproduction that is at issue here, and in doing so he uses "eissir" with precise anatomical specifications: in declaring her refusal to bear children, Polyxena in *Troie* states, "n'istra de mei fille ne fiz" (26507). Here the verb is direct and graphic, designating the passage of the child not out of the mother's side or stomach but out of her vagina. Assessed in these terms, Arlette's dream is a nightmare of horrifying delivery, and what is born is not a child but a monstrosity.[18]

---

[17] I emphasize "plausible." During the High Middle Ages, genealogical iconography usually took the form of the "virga" (rod, twig), the "arbor" appearing only in later medieval representations of bloodlines. Unlike the later "arbor," the "virga" places the sequential offspring in linear succession on the trunk rather than on the branches. On this, see Christiane Klapisch-Zuber, "Le genèse de l'arbre généalogique," in *L'arbre: Histoire naturelle et symbolique de l'arbre, du bois et du fruit au Moyen Âge*, ed. Michel Pastoureau (Paris: Léopard d'Or, 1993), pp. 41–81, and *L'ombre des ancêtres: Essai sur l'imaginaire médiévale de la parenté* (Paris: Fayard, 2000).

[18] For monstrous births in later medieval literature, see Peggy McCracken, *The Curse of Eve, the Wound of the Hero* (Philadelphia: University of Pennsylvania Press, 2003), pp. 61–76. McCracken notes several texts in which wives who were presumed to be socially inferior to their noble husbands were falsely accused of giving birth to monstrous

The monstrous imagery does not stop here. Again, let us recall that Benoît employs verbal repetition to associate what occurs in the nightmare with what immediately goes before: Arlette bears all the duke does to her ("tot li sofre"); yet, only eight couplets later, she cannot bear any more of what she is subjected to in the dream that follows ("plus sofrir neu poct"). Lexical repetition is complemented by analogies in what Arlette undergoes: on both occasions something leaves her body, and on both occasions that thing is male. Furthermore, the gynecological specificity of the verb "eissir" serves grotesquely to sexualize the circumstances of delivery itself, with the effect that the mother dreams of giving birth in a manner suggestive of the preceding experience of intercourse. The tree is described in terms not of its lateral reach (which would be logical for the extent of the Conqueror's dominion and is implied by William's "extendi et dilatari" and by Wace's "l'umbre ki entur alout") but of its vertical erection (it is "si grant, / si lonc, si dreit" [33726–27]). It is literally coming out of, retracting from the woman's body ("eisseit d['ele]" [33726]). And it looms over her to cast a shadow so dreadful that she screams in terror: "Un plaint jeta e un haut cri / dotosement se respéri / e tressailli si faitement" [She screamed and cried aloud. In terror she awoke, trembling at what she had dreamed] (33717–19). Arlette may have borne the duke's physical attentions, yet immediately after she dreams of childbirth in a manner that evokes the unbearable violence of rape.

Repressed Violence

This horrific superimposition of delivery and intercourse is quite compatible with the polymorphous, constantly shifting potential of the nightmare in which it is experienced, and it allows Benoît to imply a great deal without ever having to be explicit. Most obviously, the nightmare does not bode well for the future Anglo-Norman domains, overshadowed as they are by a monstrous presence of terrifying effect. Moreover, it further undermines the glories of the duke's birth: not only was the man who claimed paternity not the father, but the duke's mother was subjected to that man's attentions under circumstances that are metaphorically far removed from the acquiescence she allegedly showed.

It must again be emphasized that Benoît proceeds through indirection,

---

offspring, the child's deformity functioning as a visible sign of the mother's genealogical undesirability. Benoît may be working to a similar end, attempting to undermine (rather than contradict) the official version of Robert's paternity that he provides, when he earlier states, "Dex enama e maintint / L'eir qui des deus nasquié e vint" (33611–12). Arlette was indeed socially inferior to the man who was traditionally believed to have made her pregnant, and her nightmare does indeed lend the Conqueror the monstrous attributes that her inferiority would be taken to confer.

here, as in his treatment of Harold's oath, subtly contradicting the official version of events he elsewhere endorses. As I have argued elsewhere, like Wace before him, he maintained this distance from his material primarily because he found the task of unctuous glorification beneath his talents.[19] Yet, to a greater extent than Wace, he also found virtue in imposed necessity and made the *Chronique* an extended meditation on the relationship of writing to monarchic power. The pro-Norman bias of his commission is never disguised, nor are the terms of the sycophantic rhetoric through which Henry II is to be celebrated.[20] Indeed, the task of glorification becomes in itself a conspicuously self-conscious theme of the work: if history is compromised by propaganda, then it is the role of the historian to draw attention to that fact and to clarify the historical circumstances by which recourse to censorship was fostered. This Benoît magisterially achieves. In both *Troie* and the *Chronique*, he denies continuity of empire. In the first, the treachery of Antenor and Aeneas and death of Polyxena subvert any future pretense to the restoration of neo-Trojan grandeur; and, in the second, the circumstances of the Conqueror's conception expose the illegitimacy of Norman claims to England, that most recent and contextually significant location of a New Troy. In both texts, a woman's body is the site of potential violence, a physical vessel through which bloodlines will be foreclosed or usurped. And, in the *Chronique*, a woman's nightmare becomes a semiotic space through which the censored alternatives to propaganda find displaced representation. The scream with which Arlette awakens expresses a horror that reason has repressed, just as the text in which her story is told intimates potential truths that have been suppressed from the narrative of history.

---

[19] See, again, *Historical Fabrication*, pp. 226–32.

[20] See particularly *Chronique*, 42035–72, in which Benoît, having just described the Conqueror's burial, expresses his rapt anticipation of the long-delayed (and still somewhat distant) moment at which he will finally be able to write of the lofty deeds of his own monarch.

9

The Sexuality of History: The Demise of Hugh Despenser, Roger Mortimer, and Richard II in Jean Le Bel, Jean Froissart, and Jean d'Outremeuse

ZRINKA STAHULJAK

The francophone chroniclers Jean Le Bel, Jean Froissart, and Jean d'Outremeuse characterize the Franco-English Hundred Years War (1337–1453) as senseless destruction, "morteile guere" [deadly war],[1] "grandes guerres et dissolutions" [great war and annihilation],[2] "grans destructions de gens et de pays" [great destruction of people and lands], and "grant desolation" [great devastation].[3] Philippe de Mézières describes it as "une plaie ... universelle" [a wound ... universally spread].[4] They begin their histories of this particularly devastating and bloody war with the events that brought Edward III to the throne. They report that, acting upon the counsel of Hugh Despenser the Younger, Edward II forced his wife, Queen Isabella, to flee to France with their son in May 1325, accompanied by Sir Roger Mortimer and the Earl of Kent. In reality, Edward II sent Isabella to her homeland, France,

---

[1] Jean des Preis dit d'Outremeuse, *Ly myreur des histors, Chronique*, ed. Ad. Borgnet and Stanislas Bormans, 6 vols (Brussels: L'Académie royale de Belgique, 1864–80), 6:322. Henceforth cited as d'Outremeuse. All translations are my own.

[2] Jean Le Bel, *Chronique*, ed. Jules Viard and Eugène Déprez, 2 vols (Paris: Renouard, 1904–5), 1:93. Henceforth cited as Le Bel. All translations are my own.

[3] Jean Froissart, *Chroniques, Livre I, Le manuscrit d'Amiens*, ed. George T. Diller, 5 vols (Geneva: Droz, 1991–98), henceforth cited as Amiens; manuscripts A and B are published in *Chroniques de J. Froissart*, ed. Siméon Luce, Gaston Raynaud, Léon Mirot, and Albert Mirot, 15 vols (Paris: J. Renouard; H. Laurens, 1869–1975), henceforth cited as Luce; and Froissart, *Chroniques; début du premier livre: Édition du manuscrit de Rome Reg. lat. 869*, ed. George T. Diller (Geneva: Droz, 1972), henceforth cited as Rome. All citations of Book IV are from Jean Froissart, *Chroniques*, in *Œuvres de Froissart*, ed. Kervyn de Lettenhove, 25 vols (1867–77; Osnabrück, Germany: Biblio Verlag, 1967), henceforth cited as Lettenhove. All translations are my own. Quotations here are from Amiens, 1:6, and Luce, 1.2:84.

[4] Philippe de Mézières, *A Letter to King Richard II [Epistre au Roi Richart]*, ed. and trans. G. W. Coopland (New York: Barnes & Noble, 1976), p. 103. Translation modified throughout.

to negotiate the terms of Edward II's homage for Gascony with her brother, Charles IV of France; and their son, the future Edward III, later joined her there. Isabella, having been persecuted at court by Hugh Despenser,[5] returned to England only in September 1326, accompanied by the knights of Hainault, which brought about the overthrow of Edward II, the execution of his counselor and lover Hugh Despenser the Younger, and the crowning of Edward III, the war-loving king of the English whose challenge to the French throne led to the outbreak of the Hundred Years War in 1337.

Since John Boswell's *Christianity, Social Tolerance, and Homosexuality* (1980), scholars interested in the history of sexuality have been preoccupied by the elements of this story that focus on Edward II and his sexual practices and identity – perhaps excessively so.[6] Working under Boswell's influence, they have been tempted to read the capital punishment and public execution of Hugh Despenser as violence directed against a particular sexual practice and therefore an unambiguous repudiation of non-normative sex acts and desires. However, medieval francophone historians of the Hundred Years War give an interesting twist to what we have been reading as sexual violence. As I will show, they believed in general in physiology as a trigger for events that could change or shape history, regardless of the nature of sex acts.[7] It is repetition – and, specifically, the compulsion to repeat sex acts, whether

---

[5] G. A. Holmes, "Judgement on the Younger Despenser, 1326," *English Historical Review* 70.275 (1955): 266 [261–67]. On Edward II, see Mary Saaler, *Edward II, 1307–1327* (1997; London: Rubicon, 2007); Roy Martin Haines, *King Edward II: Edward of Caernarfon, His Life, His Reign, and Its Aftermath, 1284–1330* (Montreal: McGill-Queen's University Press, 2003).

[6] John Boswell, *Christianity, Social Tolerance, and Homosexuality: Gay People in Western Europe from the Beginning of the Christian Era to the Fourteenth Century* (Chicago: University of Chicago Press, 1980). Recent work on Edward's sexuality includes Claire Sponsler, "The King's Boyfriend: Froissart's Political Theater of 1326," in *Queering the Middle Ages*, ed. Glenn Burger and Steven F. Kruger (Minneapolis: University of Minnesota Press, 2001), pp. 143–67; W. M. Ormrod, "The Sexualities of Edward II," in *The Reign of Edward II: New Perspectives*, ed. Gwilym Dodd and Anthony Musson (York: York Medieval Press, 2006), pp. 22–47; and Ian Mortimer, "Sermons of Sodomy: A Reconsideration of Edward II's Sodomitical Reputation," in *The Reign of Edward II*, ed. Dodd and Musson, pp. 48–57.

[7] Instead of "homosexual(ity)," I prefer the terms "sodomy" and "sodomitical" to speak of medieval male–male relationships in their historical context and to refer to the non-normative nature of sex acts. I am aware of the imperfections and dangers of this terminology, especially in associating sodomy strictly with male–male practices (rather than to all same-sex and opposite-sex relations) or reducing male–male relationships only to this practice. On the methodology of studying sexuality *before* sexuality, see Karma Lochrie, "Presidential Improprieties and Medieval Categories: The Absurdity of Heterosexuality," in *Queering the Middle Ages*, ed. Burger and Kruger, pp. 87–96; and James A. Schultz, *Courtly Love, the Love of Courtliness, and the History of Sexuality* (Chicago: University of Chicago Press, 2006).

between men or between men and women – and not the nature of the acts themselves that provokes violent events that shape history. Historians portray the repeated sex acts in both male–male and male–female relationships as violence perpetrated against the body politic – that is, as treason. They then show how this sexual violence against the body politic is reinscribed onto "treacherous" bodies through acts of torture, castration, and public execution. In other words, for the francophone historians of the Hundred Years War, sexual violence is first and foremost political violence, treason committed against the body politic; and while castration incriminates sex acts that have led to treason, it does not specifically incriminate same-sex acts and desires.

In order to demonstrate this point, I will examine three chronicles of the Hundred Years War that are contemporaneous with the war they describe – chronicles that are often read as a set. The *Chronique* by Jean Le Bel (1290?–1369?) covers the preliminaries and the beginnings of the Hundred Years War (1325–60). This "vraye hystoire du prœu et gentil roy Edowart [III]" [true history of the valiant and noble king Edward III] (Le Bel, 1:1) served as the basis for a section (years 1325–40) in the universal history *Ly myreur des histors* (ca. 1395) by Jean d'Outremeuse (1338–99?) and for a portion of Book I, years 1325–50, of the *Chroniques* by Jean Froissart (1337–1404?). Although the first three versions of Froissart's *Chroniques*, the manuscript of Amiens (ca. 1377–81?) and manuscripts A and B (before 1391?), follow Jean Le Bel more or less closely, in the last version of the manuscript of Rome (ca. 1396–1400?) Froissart supersedes his written source with "la vraie information que je ay eu des vaillans honmes, chevaliers et esquiers" [the true information that I obtained from the brave men, knights, and squires] (Rome, p. 35). English king Edward II's deposition and the public execution of Hugh Despenser, his counselor and lover, and the subsequent public execution of Edward III's counselor, Roger Mortimer, Earl of March, lover of Queen Isabella, will be my main focus in analyzing these three chronicles in order to show how historians do not consider the nature of sex acts to be the principal trigger of major events and violence. I will end with a brief analysis of marriage as a political strategy for appeasing violence in Froissart's Book IV of the *Chroniques* and in the allegorical treatise *Epistre au Roi Richart*, which was written by Philippe de Mézières (1327?–1405) in the first half of 1395 and is devoted to the negotiations leading to the marriage of Richard II with the daughter of Charles VI of France.

Events and Sex Acts

In the retelling of the purported repudiation of Isabella, Jean d'Outremeuse uses two sources, an anonymous chronicle and Jean Le Bel's *Chronique* – sources that he understands as being "l'un contraire à l'autre" [one contrary to the other] and that he claims to have merely juxtaposed: "ilh les metit tous ensemble" [he put them together] (d'Outremeuse, 6:315).[8] According to the anonymous source, in 1323, "Hue, li dispensiers le roy, qui astoit li plus riches hons de tout le royalme, requist la damme d'amours le femme le roy d'Engleterre" [Hugh, king's dispenser, who was the richest man in the kingdom, sought the love of the lady, the wife of the King of England] (6:270). Because Isabella rejected him, Hugh sought an appropriate vengeance and "achat à I marchant le venien d'on serpent amerois et en donnat à boire le roy Eduart ... si que li roy enamat mult fort le despensiers par le forche de venien" [bought from a merchant the poison of the love snake and gave it to drink to King Edward ... so that the king, on account of the poison's power, fell madly in love with Despenser] (6:270). Despenser takes his revenge on the queen by making the king fall in love with him. The effects of the serpent's venom gesture to the sodomitical love of Edward for Hugh, but the figure of a love potion exculpates Edward from triggering the major events that follow. Rather, it is Despenser's wounded pride that leads to the repetition of vengeful acts: "Tous jours pensoit à trahison, comment ilh posist greveir la royne" [He always was thinking of treachery, of how to hurt the queen]. These acts culminate in his accusation to the king: "Je l'ay troveit aveque I homme charnelment gesante" [I found her lying carnally with a man] (6:301). A spurned lover's desire for vengeance leads to the queen's exile in France and Hainaut in 1325, and ultimately to the deposition and imprisonment of Edward II in 1326.

At this point Jean d'Outremeuse returns to the year 1325 and retells the events from his other source, Jean Le Bel's *Chronique*. D'Outremeuse faithfully copies Le Bel, reporting that it was Despenser's "malisse" (6:326; cf. Le Bel, 1:10) that led to the queen's exile; but then he interpolates the explanation of the cause of her exile from the anonymous chronicle: "Et enamat Hue la damme ... et li requist de son amour: et elle li escondit ...; et chu dont j'ay fait mention, che fut la cause por quoy ilh covient vuidier la royne la royalme d'Engleterre" [And Hugh fell in love with the lady ... and sought her love but she refused. ... And this of which I spoke was the cause why the queen had to leave the kingdom of England] (6:326–27). D'Outremeuse's interpolation – that is, the insistence on Despenser's love for the queen – overrides the other implied cause for the queen's banishment, the sodomitical love of Hugh and Edward. D'Outremeuse refers to this love as well, in a single instance drawn from Jean Le Bel's *Chronique*: "Ilh astoit sodomites, maiement del

---

[8] D'Outremeuse is not speaking of himself in the third person here. Rather, this is the voice of Jean de Stavelot, who transcribed and continued d'Outremeuse's original compilation. See Stanislas Bormans, *Chronique et geste de Jean des Preis dit d'Outremeuse: Introduction et table des matières* (Brussels: L'Académie royale de Belgique, 1887), pp. xc–xci. On Jean d'Outremeuse, see Marie-Thérèse de Medeiros, "Dans le sillage de Jean le Bel: La chute d'Edouard II chez Jean d'Outremeuse et chez Froissart," *Cahiers de recherches médiévales* 10 (2003): 131–42.

roy meisme" [He was a sodomite and likewise the king himself] (6:333). D'Outremeuse, however, does not copy the rest of Le Bel's sentence, "pour tant avoit le roy dechassé la royne par son enhortement" [and for this reason the king exiled the queen, at his (Despenser's) urging].[9] D'Outremeuse thus does not simply juxtapose but attempts to reconcile the two chronicles: "Ilh les metit tous *ensemble*." D'Outremeuse's interpolation designates Despenser's love for the queen, not the king's love for Hugh, as the trigger for the subsequent chain of events.

It can be argued, then, that d'Outremeuse uses both the anonymous source and the interpolation to occult the sodomitical love explicit in Le Bel because something is inherently wrong with this kind of love. D'Outremeuse's process of compilation and juxtaposition "straightens" the story out, as it were, such that Despenser's love for the queen, not for the king, sets the momentous events into motion. Moreover, the king falls in love with Hugh only because of the serpent's venom, under circumstances beyond his control that exonerate him from any blame. At the metahistorical level, however, the juxtaposition and interpolation give the exact measure of the extent to which historians of the Hundred Years War generally used physiology as a credible means of historical representation of events that shaped history in a significant way. The king's and Despenser's sodomitical acts *and* the unfulfilled desire of Despenser for the queen can have exactly the same result: the banishment of the queen and ultimately the deposition of Edward II. The damage lies in the duration and repetition of Hugh's love, be it for queen or king, not in the nature of the act through which love is expressed. Repetition and the compulsion to repeat, whether sex acts occur between men or between men and women, trigger major events, and violent ones at that, and shape and transform history.

Castration: Sodomy and Adultery

Similar conclusions can be reached in reading the execution of Hugh Despenser the Younger, which took place on 24 November 1326 in Hereford, following his and Edward II's capture by Isabella's army. The record of his judgment specifies:

---

[9] Le Bel, 1:28 (the full passage is cited below). In the last version of the Rome manuscript, Froissart makes the link explicit: "Et pour ce vilain et ort pechiet, li rois avoit escaciet la roine sa fenme en sus de lui" [And because of this vile and foul sin, the king had banished the queen, his wife, from him] (Rome, p. 92). For a study of Froissart's *Chroniques*, see Peter F. Ainsworth, *Jean Froissart and the Fabric of History: Truth, Myth, and Fiction in the "Chroniques"* (Oxford: Clarendon, 1990); and Michel Zink, *Froissart et le temps* (Paris: Presses Universitaires de France, 1998).

> Hughe come traitour vous estes troue par quay vous agardent touz les bones gentz du Roialme graindres et mayndres, riches et poures, et par commune assent que vous come laron estes troue et atteynt, par quay vous serrez pendu. Et come traitour vous estes troue par quay vous serrez trayne et quartere et enuoye par mye le Roialme. Et pur ceo que vous fustes vtlage par notre seignour le Roi et par commune assent et estes reuenu en court sanz garrant vous serrez decole. Et pur ceo que vous fustes tot temps desloyaut et procurant descord entre notre seignour le Roi et notre treshonurable dame la Roigne et entre les autres gentz du Roialme si enserrez vous debouwelle, et puys ils serront ars. (Holmes, "Judgement," 266–67)[10]

> [Hugh, you are found to be guilty of treason on account of which all the good people of the kingdom, great and small, rich and poor, examine you and by common assent accuse you and find you guilty of robbery, for which you are to be hanged. And, as guilty of treason, you will be drawn and quartered and your body parts sent all over the kingdom. And because you were outlawed from the court by our lord the king and by common assent, and you came back to court without consent, you will be decapitated. And because you were always disloyal and sowing discord between our lord the king and our most honorable lady the queen, and between all other people of the kingdom, you will be disemboweled and your intestines will be burnt.]

Jean Le Bel, and later Jean Froissart and Jean d'Outremeuse, report the execution sequence in this order, following Hugh's being drawn upon a hurdle through the streets of Hereford:

> On luy couppa tout premierement le vit et les coulles pour tant qu'il estoit herites et sodomites, ainsy comme on disoit, et mesmement du roy mesmes, et pour tant avoit le roy dechassé la royne par son enhortement. Quant le vit et les coulles luy furent couppez, on les jetta au feu et furent arses; aprez, on luy fendi le ventre et luy osta on le cuer et le jetta on ou feu pour ardoir, pour tant qu'il estoit faulx de cueur et traitre, et que, par son traitre conseil et enhort, le roy avoit honny et gasté son royaume, et mis à meschief.... Et, avecques ce, il avoit tellement enhorté le roy qu'il ne pouoit ne ne vouloit veoir la royne ne son aisné fil. ... Aprez ... on luy couppa la teste, et fu envoyée à Londres, et puis fu taillié en quatre quartiers, et furent envoyez aux quatre meilleurs citez d'Angleterre aprez Londres.[11]

> [First, he had his penis and testicles cut off, because he was said to be a heretic and a sodomite and likewise was said about the king himself. And for this reason the king exiled the queen, at his [Despenser's] urging. When his penis and testicles were severed, they were thrown into the fire

---

[10] The accusation of robbery comes from the fact that Despenser engaged in a widespread campaign of dispossession of lands and titles from nobles and widows. See Holmes, "Judgement."

[11] Le Bel, 1:28. See d'Outremeuse, 6:333; Amiens, 1:34; and Rome, p. 92.

and burnt. After which, he had his chest cut open and his heart torn out and thrown into the fire to burn. This was so because he had a false heart and was a traitor and because, on account of his treacherous counsel and encouragements, the king had degraded, devastated, and neglected his kingdom.... And, moreover, Hugh had so pressed the king that he couldn't and wouldn't see the queen and his eldest son.... Afterward ... he was beheaded and the head was sent to London; then his body was quartered and the quarters immediately sent to England's four foremost cities after London.]

Our three francophone historians are the only ones to add genital mutilation to the torture and public execution of Hugh Despenser. This new element of sexual violence against Despenser's body could be taken as a moral condemnation of sodomy. This conclusion can be supported by word choice and certain reported attitudes in several other instances: Edward and Hugh cannot escape by boat from Bristol because "lors pechiés leur encombra" [their sin stood in the way];[12] the Earl of Lancaster "desplaisoit li usages que li rois avoit empris" [disliked the habits the king had adopted] (Luce, 1.2:13); the people disliked "tous ses usaiges et ses maintiens" [all his customs and manners] (Amiens, 1:37); and "conmenchierent a murmurer li prelat, li baron et li honmes des chités ... que on l'avoit tant tenu en wiseusses et en delisces que li roiaulmes d'Engleterre avoit recheu blame et damage oultre mesure" [priests, nobles, and burghers ... began to complain that he had been held in idleness and pleasure to the point that the kingdom of England had received blame and damage beyond measure] (Rome, pp. 47–48).[13] Since John Boswell, modern scholars of the history of medieval sexuality have also focused on this apparent accusation and condemnation of sodomitical practice, reinforced, furthermore, with the well-known narrative of the manner of Edward II's death, caused by the insertion of the red-hot poker in his anus: "On volt dire que cheaz qui le gardoient l'avoient ... ochis par-desouz d'on chaut fier qu'ilh li butarent en cul" [It is purported that his gaolers had killed him with a hot rod that they thrust in his arse] (d'Outremeuse, 6:322). If the two distinct historiographical traditions of the "corresponding" punishments of Hugh Despenser and Edward II, suggestive of "a meeting between Hugh's genitals and Edward's anus," are read as complementary, the question of

---

[12] Amiens, 1:31. See Rome, p. 87; d'Outremeuse, 6:332; and Le Bel, 1:24.

[13] Le Bel's accusation of "herites et sodomites" was, by the fourteenth century, a fairly standard libel against one's political enemies. The widespread use of the heresy–sodomy formula may indicate that Despenser (and the king) did not practice sodomy, as Danielle Westerhof suggests in "Deconstructing Identities on the Scaffold: The Execution of Hugh Despenser the Younger, 1326," *Journal of Medieval History* 33 (2007): 89n4 [87–106]. I argue that Le Bel's rendition of the execution is grounded in reality. The text of the judgment gives reasons for the charge of heresy (pp. 265–66), and in the final sentence Despenser is called a "traitour, tyrant, Reneye" (Holmes, "Judgement," 267).

where medieval culture drew the line between normative and non-normative appears clear-cut.[14]

All three chronicles, however, rebut the initial conclusion that the penalty is inherently tied to the crime it punishes and that this royally sanctioned violence singles out sodomy as uniquely responsible for the damage done to the body politic.[15] Jean Le Bel, to whom both Jean Froissart and Jean d'Outremeuse adhere closely, reports another public execution, under the young Edward III. Roger Mortimer, Earl of March, was Edward III's chief counselor, de facto king during Edward's minority, and lover of Queen Isabella. He was executed on 29 November 1330, on charges of treason and usurpation of royal power:

> Toutesfois, le jugement fut ainsy ordonné que il morroit par telle maniere que messire Hue le Despensier. Ainsy fu fait ... luy fut le vit couppé et les coulles, et puis aprez le ventre fendu et toutes les entrailles ostées et arses, et puis on lui couppa la teste, et puis fut pendu par les hanches.[16]

> [Nevertheless, the sentence was given that he would die in the same way as Sir Hugh Despenser. So it was done ... his penis and testicles were cut off, and his chest was cut open and his intestines torn out and burnt, then he was decapitated, and finally he was hung by the hips.]

Mortimer is sentenced "to be drawn and hanged" (Mortimer, *Greatest Traitor*, p. 240), but our three historians describe the same punishment and execution sequence as for Hugh Despenser. Identical torture is applied, and in the same order, and yet Sir Mortimer is not accused of sodomy. Rather than singling out sodomy, the cause for this particular form of execution – castration, then the removal of the internal organs – lies in the sexual violence committed against the body politic. In the case of Mortimer's execution, the

---

[14] Ormrod, "Sexualities of Edward II," p. 39. On the creation of the narrative of Edward II's manner of death in the *Brut* continuations after 1333, see Mortimer, "Sermons of Sodomy." D'Outremeuse reports the death of Edward II from the anonymous source and not Le Bel; indeed, this narrative is missing in Le Bel and therefore in Froissart.

[15] For an analysis of sodomy as that which "always signifies social disorder" and as a "means to power for the socially inferior member of the partnership," see Danielle Clarke, "'The sovereign's vice begets the subject's error': The Duke of Buckingham, 'Sodomy,' and Narratives of Edward II, 1622–28," in *Sodomy in Early Modern Europe*, ed. Tom Betteridge (Manchester: Manchester University Press, 2002), p. 48 [46–63]. My point here is different: both sodomy and adultery can cause social disorder. On neutrality and sodomy in Froissart, see my "Neutrality Affects: Froissart and the Practice of Historiographic Authorship," in *The Medieval Author in Medieval French Literature*, ed. Virginie Greene (New York: Palgrave Macmillan, 2006), pp. 137–56.

[16] Le Bel, 1:103. See d'Outremeuse, 6:355; Amiens, 1:114; and Rome, p. 186. For the account of Mortimer's life and execution, see Ian Mortimer, *The Greatest Traitor: The Life of Sir Roger Mortimer, 1st Earl of March, Ruler of England, 1327–1330* (London: J. Cape, 2003), especially pp. 239–40.

sexual violence against the body politic is caused not by sex acts between men but by sex acts between Mortimer and Queen Isabella, who were lovers.

Edward III was crowned on the condition that "il preist entour luy bon conseil et sages et feables gens" [he surround himself with good counsel and wise and trustworthy counselors] (Le Bel, 1:32), including his mother, the Earl of Kent (Edward II's half brother), and Sir Roger Mortimer, so as to avoid the bad governance to which the kingdom was subject under his father's rule. But Mortimer, leagued with Isabella against the Earl of Kent, "enfourma tant et enhorta le roy par le consentement madame la royne sa mere, que le dit conte de Cayn le vouloit emprisonner, et le feroit moult tost morir pour avoir son royaume" [so misinformed and pressed the king, with the consent of the queen, his mother, telling him that the Earl of Kent wanted to imprison him and have him die to take over his reign] (Le Bel, 1:101). In addition, "encoulpoit on le sire de Mortemer plus que nul aultre" [Sir Mortimer was blamed more than any other] (Le Bel, 1:102) in the circulation of a rumor that the Queen Mother was pregnant. In other words, because Mortimer had regular and repeated sexual intercourse with Isabella, he was able to cause the Earl of Kent's death: "Par cuy procuration ilh estoit mort" [He (the Earl of Kent) was dead by Mortimer's proxy] (d'Outremeuse, 6:354). Elsewhere d'Outremeuse insists that Mortimer "estoit priveis de la meire le roy secreement" [was secretly intimate with the king's mother] (6:354). Froissart makes the link between sexual intercourse and Mortimer's influence most explicit in the Rome manuscript. The young king consults his mother, "qui mieuls amoit messire Rogier que le conte de Qent" [who preferred Sir Roger to the Earl of Kent], with the result that "ne l'escusa aultrement que elle dist: 'Ce poroit bien estre, biaus fils. On ne scet en qui avoir fiance aujourd'ui'" [she did not excuse him except to say: "That could well be, fair son. One does not know whom to trust these days"] (Rome, p. 183). Though initially it seemed that sodomitical practice was singled out in the act of castration, the identical punishment for Despenser and Mortimer tells us that what is reprehensible is genital penetration that leads to treasonous counsel penetrating to the heart of power: "Il devoit morir de la mort parelle a messire Hue l'Esp[ens]ier, car il estoit fauls, mauvais et traites contre son signeur" [He was to die the same death as Sir Hugh Despenser because he was false, evil, and a traitor to his lord] (Rome, p. 186). Mortimer was false, evil, and a traitor by means of the access to the queen that his genitals obtained for him – the queen by whose proxy Mortimer held sway over Edward III, exactly like the traitor Despenser held sway over Edward II. Just as Despenser "avoit ainsy le roy à sa voulenté attrait" [had so submitted the king to his will],[17] Mortimer had Edward III believe him: "Le rois crut ces paroles legierement, et en parla a madame sa

---

[17] Le Bel, 1:11. See Amiens, 1:11; Luce, 1.2:12; and d'Outremeuse, 6:327. See also repeated references to "votre Roial poer que vous auiez purpris contre notre seigneur le Roi" (Holmes, "Judgement," 264, 265).

mere" [The king believed him easily and spoke to milady his mother] (Rome, p. 183). The distinguishing feature of Despenser's punishment and public execution does not single out and incriminate male sodomy. Rather, what unites the two punishments is that sexual intercourse provides the platform for verbal intercourse: the punishment suggests that the counsel infiltrates the mind thanks to the sexual penetration of the body. Sexual intercourse facilitates the reception of counsel and breeds its worst kind: treason against king, kingdom, and body politic. Sexual penetration of the king's or queen's natural body betrays the king and violates the body politic; intercourse, sexual and verbal, foments disorder and treason. Castration, then, punishes treason that results from sexual intercourse: it condemns undue influence, proxy kingship, and the interruption of networks of patronage and access to the king. However, it does not discriminate between male–male and male–female sex acts, nor does it incriminate a particular sex practice.

Intercourse: Sex and Speech

These three histories reveal, then, an intimate link between sex and speech – that is, sexual and verbal intercourse. Le Bel, Froissart, and d'Outremeuse follow a clear order of crimes: the penis, which is cut off first, opens the way for the counsel emanating from the treacherous heart, which is subsequently removed.[18] Despenser's heart is removed only after the castration because "he had a false heart and was a traitor," just like Mortimer's heart is removed after castration because he was also "false, evil, and a traitor to his lord." Sexual penetration provided access to the king's ears and created the opportunity for "mauvais enort et consel" [misguided exhortation and counsel] (Rome, p. 89).[19] Edward's infamy indeed stemmed from neglect

---

[18] Claire Sponsler's argument, in an otherwise elegant and powerful article, that the punishment of the different parts of the body renders ambiguous "just what Despenser is guilty of – treason, heresy, or sodomy, all of which Froissart conflates when reckoning up Despenser's crimes" (p. 155), does not withstand scrutiny. On execution rituals, see Esther Cohen, "'To Die a Criminal for the Public Good': The Execution Ritual in Late Medieval Paris," in *Law, Custom, and the Social Fabric in Medieval Europe*, ed. Bernard S. Bachrach and David Nicholas (Kalamazoo, MI: Medieval Institute Publications, 1990), pp. 285–304; as well as Matthew Fisher's essay in this volume. It should be noted that d'Outremeuse follows Le Bel closely in the descriptions of Despenser's and Mortimer's judgments and executions, but in retelling Despenser's execution he omits the removal of the "treacherous heart."

[19] There are many repeated instances of this. See, for example, "par son traitre conseil et enhort" (Le Bel, 1:28; also Amiens, 1:34; Luce, 1.2:34), "le maistre conseiller du roy, qui tous les mauvaiz faits conseilloit" (Le Bel, 1:20), "mauvais conseil" (Le Bel, 1:13, 31; also Amiens, 1:3, 37; Rome, pp. 47, 50, 101), "par hastieu conseil et male information" (Luce, 1.2:14; also Rome, pp. 12, 13). See also "par votre malueis conseil," "par vostre malueste" (Holmes, "Judgement," 266).

and bad counsel: "Si fu moult diffammés et deparlés ... et, disoit on, que par se noncallieuseté et le mauvais consseil qu'il creoit, il avoit recheub ce doummaige" [He was much defamed and slandered ... and it was said that he suffered a loss (against the Scots) because of nonchalance and bad counsel that he believed] (Amiens, 1:3). Bad counsel was the cause of social disorder, a violation of social hierarchies, and an injustice. Under Edward II, "justice n'i avoit point de lieu ne de audiense, ne li marceant n'osoient aler ne ceminer ne ne pooient, fors en grant peril et aventure de perdre lors corps et lors biens parmi le roiaulme d'Engleterre" [justice was neither given a place nor a hearing, nor did the merchants dare travel in the kingdom of England, nor were they able to, except at great peril and risk of losing their life and possessions] (Rome, p. 54). Edward II's actions that followed Despenser's counsel made him "point dignes de jamais porter couronne ne de gouvrener roiaulme, ne de estre veus au monde" [not at all worthy of wearing the crown or governing the kingdom or being seen in public] (Rome, p. 101). Likewise, Mortimer's counsel compromised Edward III's reign: "De la mort et decolation le conte Ainmon de Qent fu li roiaulmes d'Engleterre moult afoiblis, et li rois en pluissiers lieus grandement blamés" [The kingdom of England was much weakened by the death and execution of Earl Edmond of Kent, and the king was greatly blamed in many places] (Rome, p. 185). Despenser's and Mortimer's torture reveals the performative nature of the sex act; intercourse is seen as a political speech act because, as the penis penetrates the natural body of the king or the queen, the counselor's speech penetrates the mind of King Edward II and of Edward III, via Queen Isabella, "par ... procuration."[20] This link between sex and speech highlights the political nature of the sex act; it is the political effect of sex acts that interests Despenser's and Mortimer's historians. For them, the sexual is always already the political. Without distinction of sex acts, sex between men *and* sex between men and women in positions of power can become an act of sexual violence perpetrated against the body politic.

The fact that Despenser and Mortimer were punished in identical ways tell us that what is at stake is not the nature of the sex act, but the effect it has – what it does as a political speech act.[21] And its effectiveness comes from the

---

[20] According to Mark Jordan, in the eleventh century Peter Damian modeled the term "sodomy" on "blasphemy," "on analogy to the most explicit sin of denying God." See *The Invention of Sodomy in Christian Theology* (Chicago: University of Chicago Press, 1997), p. 29. He argues, moreover, that, as a sin, sodomy entered the confessional. The act had to be confessed, but the paradox was that a sodomite could not name his sin, and repent of it, without polluting himself further (pp. 92–113). In other words, sodomy was performed as a speech act during a confession. To name and confess sodomy is to sodomize and blaspheme; sodomy is a speech act that denies God.

[21] The debate about acts versus identities in the medieval period has split scholars of the premodern. As David Halperin argues, the debate originates in "the reception and deployment of Foucault's distinction between the sodomite and the homosexual – a

repetition and reiteration of intercourse. From our modern perspective, it is tempting to think that only sodomy is implied in the description of Edward's acts as "folies": the Earl of Kent "ne s'ose tenir en ce pais pour tant que il a parlé a son frere le roi et a messire Hue le Espensier et leur a blamet leurs folies" [does not dare stay in the kingdom because he spoke to his brother the king and to Sir Hugh Despenser and reproached them for their follies] (Rome, p. 54). But we should not ignore the political context; sodomy is recriminated only because of repeated abuses of power over a long period of time due to bad counsel: "On ne li remonstra pas ses folies sitretos avant ot il fait moult de grans mauls et de crueuses justices des nobles" [His follies were not so quickly reproached to him before he had already committed many a wrong and cruel justice against his nobles] (Rome, p. 41). Likewise, the cumulative effect of Mortimer's actions – "tous les fais a messire Rogier de Mortemer" [all of Sir Roger Mortimer's deeds] (Rome, p. 185) – causes his downfall. Treason could thus be defined here as sexual intercourse between men and between men and women, as acts whose repetition cultivates bad counsel, forecloses the possibility of good governance with proxy kingship, and elicits political violence and events of a magnitude warranting commemoration. Thus the sex act by itself is neither "natural" nor "unnatural." Sodomitical *and* adulterous intercourse in themselves do not menace the social order and the body politic; they do so only when the bad counsel they are capable of fostering unsettles the social order and violates the body politic repeatedly and over a long period of time. This is the case for Despenser as for Mortimer. For our historians and their histories, sex acts, whether male–male or male–female, become relevant and worthy of historical commemoration not when they are singular occurrences, but only when they entail repetition and a disastrous political outcome – or several.

Illicit and Licit

The three types of love I have described above (Despenser and the queen, Despenser and the king, and Mortimer and the queen) underscore the fact that sex acts between persons with power are political speech acts that have the capacity to violate the body politic to the point of being judged and

---

distinction often taken to be synonymous with the distinction between sexual acts and sexual identities" ("Forgetting Foucault: Acts, Identities, and the History of Sexuality," *Representations* 63 [1998]: 95 [93–120]). Thus in proposing a supersession of acts (sodomy) by identities (homosexuality), Foucault would also have reified the divide between the medieval and the modern. On this point, see Eve Kosofsky Sedgwick, *Epistemology of the Closet* (Berkeley: University of California Press, 1990). For medieval studies, see the groundbreaking analysis of acts, identities, and periodization in Carolyn Dinshaw, *Getting Medieval: Sexualities and Communities, Pre- and Postmodern* (Durham, NC: Duke University Press, 1999).

condemned as treason. Medieval francophone historians of the Hundred Years War thus link sex acts to treason, highlighting the fact that the only sexuality deserving of commemoration is necessarily political. The nature of the sex act is neither condemned nor commemorated for its intrinsic value, but only because of the long-term, repetitive damage it does to the body politic.

One could object that medieval francophone historians attack adultery and sodomy as causes of social disorder and that they link sexual intercourse to treason because sodomy and adultery are illicit sexual behaviors. But it is worth pointing out that, in the historiographical universe of the Hundred Years War, unions sanctioned by marriage were equally troubled and troublesome. Isabella and Edward's marriage was universally seen as the cause of the Hundred Years War: "Il vous devroit souvenir … du mariage, lors bieneure repute … et des morteles espines qui sont issus du dit mariage trop poingnans, qui ont point lx. ans par tele malediction" [You should remember … the marriage, then thought a fortunate one … and deadly and piercing thorns resulting from that union, which have pierced for sixty years in such a cursed way] (Mézières, p. 112).[22] The subsequent dynastic struggle over the French throne led to Edward III of England being excluded from inheriting the French throne in 1328, even though he was Philip IV's grandson by his mother Isabella, while Philip's nephew, Philip of Valois, was crowned as Philip VI because his inherited right to the throne could be justified through the male bloodline: "C'est li poins par quoi les guerres, les pestilenses et les tribulations sont de puis incourutes et eslevées, et li grant meschief avenu par le cause dou calenge et de le deffense" [Because of this issue, wars, plagues, and tribulations have come about and arisen and the great misfortune was caused by the forbidden inheritance and the challenge of it] (Luce, 1.2:11; see also Rome, p. 46). The contracting of Richard II's marriage with Charles VI's daughter in the mid-1390s was a peace strategy intended to conclude the Franco-English war; however, there "est un grant peril de prendre teles medicines … voire se la medicine preparative n'aura este bien ordenee devant, et se la garde des contraires, apres la medicine prise, ne sera bien observee et regulee" [is great danger in taking such medicines … unless some preliminary medicine has been given before and unless, once taken, precautions against contraindications have been respected and regulated] (Mézières, p. 107). Marriage as appeasement and conclusion of a stable peace is a strategy that can either infect the wound further or cure it. If the "electuary" of marriage is "pesee" [well balanced], the great wound will be "sanee" [cured]; otherwise, it will reopen, "de nouvel et de mortel venim envenimee" [poisoned by the new and deadly venom] (Mézières, p. 112).

---

[22] Medieval historians present the dynastic struggle as the unique cause of the war. Modern historians have shown that English economic interests in Gascony and Flanders also played a significant role in the outbreak of the war.

It is thus not in the essence of marriage, and licit sexual relations, to pacify and appease conflict, since they may actually exacerbate it; what is needed is a well-crafted prenuptial agreement. In its absence, Richard's marriage to Charles VI's daughter is England's loss: "Nostre chief le roy ... s'est alyé par mariage à son adversaire: ce n'est pas signe que il le veuille guerroier" [Our leader the king ... allied himself to his enemy by marriage. This is no sign that he wishes to make war on him] (Lettenhove, 16:3). Richard's marriage submitted him to the French king, and hence England to France: "Vous avés toujours esté encliné à la plaisance des François et à vouloir traittier avecques eulx paix à la confusion et grant déshonneur du royaulme d'Angleterre" [You have always bent to the will of the French and wished to negotiate peace with them, to the confusion and great dishonor of the kingdom of England] (Lettenhove, 16:200), as well as its "débilitation" [debility] (Lettenhove, 16:163). Richard II followed bad counsel, just like his great-grandfather, Edward II:

> Jamais n'en retournera à joye non plus que ne fist Édouard son tayon, qui se gouverna si follement que il le compara, et par trop croire le seigneur Despensier. Aussi Richard de Bourdeaulx a tant creu povre conseil et mauvais que ce ne se peut celler, ne souffrir longuement et que il ne conviègne que il le compère. (Lettenhove, 16:152)

> [He will never return from (Ireland) to happiness, not any more than did Edward, his great-grandfather, who governed himself so foolishly that he paid for it, by trusting Sir Despenser too much. Likewise, Richard of Bordeaux has trusted poor and bad counsel so much that this cannot be hidden nor suffered much longer, without it being advisable that he pay for it.]

Richard's counselors "fourconseilloient le roy et le tenoient en oyseuses et despendoient et alouoient les revenues d'Angleterre" [misguided the king, kept him idle, and spent and distributed the revenues of the kingdom] (Lettenhove, 16:6), and the king "créoit si légièrement ce que on luy disoit et conseilloit que oncques roy qui euist esté en Angleterre" [believed easily, like no other King of England, what he was told and counseled] (Lettenhove, 16:89). Because of poor counsel, England's internal wealth was dissipated and its international possessions were diminished. Richard's marriage delivered the final blow and put the kingdom "en péril d'estre perdu sans recouvrier" [in danger of being lost without return] (Lettenhove, 16:194).

The Sexuality of History

In medieval francophone historiography of the Hundred Years War, sodomy, adultery, and marriage are problematic when they encourage the repetition of bad counsel and, ultimately, treason. Male–male sex acts are not singled out any more than male–female ones; they are equally problematic precisely as political sexualities, and not because an intrinsic value is attached to them.

The three decades since John Boswell's groundbreaking study have witnessed a heightened interest in Edward II's sexuality, for excellent social and disciplinary reasons, which, moreover, continue to be urgent. Historians of sexuality have turned to medieval historiographical texts seeking for information about the sexual desires and practices of historical figures and for evidence in the acts versus identities debate. In large part, their attempt has been to legitimate the interrogation of modern sexual norms by providing historical evidence for different configurations and deployments of sexuality from the past and thereby to counter the claim of a transhistorical heteronormative order. But studying same-sex relations in relative isolation from contemporaneous representations of other, opposite-sex practices has in some cases occulted the ways in which medieval historians use different sexualities to elucidate (similar) historical events and has precluded us from asking to what purpose they choose to include issues of sex in their historiographical representations. Thus what we have been reading as the oppression of a sexual minority belongs in a larger framework of historiographical strategies for depicting political events, including brutally violent ones.

We must therefore analyze normative and non-normative sexualities in a comparative framework in order to understand how medieval historians deploy sexual acts and sexual rhetoric in writing history. In this way, sexuality will serve not only to trace the historical modulations in the discursive and cultural construction of sex and desire (the traditional province of the history of sexuality) but also as a category of analysis for understanding historiographical techniques. We must take seriously questions of how medieval historians represent sex acts as impacting the course of history, why they link those acts to historical events and violence, and how and why they sexualize history and violence. A comparative view of medieval sexualities would thus advance the goals of an ethics of history as well as an ethics of sexuality. Ultimately, it may give not only a history to sexuality but also a sexuality to history.

PART IV
TRAUMA, MEMORY, AND HEALING

10
"Guerre ne sert que de tourment": Remembering War in the Poetic Correspondence of Charles d'Orléans

Deborah McGrady

> Conveying the felt and complex experience of terror – which includes its conceptual antonym "peace" within it – is what poetry is all about.
>
> Rukmini Bhaya Nair, *Poetry in a Time of Terror*

During the Hundred Years War (1337–1453), the lyric voice dramatically changed registers to express the violence and trauma suffered by the social psyche. Confirming Rukmini Nair's claim that poetry can uniquely convey the complexity of terror, late medieval francophone writers reshaped courtly poetry, a genre previously dominated by love, to give voice to contemporary anxieties concerning the matter of war. War invaded the lyric world, redrawing generic, thematic, and affective boundaries, resulting in what one scholar has referred to as a "schizophrénie littéraire."[1] For Adrian Armstrong and Sarah Kay, lyric accounts of social events differed markedly from traditional historical reflection in that "the presence of verse conjures an absent meaning: a 'truth' about history that is not to be equated with factual detail because it is located not in external reality but in (not necessarily explicit or even conscious) subjective processes of reflection, sentiment, commitment, or memory."[2] For these two scholars, verse allows for an alternative and personalized version of writing history and remembering the past, but in

---

[1] Florence Bouchet, "Introduction," in Alain Chartier, *Quadrilogue invectif*, ed. Bouchet (Paris: Honoré Champion, 2002), p. 27 [7–40]. On the changing field of poetry owing to wartime events, see Isabelle Bétemps, "Écrivains médiévaux de la Guerre de Cent Ans: Alain Chartier, Pierre de Nesson, Charles d'Orléans," in *Images de la Guerre de Cent Ans*, ed. Jean Maurice, Daniel Couty, and Michèle Guéret-Laferté (Paris: Presses Universitaires de France, 2002), pp. 113–24.

[2] Adrian Armstrong and Sarah Kay, *Knowing Poetry: Verse in Medieval France from the Rose to the Rhétoriqueurs* (Ithaca, NY: Cornell University Press, 2011), p. 60.

the commemorative act of lyric expression we may go a step further and claim that, through the process of transforming history into a poetic event, late medieval lyric influenced and shaped events. According to Robert J. Jaeger, late medieval verse generated a new outlook on violence via a *pax poetica*, a doctrine of peace that took shape in this period.³ Nicolas Offenstadt failed to recognize the distinctiveness of lyric in his recent important study on late medieval peace theory (a study that gives individual attention to other discourses, including chronicles, pamphlets, official correspondence, sermons, and staged ceremonies),⁴ but it is nonetheless appropriate to speak of peace poetry as a genre unto itself. Attesting to this growing trend are John Gower's "To King Henry IV, in Praise of Peace" (1399–1400), Christine de Pizan's *Livre de la paix* (1412–13), Alain Chartier's *Lai de paix* (ca. 1429), and Charles d'Orléans's "Priez pour paix, doulce Vierge Marie" (ca. 1434) and his poetic correspondence with Philip the Good, Duke of Burgundy, during peace negotiations (1439–40). These writings break with established "just war" doctrine to claim that war was not a logical precursor to peace but its contradiction. What this evidence suggests is that the late medieval poetic engagement with political and social realities forged a new *memoria* – meaning both memory and memorial – that had the capacity to reshape history.

To explore poetry's power to change both the reception of wartime experiences and the course of political events, let us consider the work of the quintessential wartime poet, Charles d'Orléans (1394–1465), who lived for twenty-five years as a political prisoner of the English (1415–40). The choice may strike readers as curious given that Charles's personal experiences with the humiliation of defeat, the trauma of the battlefield, and his powerlessness to evade captivity were never given full expression in his poetry. In fact, in contrast to Jean Regnier, a contemporary prisoner of the Burgundians who poignantly detailed his suffering in captivity,⁵ Charles wrote only obliquely in his poetry of his imprisonment, preferring to focus on his status as a prisoner of love rather than as the king's captive. And whereas Alain Chartier and Christine de Pizan commemorated the communal trauma endured at the 1415 Battle of Agincourt, Charles d'Orléans remained mute on the battle he triggered when he cosigned with two other royal princes an invitation to battle addressed to Henry V on 20 October 1415.⁶ Even Joan of Arc's liberation of his city of Orléans is hauntingly absent from his writings, although both

---

   ³ Robert F. Yeager, "*Pax Poetica*: On the Pacifism of Chaucer and Gower," *Studies in the Age of Chaucer* 9 (1987): 87–121.
   ⁴ Nicolas Offenstadt, *Faire la paix au Moyen Âge* (Paris: Odile Jacob, 2007).
   ⁵ Jean Regnier, *Les fortunes et adversitez de Jean Regnier*, ed. Eugène Droz (Paris: SATF, 1923).
   ⁶ Pierre Champion, *Vie de Charles d'Orléans (1394–1456)* (Paris: Honoré Champion, 1969), p. 144.

Christine and Chartier celebrated her success. Although these silences may justify Joël Blanchard and Jean-Claude Mühlethaler's exclusion of Charles from their study of *poètes engagés*,[7] it is nonetheless crucial to acknowledge that his verse bears the deep psychological wounds caused by wartime trauma.

Even Charles's poetic silence may be interpreted as a direct result of wartime realities. Witness, for example, Hue of Lannoy's 1433 letter to his lord, Duke Philip the Good of Burgundy, in which he detailed his recent visit with Charles in England and the strict surveillance by captors of the prince's communication. Beyond describing the duke's inability to move freely, Hue notes that, when discussing peace negotiations, Charles resorted to physical gestures to counter his public statements. He also reports that Charles was denied by his jailer, the Earl of Suffolk, the right to address a letter to Duke Philip.[8] Such documented constraints on the duke's freedom of expression reinforce A. C. Spearing's astute observation that the historic Charles undoubtedly "was divided from himself as well as from others; his life was no more than a document devised not so much to express as to conceal its inner meaning."[9] Moreover, it is a political reality explicitly treated in Charles's poem to the same Duke of Burgundy around 1430 concerning the political necessity to disguise his true feelings for the duke at court (discussed below). As is implied by both the thwarted request to write to Duke Philip in 1433 and subsequent verse epistles addressed to the same duke, political realities affected Charles's writing, sometimes by silencing textual expression and other times by inspiring covert poetry that contained embedded political commentary likely hidden from the duke's jailers.

These politically charged moments, however, are generally designated by literary scholars as uninteresting and even unpoetic exceptions to Charles's corpus. Julia Kristeva's treatment of subjectivity and its relation to the unconscious as both a psychological and literary enterprise can help us move beyond this impasse to recognize the incomparable, albeit understated and even sometimes silenced, commemoration of war and writing. In her study of Louis-Ferdinand Céline's literary treatment of the Second World War, Kristeva explores literary acts of abjection (equivalent to vomiting or gagging) that

---

[7] Joël Blanchard and Jean-Claude Mühlethaler, *Écriture et pouvoir à l'aube des temps modernes* (Paris: Presses Universitaires de France, 2002).

[8] Joseph Stevenson, ed., *Letters and Papers Illustrative of the Wars of the English in France during the Reign of Henry VI, King of England* (London: Longman and Co., 1864), vol. 2, part 1, pp. 230–38, 234.

[9] Anthony C. Spearing, *Textual Subjectivities* (Oxford: Oxford University Press, 2005), pp. 233–34. See also Spearing, "Prison, Writing, Absence: Representing the Subject in the English Poems of Charles d'Orléans," *Modern Language Quarterly* 53.1 (1992): 83–99. On the overriding absence of treatment of political issues in his English compositions, see Robert Epstein, "Prisoners of Reflection: The Fifteenth-Century Poetry of Exile and Imprisonment," *Exemplaria* 15 (2003): 159–98, esp. 177–79.

often mark the encounter with the unconscious in Céline's literary style.[10] In his case, transgressive thematic crossings between sex and death, violence and desire, and horror and pleasure are stylistically enhanced via exclamations and ellipses that allow for the unconscious to surge forward. Although Charles's poetic treatment of war in no way compares to the brutality of Céline's writings, it nevertheless reveals the power of textual transgressions – whether entailing treatment of "unpoetic" topics in verse, textual outbursts that allow for the repressed to surface, or the material commemoration of prohibited poetic and political collaboration – to give poetic form to wartime trauma and voice to a peace doctrine. Where Kristeva claims for Céline's writings the power to bring into full view the horror of war, we might see in the prince's lyric record of wartime events rare insight not only into the torment of war and imprisonment but also into poetry's effect on history. His personal manuscript further documents how the material commemoration of both poetry and the experience of its reception can transform lived trauma into a literary monument that memorializes poetic collaboration and the changes it instigates.

A small cluster of politically engaged poems composed primarily during Charles's imprisonment – seven of which register a lyric correspondence with Philip the Good – and later grouped together in his personal manuscript, Bibliothèque nationale de France, MS fr. 25458, will serve as the focus of this chapter. They merit scrutiny because of the way their material history records layered reception of both the historical events detailed and the experience of writing and reading about those events. According to the prince's modern editor, Pierre Champion, these works were most likely composed between 1433 and 1440.[11] But these dates can be deceptive since they signal only a first phase of composition, whereas the codex suggests an extended engagement with these works over many years. The most obvious manifestation of this ongoing engagement is the inclusion in the codex of two lyric replies written by Philip the Good. These responses provide an unparalleled opportunity to study both a contemporary reader's reception of Charles's politically engaged writings and the poet's reaction to this reception via his return missives.[12] Second, although the initial phase of scribal activity in MS fr. 25458 is believed to have been undertaken in England near the end of Charles's imprisonment, the codex bears ample traces of later additions incorporated after his liberation and return to France. Of specific

---

[10] Julia Kristeva, *Pouvoirs de l'horreur* (Paris: Seuil, 1980), pp. 157–82.

[11] *Charles d'Orléans: Poésies*, ed. Pierre Champion, 2 vols (Paris: Honoré Champion, 1971), 1:xxiii–xxv.

[12] In his otherwise insightful reading of the reception (or lack thereof) of Charles's political poetry, Jean-Claude Mühlethaler curiously ignores Duke Philip's engaged response to these works. See *Charles d'Orléans: Un lyrisme entre Moyen Âge et modernité* (Paris: Garnier, 2010), pp. 193–210.

interest to this study is the continued activity centered on the cluster of peace poems that are among the final entries in the English-produced portion of the manuscript. In fact, as we shall see, the last poem addressed to Duke Philip was ostensibly added to the codex by a second scribe after Charles's liberation. Furthermore, lyric continuations and added rubrication in MS fr. 25458, some in the prince's own hand, suggest a sustained preoccupation with these texts and a compulsive return not to the site of trauma but to the site of a collaborative response to it that entails first giving poetic expression to Charles's suffering before then joining forces to secure his freedom. As a healing memory, this strategy entails transforming the poetic record of wartime suffering into a literary monument to peace and friendship. In this respect, the material expression of these poems offers a unique form of history writing in which the past can be recuperated to articulate new terms of engagement, both political and poetic.

Rewriting War through Peace

That peace should play an important role in Charles's wartime writing comes as little surprise given that his freedom was regularly explained as contingent on peace, especially from the signing of the 1420 Treaty of Troyes until his freedom in 1440. In declaring that upon the death of Charles VI the King of England would be formally recognized as King of France, this treaty promised what many in English circles referred to as the "final peace." With the sudden death of both kings in 1422 and the ascension of the one-year-old Henry VI, the treaty's future was profoundly destabilized. From this moment on, Charles's fate was publicly yoked to the treaty's realization. Henry V's younger brother, the Duke of Gloucester, claimed that the king on his deathbed had decreed that Charles would remain a prisoner until peace was achieved, which entailed the successful enactment of the Treaty of Troyes.[13] In all negotiations put before England during this time, Charles's liberation was listed as a key point of interest. Indeed, in one version Charles's freedom was presented not as contingent on "final peace" but as proof that such peace had been achieved. Amid this debate, the young Henry VI eventually disagreed with his uncle and granted the prince's temporary release in 1439 to

---

[13] See Thomas Rymer, ed., *Foedera, Conventiones, Litterae, et ... Acta Publica*, 20 vols (London, 1704–35), 10:782–86. See also Christopher T. Allmand, "Documents Relating to the Anglo-French Negotiations of 1439," *Camden Miscellany* 24 (1972): 79–149. For a full reassessment of Charles d'Orléans's political role, see two chapters in Mary-Jo Arn, ed., *Charles d'Orléans in England (1415–1440)* (Cambridge: D. S. Brewer, 2000): Michael K. Jones, "'Gardez mon corps, sauvez ma terre' – Immunity from War and the Lands of a Captive Knight: The Siege of Orléans (1428–29) Revisited," pp. 9–26; and William Askins, "The Brothers Orléans and Their Keepers," pp. 27–46.

participate in a new round of peace negotiations orchestrated by the Duchess of Burgundy, Isabelle of Portugal. Archival records suggest that Charles fulfilled a crucial role even while being prohibited from direct involvement in discussions. For even though he was not allowed to attend talks in person at Saint-Omer, he was transported from England and lodged in English-controlled Calais, where he enjoyed frequent visits from the duchess during negotiations. During this time, the Duke of Burgundy was also in Saint-Omer, but he avoided public involvement in the talks given his problematic relations with both parties since his break with the English and his reconciliation with the French king through the 1435 Treaty of Arras. Nonetheless, as we shall see, the dukes exchanged lyric missives – most likely written in great secrecy – that document their efforts to rewrite the politics of war through a poetics of peace.

In Bibliothèque nationale de France, MS fr. 25458, Charles's peace writings are grouped closely together in quires Q through S. Confectioned in England upon the duke's request around 1440, these quires were apparently always viewed as a sequential unit, even though they remained unbound for a time.[14] For Champion, the three undated poems that open quire Q are thematically organized around the poet's call for peace:

"La complainte de France," pp. 191–93 (C1)[15]
"En regardant vers le pais de France," p. 194 (B75)
"Priez pour paix, doulce Vierge Marie," pp. 195–96 (B76)

Contrary to Champion's assertion that the lyric series contained in the next two quires "se distinguait … des ballades politiques" (*Manuscrit autographe*, p. 45), these subsequent texts register a compulsive return to wartime issues. Indeed, only six pages into quire R we discover another constellation of political poems. On page 210 Charles writes of his rumored death (B82), and then in the next ballade he addresses his fellow prisoner, the Duke of Bourbon, regarding his recent permission to visit France while the poet must remain behind as a "prisonnier" (B83, 27). A few pages later, in quires R

---

[14] Determining the original order and the chronology of additions to this manuscript has triggered much debate. Pierre Champion offered an important blueprint in *Le manuscrit autographe des poésies de Charles d'Orléans* (Paris: Honoré Champion, 1907). More recently, Mary-Jo Arn has corrected a number of Champion's claims in *The Poet's Notebook: The Personal Manuscript of Charles d'Orléans (Paris BnF MS fr. 25458)* (Turnhout, Belgium: Brepols, 2008). See especially table 3, p. 187.

[15] I use here the consecutive pagination used in MS fr. 25458 and the nomenclature and line numbering introduced by Pierre Champion in *Charles d'Orléans: Poésies*. All quotes in the original language are from Champion. With occasional alterations, translations are from *Poetry of Charles d'Orléans and His Circle: A Critical Edition of BnF MS. fr. 25458, Charles d'Orléans's Personal Manuscript*, ed. John Fox and Mary-Jo Arn, trans. R. Barton Palmer (Turnhout, Belgium: ACMRS and Brepols, 2010).

through S, pages 215–27, the poetic exchange with the Duke of Burgundy documents a sustained lyric discussion that deals in real time with the 1439 peace negotiations.

The first three poems that Champion identified as a clear peace sequence are distinguished from the peace writings exchanged between the dukes by their pessimistic outlook on the current state of affairs. Addressing France in the opening complaint, the poet rhetorically inquires, "Congnois tu point pourquoy es en tristesse?" [Do you not see why you are saddened?] (11), and he proceeds to detail God's punishing of France for its "grant ourgueil, glotonnie, peresse, / Couvoitise, sans justice tenir, / et luxure" [great arrogance, gluttony, sloth, / Greed, maintained without justice, / And desire for rich living] (14–16). To turn the tide, the poet addresses all members of the kingdom – clergy, nobility, laborers, and merchants – in "Priez pour paix" and urges them to pray for a return to peaceful times. Linking these two works is B75, where the poet staves off personal sorrow before the sight of France's distant shoreline by reminding himself of current efforts to secure "bonne paix."

In spite of the fact that these poems place the poetic voice against the backdrop of current political realities and invite us to read them as a sequence, they fail to provide historical precision that would identify them as targeted responses to datable events. In fact, these works insist on their atemporality. In B75, the precise spatial reference to the poet gazing on France from Dover is destabilized by internal temporal conflations. That is, if the poem begins by mapping location, the registered experience transports the poet to a lost time in France:

> En regardant vers le païs de France,
> Un jour m'avint, a Dovre sur la mer,
> Qu'il souvint de la doulce plaisance
> Que souloye oudit pays trouver;
> Si commençay de cueur a souspirer. (1–5)

> [While gazing toward the country of France
> One day at Dover by the sea
> I recalled the sweet pleasure
> I used to find in that country.
> And so from the heart I began to sigh.]

The poet further disturbs our reading through destabilizing thematic clashes. As Mühlethaler remarks, the ambiguous use of "doulce plaisance" draws attention to the fact that "la patrie lointaine se substitue à la femme aimée" [the distant fatherland substitutes for the beloved woman] (*Charles d'Orléans*, p. 200). Here conventional love discourse expresses the nostalgic longing of a political prisoner for a country that is no longer. Indeed, let us not forget that had the poet truly gazed on the distant shoreline from Dover, he would see not France but the English-controlled Calais region. Having thus conflated the sorrows of amorous separation with the prisoner's temporal and physical distancing from a longed-for countryside, the poetic voice defers lyric development of this painful memory by literally shifting the gaze from the shoreline to contemplate the imagined "voye ... de bonne paix" [path ... of good peace] (10–11). This allegorical path offers him comfort: "Tournay en confort mon penser" [I turned my thoughts toward consolation] (12). And yet the lyric voice registers that these efforts to concentrate on imagined peace had no effect on his true sentiments: "Mais non pourtant mon cueur ne se lassoit / de voir France que mon cueur amer doit" [Yet my heart never did tire / from seeing France, which my heart rightly loves] (13–14). Fusing the real and the metaphorical, the poet plans to load his "nef d'esperance" [ship of hope] (17) with his wishes and prayers that peace might soon be achieved, trusting that, in his stead, it will cross the sea to communicate his message.

The envoi exposes the failure of these lyric strategies to drown out the poet's sorrow. Here, for the first time, this sorrow surfaces with sudden poetic pathos:

> Paix est tresor qu'on ne peut trop loer.
> Je hé guerre, point ne la doy prisier;
> Destourbé m'a long temps, soit tort ou droit,
> De voir France que mon cueur amer doit! (22–25)

> [Peace is a treasure that cannot be overpraised.
> I hate war, no one should value it;
> War has, rightly or wrongly, long made it difficult for me
> To look at France, which my heart rightly loves!]

If the first line buoys the cause of peace by equating it with a coveted treasure, the next line interrupts with a coarse, stripped-down, and decidedly unpoetic outburst that exposes the poet's true sentiments: "Je hé guerre" [I hate war] (23). There is an obvious attempt in the second half of the hemistich to recuperate into the poetic realm this unadorned burst of anger. Recycling the negation and lexicon of praise used to celebrate peace, the poet portrays war as its radical opposite. Where praising peace is a natural reaction that one cannot resist, war must not be valued by anyone. This rhetorical game should not cloud our understanding of this crucial moment where the poet breaks with both lyric convention and political decorum to counter "just war" politics with a subjective exclamation that exposes the violent personal reality of imprisonment, isolation, and alienation. In the final lines, the poet openly blames the war for his separation from his homeland. Charles tethers this accusation to the allegorical world that was so carefully constructed in the previous stanzas through his choice of the term "destourbé," which not only suggests the notion of being held back by force, being destroyed by another, or being tormented but also evokes the powerful winds – tourbillons – that are so common to this striking coastline and that would certainly throw about his "nef d'esperance" with the same force that the real war had exerted on the prisoner-poet.

Peace Negotiations: Speaking the Truth in Poetic Correspondence

Irenic preoccupations also dominate Charles's lyric correspondence with Philip the Good, and, at least at the outset of this exchange, the poet's desire for peace continues to be qualified by his yearning for freedom and his sense of powerlessness. Unlike the first cluster of peace poems found in quire Q, however, the lyric exchange between the two dukes is far less poeticized and adopts instead a pragmatic, although often ambiguous, tone. As was the case with the earlier peace poems, these compositions are not internally dated, but geographical references and political allusions give every impression that this series of seven ballades documents various stages of negotiations. References in Charles's first ballade to his arrival "en ce païs" [in this country] (B82, 2) and his command that his poem head to Saint-Omer echo the poet's actual arrival in Calais in 1439 for peace negotiations and Duke Philip's residence in Saint-Omer at that time. Knowing that Henry V never set a ransom fee for Charles's release, the poet's search for ransom funds in his third and fourth poems to Philip (B89 and B93) can only refer to the 1440 decision of Henry VI to set his ransom at 240,000 écus. The Duke of Burgundy's two ballades (B87a and B88a) also contain details that echo important aspects of the negotiations. Unnoticed by scholars, for instance, is Philip's statement in his first ballade that he would like to see Charles freed "quitte du tout" [without debt] (B87a, 7), a suggestive reference to the duchess's repeated proposal that the duke be freed without ransom.[16] Finally, Charles's opening statement in his second ballade that he writes from "Albion" or England (B89, 1) likely refers to time spent there in the intervening months between formal negotiations and his final release.

This plotting of the individual poems does not clarify whether this exchange was a public affair or a secret one. However, given the political dynamics of the negotiations, it is safe to assume that these missives were kept secret. After all, so controversial was the Duke of Burgundy at this stage that both the English and French courts considered him untrustworthy. Given that he expresses his concern with the leadership vacuum at the French court in B83a, it makes sense that he would not want this poem to circulate widely, since it certainly would have fueled French suspicions. Moreover, as noted above, as early as 1433 Charles d'Orléans had been denied the right even

---

[16] See Allmand, "Documents," 126, 136.

to direct a public letter to the duke, who at that time was still an ally of the English crown. Similarly, Charles's blunt pronouncements in B93 that he was ready to serve anyone who would pay his ransom casts doubt on his regular public pronouncements of his unwavering dedication to peace, even if it cost him his life.[17] Of no small value is this mutual testimony to the desire for reconciliation between their two houses, which had been at war since the 1407 assassination of Charles's father, Louis of Orléans, by men associated with Philip's father. What this exchange powerfully reveals is that although both men were denied direct participation in the 1439 talks they used poetry to covertly influence the present and the future. That Philip eventually paid Charles's ransom; that Charles married Philip's niece, Marie de Clèves, in the month of his release (November 1440); and that the two men enjoyed a sustained political collaboration[18] until Charles's death all provide ample proof that the dukes were not just recording history but making history in verse.

It is not only on the political front that these works prove revolutionary, regardless of literary scholars' tendency to downplay their poetic value. For Jane H. M. Taylor, these are "not poems of any lyric sophistication."[19] Ann Tukey Harrison offers only tepid praise for Philip, whom she identifies as a "competent poet," and even her acknowledgment of the "striking rearrangements" of Charles's poetry by his cousin fails to recognize the profound impact Philip has on the former's poetry.[20] If, however, we treat this exchange seriously as a lyric dialogue, it becomes apparent that, while making history, these two men were also rewriting lyric convention.

The inaugural missive (B82) composed by Charles contains much recycled material from B75. In B75, peace was identified as a "trésor" (B75, 22), and here in B82, which is addressed to Philip, "Peace" as an allegorical figure offers to those who celebrate her a "butin / de grans biens" [booty / of great worth] (B82, 19–20). In addition, Charles's earlier unadorned declaration of hatred for War is reiterated: "Je la hé" [I hate her] (B82, 22). War, who rendered the B75 poet powerless, is now more bluntly blamed as the source of personal torment: "Guerre ne sert que de tourment" [War brings only torment] (B82, 21). Again we encounter the poet's wishes couched in a metaphoric world and contrasted with his inability to change events in real life when he proclaims his desire to "banish" War had he the power: "Bannie

---

[17] See Stevenson, *Letters and Papers*, pp. 232–33.

[18] A case in point is Charles's lobbying on Philip's behalf for his proposed crusade in 1455. See Champion, *Vie*, pp. 458–63.

[19] Jane H. M. Taylor, *The Making of Poetry: Late Medieval French Poetic Anthologies* (Turnhout, Belgium: Brepols, 2007), p. 102.

[20] Ann Tukey Harrison, "Orléans and Burgundy: The Literary Relationship," *Stanford French Review* 4 (1980): 481, 483 [475–84]. Harrison also refers to Philip's metaphors as "imprecise," which caused his message to be "weakened" (480).

seroit plainement / S'il en estoit a mon vouloir" [She would be banished / if I had my wish] (B82, 23–24). In this lyrically rich account, allegory allows him to propose to Philip a new world order in which War is banished and Peace divvies out booty once reserved for war victors.

In Philip's response to Charles (87a), however, a new perspective is self-consciously engineered. Philip appropriates Charles's refrain as his opening line to evoke his own desire to see Charles free. In the process, he references what Charles has compulsively avoided in his writings – explicit acknowl-edgment of his prisoner status:

> S'il en estoit a mon vouloir,
> Mon maistre et amy sans changier,
> Je vous asseure, pour tout voir,
> Qu'en vo fait n'auroit nul dangier;
> Mais par deça, sans attargier,
> Vous verroye hors de prison,
> Quitte de tout, pour abregier
> En ceste presente saison. (B87a, 1–8)

> [If I had my wish,
> My master and faithful friend,
> I assure you, in all honesty,
> You would be facing no threat,
> For on this side, with no delay
> I should see you out of prison
> Quit of everything, in a word,
> In this present season.]

Philip adroitly manipulates his cousin's flaccid refrain by structuring each of his own stanzas around a call to action. First he chooses as his refrain "en ceste presente saison" [in this present season] to anchor his proposals in time, thereby countering Charles's repeated reference in his refrain to a time that can never be ("S'il en estoit," B82). Second, having cited his cousin's refrain in the first stanza, he uses the first line of subsequent stanzas to revise the impotence it expresses. Thus the second stanza opens with a call for divine intervention: "Se tel don povez recevoir / Par la grace Dieu" [If you can receive such a gift / through God's grace] (9–10). By the third stanza, the imperative underscores the action to be taken by the two men. Philip proposes that they join forces to assure universal peace and individual liberty – "Mettons nous en nostre devoir" [Let us get on with our work] (17) – and he begins the envoi by referring to planning Charles's liberation – "Or pensons de vous allegier de prison" [Now let us see about freeing you from prison] (25). Philip then closes with a promise to do all he can immediately: "Et du tout m'y vueil obligier, / En ceste presente saison" [And I'll commit myself to accomplishing all this / in this present season] (28–29). Harrison has observed that Philip moves from wishful thinking (expressed through the imperfect conditional) to action over the course of this ballade ("Orléans and Burgundy," 481), but we need to understand this development as a rhetorically strategic rewriting of Charles's typical lyrical treatment of his prisoner status. Philip's poetic call to action has important repercussions for Charles's poetry. Disposing of Charles's common theme of impotence, Philip demands that he acknowledge instead his personal role in events. Charles's response, Ballade 88, is surprisingly action-oriented, as it specifies what each man must accomplish in the coming months. For his part, Charles promises to send secret messages to the duke concerning affairs, and he expects that Philip will work on the French side of things in turn.

Philip's second and final recorded response to Charles again cites the refrain of his cousin's recent ballade as his first line. Here Charles's repeated promise of allegiance – "de cueur, de corps et de puissance" [with heart, body, and might] (B88a, 1) – allows his cousin the opportunity to return the oath. But now it is Philip's turn to defer action when he reminds Charles that France is in a pitiful state, thereby suggesting that he will be able to do little on his side as requested by Charles in B88. In the third stanza Philip again urges his cousin to think of his future liberty, and he reiterates that it can only be through Charles's efforts that peace will be achieved. His envoi returns yet again to the topic so often avoided by Charles himself when he closes with a prayer that God deliver Charles from his great suffering:

> Or prions Dieu, par sa doulceur
> Qu'a vous delivrer se dispose,
> Car trop avez souffert douleur
> Quoy que nul dye ne deppose. (28–31)

> [Now let us pray God that in his grace
> He determines to deliver you,
> For you have suffered too much grief
> No matter what anyone says or affirms.]

The refrain highlights that this suffering has been regularly censored. Although Philip was most likely referencing the public downplaying of his cousin's predicament, this observation draws attention to Charles's constant resistance to treating personal trauma directly in his writings.

The remaining poems to Duke Philip that Charles penned (B89, B93, and B94) maintain an action-oriented stance as Charles searches for individuals who might contribute to his ransom. The dominance of present and future tenses in these poems obliterates the nostalgia so common to Charles's poetry. In these ballades the poet speaks of his imminent release by the king to "pourchasser / La paix aussi ma raençon" [work for / peace and my ransom as well] (B89, 10–11) and his willingness to serve any and all who will provide ransom funds: "Metroye corps et ame en gage" [I would leave my body and soul as a pledge] (B93, refrain). With his focus on pursuing freedom, the poet mentions his prisoner status on only one occasion. Instead of lamenting his powerlessness, he looks forward and proclaims, "Qui m'ostera de ce tourment, / Il m'achetera plainement" [Whoever rescues me from this torture / will have purchased all of me] (B93, 25–26). Where Charles's inaugural poem in the exchange registered his true sentiments concerning war only as an outburst – "Je la hé" – or through reference to his powerlessness, these later compositions detail plans for his liberation. Returning to the scholarly tendency to downplay the value of this poetic exchange, it is essential to recognize that these lyric missives represent a true dialogue between the two dukes. This dialogue not only results in real political action culminating in Charles's eventual liberation, but it also reveals the ability of political action to effect change in lyric expression. In the final case, Philip's responses instigate a new way of writing that is far less nostalgic and more inclined to replace fantasy with real action, strategies that make space for Charles to inhabit the present and to assume control of his fate.

Past Poetry and Book Commemoration

It is, however, during the process of transforming his poetry into a material artifact that Charles truly anchors his lyric experience in historic events. Editorial practices in MS fr. 25458, sometimes inscribed in the poet's very hand, document efforts to transform the memory of writing about his torment into a new narrative of poetic coherence. One hundred years of scholarship on the production of this codex, most notably by Pierre Champion, Patricia Stirnemann, and Mary-Jo Arn, have repeatedly confirmed Charles d'Orléans's direct involvement in its production. On the eve of the duke's liberation he commissioned from scribes working in London two copies of his lyric works, one containing his French compositions, the other his English writings. The late production of both collections is confirmed by the presence of the 1439–40 poetic correspondence with Philip in the final quires of the French-language manuscript.[21] Charles would return to France with the unbound pages of his French writings in hand. Documenting the myriad ways in which MS fr. 25458 changed over the next twenty-five years, Arn notes that around sixty leaves of the original 317 unbound pages were ruled but left empty, then later filled with new writings after 1439. These quires brought from England would be further expanded through the addition of new quires of poetry produced in France until Charles's death in 1465.[22]

---

[21] Note that two English ballades (B111 and B113) found in British Library, MS Harley 682, are generally viewed as reworked translations of Duke Philip's compositions. For the poems, see Mary Jo Arn, ed., *"Fortunes Stabilnes": Charles of Orléans's English Book of Love: A Critical Edition* (Binghamton, NY: Medieval and Renaissance Texts, 1994).

[22] See Arn, *Poet's Notebook*, p. 57 and table 3, p. 187.

Through this additive process, the collection's message would repeatedly undergo important alterations. Regarding the base version, Champion believed that the central classification principle was genre; and yet even he was required to recognize that a thematic motivation dictated much of the contents of quire Q, which, as I have argued here, extended into the next two quires, in which the lyric exchange between Charles and Philip appears. If we compare this organization to the layout of Jean Regnier's collection of poems composed during imprisonment, the failure to package these writings as a coherent narrative is striking. Regnier chose a common overarching organizing principle that entailed framing his work with a verse narrative detailing his prisoner status. In Charles's case, no narrative frame is offered to situate his writings in time and space. Instead he opens with allegorical writings that locate themes of imprisonment, isolation, and impotence in an amorous context absent of historical or geographic indicators. For a reader unfamiliar with Charles's life story, it would be impossible before arriving at at least quire Q to appreciate the thematic overlap between the poet's lyric world and the author's historical reality or between his love lyrics and his political poems. Having observed Charles's general avoidance of such conflation in his poetry, it comes as little surprise that the material artifact, at least initially, imitates the poetic drive.

There is, however, intriguing material evidence that points to the author's later efforts to historically ground these compositions. Taylor offers a compelling study of the progressive transformation of MS fr. 25458 from what might be identified as an author-centered collection into what she describes as a "miscellany" that comes to include poetic contributions written by visitors to Blois in the late 1450s and 1460s who recorded their poems in the duke's book. But, as Taylor acknowledges, the move toward a "plurivocal" rather than a "univocal" collection began when Charles ostensibly set about revising the quires copied in England.[23] Taylor's argument is based on Champion's listing of these retrospective revisions made to the base collection, which he contended were written predominantly by Charles himself. Although the majority of alterations concern textual corrections, emendations to the poems that have preoccupied us thus far testify to a concerted interest in recording the social and historical context in which they were produced.[24]

---

[23] Taylor, *Making of Poetry*, p. 103. See also Arn's description of the changing codex in *Poet's Notebook*, pp. 4–5. Both authors draw heavily on Champion's detailed analysis of the various hands throughout MS fr. 25458. Drawing on comparative analysis with legal documents bearing Charles's signature, Champion argues that the poet regularly corrected and added rubrics to the English quires.

[24] In *Canon, Period, and the Poetry of Charles of Orleans: Found in Translation* (Ann Arbor: University of Michigan Press, 2000), Anne E. B. Coldiron argues convincingly that Charles willingly acknowledged the need to change the ordering of his poetry according to the intended audience.

When Charles reviewed the base transcription of his compositions, he took action to commemorate the lyric exchange that had profound political and poetic repercussions for him. Specifically, he personally added headings to each entry of this exchange to identify author and recipient. The first entry is thus prefaced by "Orlians a Bourgogne," and so on. Although this is not the only lyric exchange that was transcribed in the base collection and subsequently notated by Charles, the act of naming the two dukes in this exchange brings a necessarily political slant to bear on its reading.[25] It should be noted that without these references there would have been little possibility that even the most informed reader would deduce that Philip was the author of B87a and B88a. Furthermore, Charles's references to "mon frère et mon compaignon" [my brother and my companion] (B87, 3) or to his "beau frère" [fair brother] (B93, 1) are too vague to have been identified as clear references to Philip. Further confusion would have marked readings of B94, where references to the need to disguise one's love (2–3) so that no one will detect shared affections – "que nul n'espye / nostre amour [that no man spies / our love] (18–19) – would have very likely been read as a poem to a lady rather than a political message to his cousin. Thus had Charles not written in these headings, the relationship forged therein and the ways in which a single reader altered the development of his literary portrait would have remained muted.

The transformative effect of this poetic partnership is further manifested in the body of the material artifact, where the lyric exchange sutures the gap between poetic transcriptions that precede liberation and those poems added to the quires brought back from England after captivity. As Patricia Stirnemann has argued, the last text attributed to the first scribe located in England is B93, in which Charles speaks of his need of ransom funds. The final ballade composed for Philip, B94, which immediately follows, represents the first entry written in a new scribal hand associated with later additions to the codex postdating Charles's return to France.[26] As such, the material rendering of the poetic correspondence literally confirms the passage of Charles's writings from England to France. In the process, it commemorates the men's voiced desire and ultimate shared success in realizing Charles's liberation. Moreover, this final poem asserts the poet's unwavering and eternal fidelity to his cousin – "Vostre loyaument, sans faulser" [Yours faithfully, never to prove false] (B94, refrain) – a fidelity that bridges past, present, and future and that proclaims a new history for these previously warring houses.

The retrospective treatment of the dukes' lyric exchange is not the only example of Charles returning to his transcribed political writings to document

---

[25] He also identifies, for example, poems exchanged with Garancières, *chambellan* to Louis of Orléans, who died at Agincourt fighting alongside Charles (B77 and B77a).
[26] Patricia Stirnemann and François Avril, *Manuscrits enluminés d'origine insulaire VIIe XXe siècle* (Paris, Bibliothèque nationale, 1987), p. 181.

and commemorate the experience of writing about wartime events. Charles's *Complainte de France* (C1) ends on page 193 of quire Q before the peace ballades begin on a clean page 194. The first nine stanzas of this complaint evoke a lost time when harmony reigned in France, in contrast to the current dire state of the kingdom. But a final tenth stanza adopts a retrospective gaze that reveals the poet rereading the work in his old age:

> Et je, Charles, duc d'Orlians, rimer
> Voulu ces vers ou temps de ma jeunesse,
> Devant chascun les vueil bien advouer,
> Car prisonnier les fis, je le confesse;
> Priant a Dieu, qu'avant qu'ay vieillesse,
> Le temps de paix partout puist avenir,
> Comme de cueur j'en ay la desirance,
> Et que voye tous tes maulx brief finir,
> Trescrestian, franc royaume de France! (82–90)
>
> [And I, Charles, Duke of Orleans, was pleased
> To compose these verses in the time of my youth;
> Before one and all I acknowledge
> That as a prisoner I wrote them, this I confess
> Praying to God, that before old age falls upon me,
> A time of peace might everywhere come to pass,
> As is the desire of my heart,
> And I see all your ills soon end,
> Kingdom of France so Christian and noble!]

Although paleographic studies have not treated this addition, it is very likely that the stanza was composed, as Daniel Poirion speculated, upon Charles's return to France, as it sets the poet's imprisonment in the past.[27]

As a retrospective epilogue, this closing stanza captures a distinctive moment when the poet reflects back on the memory of writing these words. He presents himself in the stanza's first line as a powerful figure through his triple self-naming as a speaking subject, a named individual, and one with princely authority. He then tellingly links himself to the voice of the previous stanzas through an enjambment introduced via the term "rimer" (to rhyme). Although poetic activity may link the two voices, they are also sharply contrasted in the subsequent lines through references to "jeunesse" and "veillesse," along with the contrast between the named prince of the present and the "prisonnier" of the past. The poetic voice of the final stanza takes ownership of the suffering and isolation expressed in this past complaint and confesses his past identity as a prisoner as he makes room for a final

---

[27] Daniel Poirion, *Le poète et le prince: L'évolution du lyrisme courtois de Guillaume de Machaut à Charles d'Orléans* (Paris: Presses Universitaires de France, 1965), p. 283.

prayer of peace. Whereas the complaint itself originally pleaded with France to submit to God, the added stanza announces that the poet's own prayers at that time were always for the peace he continues to seek.

Rewriting past suffering to commemorate an extended discourse of peace in this passage, Charles d'Orléans engages in "enchantment" politics – the tendency, according to Sarah Cole, of victims to speak of the "transformative power" of past violence, a tactic that "steers as clear from the violated body as it can."[28] Indeed, in this very instance where we see Charles appropriate not simply past poetry but the suffering from whence it issued, we also see him yet again replace the expression of that past torment with an evocation of peace. This strategy allows him to wrap the wounds of wartime trauma in a textual promise of peace. In essence, we witness the poet in the act of organizing and amending past poetry to create a collection that transforms imprisonment, isolation, torment, and suffering into a commemorative collaborative artifact in which lyricized memories of past violence forge a new history.

For Charles, "guerre ne sert que de torment," but the poetic expression of that torment allows him to "re-member" – both recall and reconstitute – a history of war and imprisonment that celebrates the power of lyric. That this new account redirects attention toward future peace should not lead us to conclude that he conceals past trauma or the historical violence at the origin of his prisoner poetry. Instead, the successive layers of poetic elaboration are only loosely sutured so that we never lose sight of the original wounds exposed by this wartime poetry.

---

[28] Sarah Cole, "Enchantment, Disenchantment, War, Literature," *PMLA* 124 (2009): 1633b–34a [1632–47].

11

Commemorating the Chivalric Hero: Text, Image, Violence, and Memory in the *Livre des faits de messire Jacques de Lalaing**

ROSALIND BROWN-GRANT

Just as violence was central to the reality of historical experience in late medieval France and Burgundy, so it was inevitably a key issue in the historical writings of the period whose chief aim was to preserve the memory of knights and their military deeds, to perpetuate an individual's earthly renown, and to present the reader with exemplary models of valorous conduct.[1] These aims are nowhere more apparent than in the chivalric biographies of the period,[2] of which the most famous is that devoted to the Burgundian hero Jacques de Lalaing (1421–53), who was regarded by his countrymen as the very epitome of chivalry.[3] This biography, the *Livre des faits de messire Jacques de Lalaing* (ca. 1470),[4] composed by an author whose name has not come down to us,

---

* I am, as ever, hugely indebted to S. H. Rigby for his insightful comments on successive drafts of this chapter. I would also like to thank the editors of this volume for their suggestions for improvements to it, as well as Ralph Moffat and Pascal Schandel for their guidance on certain technical points.

[1] See Bernard Guenée, *Histoire et culture historique dans l'Occident médiéval* (Paris: Éditions Aubier-Montaigne, 1980); and Claude Thiry, "Historiographie et actualité (XIVe et XVe siècles)," *Grundriss der Romanischen Literaturen des Mittelalters*, vol. 11.1, *La littérature historiographique des origines à 1500* (Heidelberg: Carl Winter, 1986), pp. 1025–63.

[2] See Sumner Ferris, "Chronicle, Chivalric Biography, and Family Tradition in Fourteenth-Century England," in *Chivalric Literature: Essays on Relations between Literature and Life in the Later Middle Ages*, ed. Larry D. Benson and John Leyerle (Toronto: University of Toronto Press, 1980), pp. 25–38; Ruth Morse, "Historical Fiction in Fifteenth-Century Burgundy," *Modern Language Review* 75 (1980): 48–64; and Elisabeth Gaucher, *La biographie chevaleresque: Typologie d'un genre (XIIIe–XVe siècle)* (Paris: Champion, 1994).

[3] Richard Barber, *The Knight and Chivalry* (London: Cardinal Books, 1974), p. 151.

[4] Citations of the *Livre des faits* will be made parenthetically within the text and will refer to page numbers in Emmy Springer's critical edition, "Les Fais de messire Jacques de Lalaing," PhD diss., Université de Paris III, 1982. All translations are my own.

draws on a variety of fictional motifs and historical sources for its subject matter:[5] the romance theme of the hero's early chivalric and sentimental education; a fragment of a chronicle of the Ghent War that, until recently, was thought to be by Georges Chastellain but is now unattributed;[6] an epitaph on Lalaing that definitely *is* by Chastellain; and contemporary heraldic reports of the jousts that the hero fought between 1445 and 1450 during his *errances* across Europe. These reports were composed by a number of heralds who had witnessed Lalaing's deeds at first hand, including Jean Le Fèvre de Saint-Rémy, known as "Toison d'Or" from his official capacity as king of arms of the Burgundian Order of the Golden Fleece. Le Fèvre advised the hero in many of his chivalric undertakings, officiated as a judge for part of the year-long *pas d'armes* known as the Pas de la Fontaine des Pleurs that Lalaing organized at Chalon-sur-Saône between 1449 and 1450, and was with the knight when he died at the siege of Poeke during the Ghent War.

The *Livre des faits* found favor not only among Burgundian nobles but also among pro-Burgundian English readers at the court of Edward IV, notably William, Lord Hastings, who appears to have commissioned what is now the earliest extant manuscript of the biography: Paris, BnF fr. 16830.[7] This deluxe parchment codex contains eighteen miniatures (an author portrait, three scenes of interiors at court, nine scenes of jousting, and five scenes of warfare) that have recently been identified as the work of two different artists: the "Maître aux inscriptions blanches" (Master of the White Inscriptions) for the authorial frontispiece and the "Maître aux mains volubiles" (Master of the Chattering Hands) for the others.[8] While Elisabeth Gaucher has argued that these miniatures offer a fairly literal interpretation of the key episodes of Lalaing's chivalric career but are also informed by a symbolic

---

[5] See Georges Doutrepont, "Le *Livre des faits du bon chevalier messire Jacques de Lalaing*: Une biographie romancée du XVe siècle," *Journal des savants*, 1939, 221–32; and Elisabeth Gaucher, "Le vrai et le faux dans l'écriture de quelques biographies du XVe siècle: 'Écrire la vie, une autre histoire,'" in *Écritures de l'histoire (XIVe – XVIe siècle): Actes du colloque du Centre Montaigne, Bordeaux, 19–21 septembre 2002*, ed. Danièle Bohler and Catherine Magnien-Simonin (Geneva: Droz, 2005), pp. 205–17.

[6] See Graeme Small, *George Chastelain and the Shaping of Valois Burgundy: Political and Historical Culture at Court in the Fifteenth Century* (London: The Royal Historical Society, 1997), p. 154.

[7] See Hanno Wijsman, "William Lord Hastings, *Les Fais de Jacques de Lalaing*, et le Maître aux Inscriptions Blanches à propos du manuscrit français 16830 de la Bibliothèque nationale de France," in *"Als ich can": Liber amicorum in Memory of Professor Dr. Maurits Smeyers*, ed. Bert Cardon et al., 2 vols (Paris: Uitgeverij Peeters, 2002), 2:1641–64.

[8] See Ilona Hans-Collas and Pascal Schandel, with the collaboration of Hanno Wijsman, *Manuscrits enluminés des anciens Pays-Bas méridionaux: I. Manuscrits de Louis de Bruges* (Paris: Bibliothèque nationale de France, 2009), pp. 72–77.

attempt to "resurrect" the dead hero for the reader,[9] for Michelle Szkilnik the image of the setting of the Pas de la Fontaine des Pleurs, with its pavilion topped by an image of the Virgin Mary (fol. 124r), is a symbolic expression of Lalaing's aspiration to go on crusade.[10]

In common with other chivalric biographies of the period, such as that of the French hero Boucicaut or the pseudoautobiographical *Jouvencel*, the *Livre des faits* was designed to exalt Lalaing's achievements as an exceptional member of the caste of knights who were "the privileged practitioners of violence in their society."[11] Yet no matter how familiar with the idea of violence as a way of life his contemporaries may have been, the hero's death at the age of thirty-two is described in this text as being traumatic for those who witnessed it, and his loss is portrayed as being deeply felt by his fellow troops, sovereign, family, and friends (pp. 553–54). Moreover, the violent manner of his death was deemed to be particularly shocking since it resulted from part of his head being blown off by a shattered fragment from the wooden mantle of a Burgundian bombard that had been struck by a cannonball shot from the *veuglaire* of a Ghentish burgher. Lalaing, the ultimate chivalric figure, was thus brought down not in hand-to-hand combat but by an unfortunate ricochet caused by an unchivalric foe. Nevertheless, although modern commentators have often seen Lalaing's demise as being ironically prosaic or even as a convenient metaphor for the end of chivalry itself, with the hero being cast in the role of a hopeless anachronism,[12] his contemporaries made sense of his death in a very different way. As the biographer himself states by way of offering consolation to the hero's relatives and intimates, the writing of the book of his life was a chance for the fame of the dead knight to become immortal: "Tant que livres dureront, sa bonne renommee et ses nobles et haulx fais reluiront sur terre" [For as long as there are books, his good name and his great, noble deeds will shine forth on this earth] (p. 554).

There is, then, at the heart of the *Livre des faits* a tension between the celebration of a chivalric life that was predicated on violence and the need to show how this life transcended the moment of violence that brought it so abruptly to an end. This tension is negotiated in the biography principally through the complex interplay of text and image since, as we shall see, the symbolic dimension of the illuminations in fr. 16830 reveals a high degree

---

[9] Elisabeth Gaucher, "Le *Livre des Fais de Jacques de Lalain*: Texte et image," *Le Moyen Âge* 95 (1989): 503–18.

[10] Michelle Szkilnik, "Mise en mots, mise en images: *Le Livre des Faits du bon chevalier Jacques de Lalain*," *Ateliers (Cahiers de la Maison de Recherche, Université Charles de Gaulle–Lille 3)* 30 (2003): 75–87.

[11] Richard W. Kaeuper, *Chivalry and Violence in Medieval Europe* (Oxford: Oxford University Press, 1999), p. 130.

[12] See, for example, Jean Rychner, *La littérature et les moeurs chevaleresques à la cour de Bourgogne (Leçon inaugurale 30 janvier 1950)* (Neuchâtel, Switzerland: Secrétariat de l'Université, 1950).

of self-consciousness about the process of turning an individual's life into a book and, in so doing, of giving that life a significance that was more than the sum of its sequence of violent acts. This chapter thus argues that the frontispiece of the Paris manuscript furnishes the text with a putative author whose identity as authoritative eyewitness – one whose explicit role was to interpret and record for posterity the chivalric violence of the knightly caste – enhances the status of the biographer's first-person voice in the prologue.[13] Developing a key motif introduced in this author portrait, that of chivalric companions as *semblables*, or "mirrors," for each other, it then goes on to consider the ways in which text and image in the manuscript show how, under the gaze of his male peers, Lalaing constructed his chivalric reputation by conforming to, and even exceeding, contemporary expectations of knighthood. The hero's acts of violence, whether in the tournament yard or on the field of battle, are thus recast as harmonious expressions of chivalric identity and community.[14] Finally, it discusses the manner in which the image portraying Lalaing's death contributes to the narrative's emplotment of his life in terms of an exemplary chivalric career while recuperating the violence that ended it for the purpose of literary immortalization.

Prologue and Frontispiece: The Heraldic Author as Arbiter of Chivalric Violence

True to the historiographical aims of the *Livre des faits*, the authorial prologue invokes all the conventional contemporary topoi about commemoration, preservation of reputation, and exemplarity that it takes from the prologues of various "historico-realist" romances of the period. Yet, in contrast to the writers of these romances, who claimed an authority for themselves based on their role as the supposed transcribers or translators of preexisting narratives for their readers,[15] Lalaing's biographer stresses that the truth-value of *his* text lies in its being the fruit of eyewitness experience: "Et pour ce que moy, acteur de ce present traictié, ay veu de sez haulz faiz aucune partie ... ay prins plaisir de lez ramentevoir" [Because I, myself, author of the present work, saw a certain number of his great deeds at first hand ... it has

---

[13] See Rosalind Brown-Grant, "Narrative Voice and Hybrid Style in Burgundian Chivalric Biography," *Cahiers de recherches médiévales et humanistes* 22 (2011): 25–41.

[14] Although only a small number of images are reproduced here, most of those cited in this study can be accessed via the "Banque d'images" on the website of the Bibliothèque nationale de France in Paris.

[15] See Sophie Marnette, "Sources du récit et discours rapportés: L'art de la représentation dans les chroniques et les romans français des 14e et 15e siècles," *Le moyen français* 51–53 (2002–3): 435–59; and Brown-Grant, "Narrative Style in Prose Romances of the Later Middle Ages," forthcoming in *Romania* 130.2 (2012).

given me pleasure to preserve them for posterity] (pp. 13–14). However, the biographer does not go on in his prologue to specify in what precise capacity he acted as an eyewitness since, unlike the Burgundian chroniclers of the period who clearly set out their status and credentials as writers of history by means of the formula *je* + name + function (of office), as in "Je, Mathieu d'Escouchy, homme lay, natif de Quesnoy le Comte, de Haynnault" [I, Mathieu d'Escouchy, layman, native of Quesnoy le Comte, in Hainault],[16] he divulges no such information. The effect in this text, then, is to focus maximum attention on Lalaing, his subject, rather than on his own role as author, as is also the case in the life of Boucicaut, in which the biographer likewise remains unnamed.

The only source that the Lalaing biographer mentions other than his own eyewitness experience is the account of the Pas de la Fontaine des Pleurs by the Burgundian king of arms, Jean Le Fèvre/Toison d'Or. His text thus incorporates extracts from the epistle that Le Fèvre had sent to Lalaing's father shortly after his son's death, in which he offered him his "mémoires" of the tournaments at which he had himself been present or had heard about from other reliable informants. As the *Livre des faits* biographer says, "Et affin que sachiéz et crez cestuy traitiet estre vray, Thoison d'Or par l'ordonnance du duc de Bourgoingne, son prince et son souverain seigneur, le fist" [And in order that you might give credence to the truthfulness of this work (i.e., this part of the biography), you should know that it was written by Toison d'Or, by order of the Burgundian duke, his prince and sovereign lord] (p. 400).[17] In this epistle Le Fèvre had explained that the task of writing Lalaing's life story was not one he personally felt equipped to undertake, stating that his intention was merely to supply his "mémoires" to others whom he deemed worthier of the commission.[18] Moreover, that the *Livre des faits* is not the work of Le Fèvre himself is made clear by the fact that the biographer indicates that Toison d'Or was no longer alive at the time of his writing of the life of Lalaing, referring to him as "le noble roy d'armes de la Thoison que chascun nommoit Thoison d'Or, *lequel fut tenu tout son vivant* le plus sachant et vertueux et voir disant que pour son temps estoit pour un roy d'armes" [the noble king of arms of the Golden Fleece, who was known to all as Toison d'Or; *he who was regarded throughout his lifetime* as the most

---

[16] Mathieu d'Escouchy, *Chronique de Mathieu d'Escouchy*, ed. G. du Fresne de Beaucourt, 3 vols (Paris: Librairie Renouard, 1863–64), 1:2. On chronicle prologues, see Christiane Marchello-Nizia, "L'historien et son prologue: Forme littéraire et stratégies discursives," in *La chronique et l'histoire au Moyen Âge: Colloque des 24 et 25 mai 1982*, ed. Daniel Poirion (Paris: Presses Universitaires de Paris–Sorbonne, 1986), pp. 13–25; and Brown-Grant, "Narrative Style in Burgundian Chronicles of the Later Middle Ages," *Viator* 42.2 (2011): 1–49.

[17] See François Morand, "Épitre de Jean Le Fèvre, Seigneur de Saint-Remy," *Annuaire-Bulletin de la Société de l'Histoire de France* 21 (1884): 239 [177–239].

[18] See Morand, "Épitre," 181.

Fig 1. Paris, BnF fr. 16830, fol. 1r. The author depicted as Toison d'Or, Jean Le Fèvre de Saint-Rémy, king of arms of the Burgundian Order of the Golden Fleece.

knowledgeable, virtuous, and truthful king of arms of the age] (pp. 329–30; emphasis added).

Nevertheless, if Le Fèvre was not the author of the whole of the *Livre des faits* but simply a source for part of it, the frontispiece of fr. 16830 *does* offer a portrait of its supposed author, who is presented not just as a herald but as Toison d'Or himself (fol. 1r; see fig. 1). This pictorial misidentification of the herald as the author may have been the result of the illustrator's picking up on the reference to Le Fèvre within the text or it may have been the product of the biographer's desire to efface himself in favor of the person who was the chief recorder and arbiter of acts of Burgundian chivalry. Whatever its cause, this visual depiction of the author is highly significant for the way in which it confers authority on both the creator of the text and, by extension, his account of its hero. Resplendent in his herald's tabard, complete with the coat of arms of the Burgundian duke, this authorial figure acquires the status of a reliable and trustworthy eyewitness. Certainly heralds were routinely praised in this way by chroniclers such as Mathieu d'Escouchy, who called them "justes enquereurs" [just inquirers] and drew heavily on their accounts of chivalric events and warfare in their own works.[19] That this portrait is indeed meant to represent Toison d'Or is further signaled by the distinctive gold collar that he wears, one consisting of motifs of "firesteels" striking flames from black flints, from which hangs a pendant in the shape of a golden ram.[20] In reality, this collar was worn only by actual members of the Order of the Golden Fleece, not by its officers, but here it functions as a synecdochic and emblematic indicator of the wearer's heraldic name. The visual attribution of the biography to the pen of Le Fèvre in the frontispiece thus gives the deeds of violence that the text recounts the sanction of the very highest of heraldic authorities.

However, this portrait not only endows the supposed author of the *Livre des faits* with the credibility of Le Fèvre as an eyewitness but also draws the reader's attention to the process of literary immortalization that, as we have seen, the text itself sets out as one of its chief aims. This process is emphasized by the text's youthful representation of Toison d'Or, who was born around 1396 and so would have been well advanced in years if he was writing after Lalaing's death in 1453 (Le Fèvre himself died in 1468). That this depiction of him as a young man is not a mere slipup on the part of the frontispiece

---

[19] D'Escouchy, *Chronique de Mathieu d'Escouchy*, 1:3. See also the complete issue devoted to the study of medieval heralds in *Le héraut, figure européenne (XIVᵉ–XVIᵉ siècle)*, *Revue du Nord* 88 (2006).

[20] On these collars and who was entitled to wear them, see D'Arcy Jonathan Dacre Boulton, *The Knights of the Crown: The Monarchical Orders of Knighthood in Later Medieval Europe 1325–1520* (Woodbridge, UK: Boydell Press, 1987), pp. 356–96; and Françoise de Gruben, *Les chapitres de la Toison d'or à l'époque bourguignonne (1430–1477)* (Leuven, Belgium: Leuven University Press, 1997), pp. 43–48.

illustrator (who, in accordance with usual workshop practice, would have been the more experienced of the two artists working on this manuscript)[21] can be seen in the fact that the illuminator responsible for the later images in fr. 16830 *does* clearly distinguish between men of different ages. While the older noblemen of high status such as the Burgundian duke, Philippe le Bon, and the hero's own uncle, the seigneur de Créquy, are shown as having gray hair, the younger men of lower status, including Lalaing himself, are all portrayed with flowing brown locks (fol. 99r).

The effect of this depiction of Toison d'Or as being of a similar age to the hero is to make explicit the association between the herald as the putative author of the text and the knight as its subject. The biographer himself hints at this association in the prologue when he explains that, just as Lalaing desired to perform chivalric deeds that would ensure the enhancement and perpetuation of his family's good name, so he hopes to achieve the same for the hero through his act of writing, this link between them being suggested through repetition of the verb *mettre*: "Ay voulu *mettre et escripre* les haulx faiz et emprinses tresvaillans que en son temps fist et acheva messire Jacquez de Lalaing ... lequel, pour acquerir gloire immortel, *mist grant paine et labeur* durant son temps de augmenter et acroistre en tout honneur et bonne renommee la maison dont il estoit yssus" [I wanted *to put in writing* the great deeds and most worthy exploits that messire Jacques de Lalaing performed in his day ... he who, in order to attain immortal glory, *put great effort and labor* during his life to enhancing and increasing the honor and high renown of the family from whence he came] (p. 13; emphasis added). In other words, this opening image cements the symbiotic relationship that existed in late medieval chivalric culture between the knight, who furnishes the herald with his material, and the herald, who grants literary immortality to the knight through his writings,[22] by showing how the supposed author is himself preserved forever in the same youthful state as the hero. Pictorially transcending the limitations of time, knight and herald are thus conjoined in their mutual endeavor to construct a faithful record of the acts of chivalric violence accomplished by the hero, acts that will redound to the glory of his name.

---

[21] See Martine Dauzier, "L'image-porche ou la première page enluminée dans les romans médiévaux," in *From Sign to Text: A Semiotic View of Communication*, ed. Yishai Tobin (Amsterdam: John Benjamins, 1989), pp. 509–18.

[22] See Michel Stanesco, "Le héraut d'armes et la tradition littéraire chevaleresque," *Romania* 106 (1985): 233–53; G. A. Lester, "The Literary Activity of the Medieval English Heralds," *English Studies* 71.3 (1990): 222–29; and Maurice Keen, "Chivalry, Heralds, and History," in his *Nobles, Knights, and Men-at-Arms in the Middle Ages* (London: Hambledon Press, 1996), pp. 63–82.

From Violence to Harmony: The Knight as "Mirror" of His Chivalric Community

The notion symbolized in the authorial frontispiece of the physical resemblance between the knight and herald as young men in their prime also anticipates a key leitmotif in the *Livre des faits*: that of chivalric companions as each other's *semblables*. Not only does Toison d'Or emerge as an important character whose companionship, friendship, and heraldic advice underpin his relationship with Lalaing, one that lasts up until the moment of the hero's death, but also his bond with the young knight exemplifies the narrative's chief aim of showing how Lalaing earns his great reputation by imitating his peers, by seeking to surpass them, and, finally, by himself becoming a "mirror" for his contemporaries to gaze at, emulate, and resemble. This emphasis on the idea of the hero as a mirror for others is summed up with particular force in the epitaph taken from Chastellain, with its elaborate metaphors of the dark tomb barely being able to keep hidden from view the brilliant reputation of the knight within, he who was a "miroir cler de haute noble vye / Des bons spectacle" [a bright mirror of a great and noble life / A spectacle for the good] and a "lampe ardant en chambres et en salles / Dont tout oeul prinst clartéz especialles" [a burning lantern in chambers and staterooms / From which all eyes could gain extraordinary light] (pp. 555–56). Chastellain's epitaph, which was originally composed for Lalaing's funeral, encapsulates the idea that is enacted throughout the rest of the biography, that of "translating" the knight's corporeal existence into a resplendent book, one whose covers can be opened again and again to reveal the dazzling example contained in its pages, with the text thereby overcoming, through its act of commemoration, the act of violence that brought its hero's life to such a tragic close.

Making great play of the theme of Lalaing's mirroring his chivalric companions and becoming a mirror in turn, the *Livre des faits* reveals how the hero gains acceptance from his male peers by resembling them in his dress, conduct, and prowess, thus strengthening the bonds that unite them as a social group. Lalaing is first recognized as a potential *semblable*, and thus eligible to join the ranks of this illustrious, international sporting elite, when he is introduced at his family home to the young nobleman Adolphe de Clèves, who invites the adolescent "Jacquet" to join him at the court of Philippe le Bon, Adolphe's uncle, where they will finish their knightly education together. The hero more than fulfills this early promise, imitating the clothes, manners, and habits of his friend so well that they end up seeming almost as alike in their appearance as two brothers:

> Et tellement et sy bien se gouverna en toutes fachons que le jenne duc, son maistre le tenoit avec luy pour le plus prochain de son hostel, car eulx deux estoient comme d'un eage, et d'une grandeur, et de fachon de corps, et de maintieng. Parquoy le jenne duc le tint si chier que pou s'en failloit qu'il ne tenist comme son propre frere. (p. 58)

[And he governed himself so perfectly in all respects that the young duke (Adolphe), his master, regarded him as the closest member of his household, for these two were alike in age, size, build, and bearing. Hence the young duke bore him such love that he looked upon him almost as if he were his own brother.]

Like the hero's relationship with his heraldic companion, Toison d'Or, that with his near lookalike, Adolphe de Clèves, is shown as persisting right up until the instant when he was killed. It is thus principally under the gaze of his male peers – both those of his own age who are literally his *semblables* (or visually portrayed as such in the case of Toison d'Or) and those who are older and socially superior to him – that Lalaing's reputation as a chivalric paragon is forged.[23]

Biographies such as the *Livre des faits* have often been deemed rather tedious by modern readers because of their tendency to repeat episode after episode of the same sorts of chivalric events. In fact, however, it is precisely by depicting their heroes conforming to the verbal and visual norms of the knightly caste that such works are able to demonstrate how their subjects' chivalric identities were successfully constructed. In other words, through the reiteration of Lalaing's performance of appropriate conduct both on and off the field of combat the text manages to transform the literal acts of violence that he accomplishes into an expression of his harmonious integration into the chivalric community. The narrative thus regales the reader with detailed descriptions of the costly garments that the hero wears during the *monstres* or "displays of arms" preceding each tournament; provides lengthy lists of the blows given and received during combat; reports the many elegant speeches that he makes at the various courts of Europe where he seeks out challengers willing to take up his chivalric *emprise*; and records the formulaic verbal exchanges between him, his opponents, and the judges at his *pas d'armes*. Any public divergence from the norms of expected chivalric conduct, such as an ungracious or petulant comment from a knight who has lost a combat, an unorthodox choice of weapon, a failure to follow chivalric protocol in the course of a fight, or a disregard for a sovereign's ruling, is publicly reprimanded by the knight's social superiors.[24]

This process of subordinating the literal violence on which the knight's identity is based to the creation of a vision of chivalric community in which his every action and gesture are shown to be in perfect harmony with those of his peers is similarly enacted in the *Livre des faits* by the images that accom-

---

[23] See Michelle Magallanez, "Framing Narrative and Performance: Narrators' Roles in Late Medieval Burgundian Romance, Chronicle, and Chivalric Biography," *Mediaevalia* 20 (2001): 283–311.

[24] See, for example, the case of Diego Guzman, pp. 235–36.

pany the narrative. As Gaucher has pointed out, the miniatures in fr. 16830 are not only less graphic than the text itself in illustrating the wounds sustained by the hero and his opponents but they are also far less explicit in their depiction of the violence of combat (whether in tournament or battle) than manuscripts of contemporary chronicles that commemorate similar events.[25] Far from simply glorifying physical violence per se, the illuminations in the biography emphasize the high degree of conformity to the social demands of courtesy expected of the knight when judged by his fellow noblemen (and, to a far lesser extent, noblewomen). Indeed, in frequently positioning the reader/viewer of the manuscript as a direct spectator, particularly of the joust scenes (for example, fol. 31r; see fig. 2), these images adopt a visual strategy that corresponds precisely to its textual strategy of presenting the hero as a mirror for the audience to contemplate. If the depiction of Lalaing in the illumination cycle as a courtier, jouster, or warrior is therefore highly conventional, it is, once more, this very conventionality that underscores the congruity of his appearance and conduct in each situation in which he finds himself.

This impression of physical and behavioral congruity is achieved in the miniatures of the *Livre des faits* through a delicate pictorial balancing act between highlighting the hero as a distinctive individual and showing how he blends in as a fully integrated member of his social group. Thus, in the images of the scenes at court Lalaing can always be clearly identified by the deferential kneeling posture that he adopts before his superiors, such as the Count of Saint-Pol, the king of Castile, and the Duke of Burgundy (fols. 24r, 66v, and 99r, respectively). Yet the fact that the color of his robe in these miniatures is matched with that of another person in the scene reinforces the degree to which his appearance is also shown as being in keeping with his surroundings. In some of the illustrations of joust scenes Lalaing is made identifiable through some visual detail that stresses his exceptional valor, such as his choice to fight Diego Guzman with his visor raised (fol. 81v) or to fight Jehan Pitois with only one leg covered in armor (fol. 142r). In this series of images, however, it is often far more difficult to tell Lalaing apart from either his opponent, such as the Sicilian knight Jean de Boniface (fol. 47r), or his own companions, such as Simon de Lalaing and Hervé de Meriadec at the Stirling joust (fol. 107v). Nevertheless, at all times the fittingness of his chivalric performance is suggested visually by the way in which the arc of his body as he wields his weapons is echoed symmetrically by that of his adversary (see especially fols. 81v, 113v, 134v, and 142v). Finally,

---

[25] Gaucher, "Le *Livre des Fais*," 510. On violence in medieval chronicle illuminations, see Christiane Raynaud, "Le langage de la violence dans les enluminures des *Grandes chroniques de France* dites de Charles V," *Journal of Medieval History* 17 (1991): 149–70.

Fig. 2. Paris, BnF fr. 16830, fol. 31r. Lalaing displays his arms before combat begins at the Nancy joust.

in the miniatures illustrating battle scenes prior to the one that depicts his death, Lalaing is occasionally featured as having performed a particularly valorous deed. In the miniature depicting the battle for the Pont d'Espierres, for example, in which Lalaing is portrayed mounted on a striking white horse and with a trickle of blood on his face, his unfailing esprit de corps is visually underlined by his gesture of salute, which mirrors that of his commanding officer, the comte d'Estampes (fol. 157v; see fig. 3). Generally, however, it is impossible to identify Lalaing with any certainty in these scenes, as he is always shown wearing armor identical to that of his companions, as in the images of the battles of Lokeren and Barzel (fols. 165r and 182r, respectively). This uniformity of appearance again emphasizes how the hero has thoroughly assimilated his chivalric role by becoming one element among many in the ranks of Burgundian knights who staunchly defend their sovereign, the duke, against his Ghentish foe.

In tandem with the text's reiteration of the way in which Lalaing never fails to conform to the social expectations of knighthood, the miniatures in this manuscript of the *Livre des faits* represent the hero's acts of violence as the proofs of his chivalric worth by highlighting the constant appropriateness with which he performs them in terms of his dress, gestures, and bearing. By turning these acts of violence – whether in the tilting yard or in the heat of war – into socially acceptable chivalric ritual, the text and image together establish a harmonious correspondence between the hero and his *semblables*, one that bespeaks his successful integration into the chivalric community while also pointing to his qualities as an outstanding practitioner of the military arts.

Violence Transcended: The Death of Lalaing and Visual Incongruity

These pictorial and textual hints of Lalaing's exceptional status, which suggest that he not only meets the chivalric requirements that his society demands of him but even surpasses them, culminate in the final miniature of the cycle, which depicts his violent death (fol. 202r; see fig. 4). The narrative anticipates this moment by subtly building up a palpable sense of tragic irony about Lalaing's premature demise through its frequent references to people remarking of him that if he were to live to a ripe age, he would prove himself to be a worthy scion of his illustrious family (p. 106, for example). More specifically, the text prepares the reader for the fateful events at the siege of Poeke by stressing that the Ghent War, the first actual war in which the hero had fought, is a brutal conflict in which the Burgundian knights are no longer fighting their own noble *semblables*. Instead of competing in the lists according to set rules of conduct, they now have to confront the Ghentish burgher, a very different type of opponent, one who ignobly flees rather than engaging in open battle (pp. 518–19) and who fails to observe

Fig. 3. Paris, BnF fr. 16830, fol. 157v. Lalaing among the ranks of Burgundian knights pitted against their Ghentish foe in the battle for the Pont d'Espierres.

Fig. 4. Paris, BnF fr. 16830, fol. 202r. The death of Lalaing at the siege of Poeke in the Ghent War.

peace treaties (p. 540).[26] Although the images of war in fr. 16830 prior to that depicting Lalaing's death do not differentiate between the opposing sides, except through the occasional banner to signify whether the opponents are Burgundian or Ghentish, the introduction of visually incongruous elements into the final scene underscores the deadly nature of the hero's encounter with his unchivalric foe.

The first of these incongruities is the presence of artillery, since this is the only miniature in which firearms are shown, even though the text makes frequent reference to the use of artillery by both armies, such as during the Burgundian assault on the village of Moerbeke (p. 505).[27] A second, even more striking incongruity in this scene is that, for the first and only time in this cycle of illuminations in the *Livre des faits*, Lalaing's physical appearance is out of line with that of his companions and *semblables*, who are identifiable as a group, if not as individuals, by their faces being shown. Thus, while Toison d'Or, Adolphe de Clèves, and Antoine de Bourgogne, all of whom are mentioned by name in the text, are portrayed wearing identical armor, Lalaing is dressed in a long blue robe with a gold collar around his neck. One reason the artist may have chosen to depict the hero in this way is that Lalaing, as the narrative explains, was not then on active duty, having been injured in combat a few days before and been told to rest by both his doctor and Toison d'Or. The illustrator therefore showed Lalaing in nonmilitary dress, despite no mention being made in the text of his not wearing armor. The hero's incongruous attire serves a further purpose, however, by drawing the reader's eye to him in such a way as to suggest that he has unwittingly become a target. Indeed, although the text explains that Lalaing's death was an unfortunate accident caused by a piece of wood splintering off the mantle of a Burgundian bombard, what the illustrator actually shows is a Ghentish soldier taking direct aim at the hero. This representation of the young knight as a deliberate target is also emphasized by the artist's use of two other conventions of miniature composition: the diagonally descending line following the eyes of the soldier and of Lalaing as they lock on to each other; and the depiction of consecutive events in one synchronous image, as flames emerge from the end of the soldier's *veuglaire* at the same time as blood spurts from the left side of Lalaing's face when the projectile hits him, thus sealing the fateful link between the two men.

Yet in this tragico-ironic image of a hero who surpassed all of his *semblables* but was felled in such an untimely fashion by an unchivalric opponent, there are also two visual clues whose very incongruity encourages the reader

---

[26] See Malcolm Vale, *War and Chivalry: Warfare and Aristocratic Culture in England, France, and Burgundy at the End of the Middle Ages* (London: Duckworth, 1981), pp. 147–76.

[27] See Robert Douglas Smith and Kelly DeVries, *The Artillery of the Dukes of Burgundy, 1363–1477* (Woodbridge, UK: Boydell Press, 2005).

to interpret Lalaing's violent death in a more positive light. The first of these is the gold collar he wears, which both signals his high social status and reaffirms his membership of an elite chivalric caste, as it echoes the ones that he and other nobles are shown wearing in earlier miniatures, such as that in which the hero is welcomed at the court of the king of Castile (fol. 66v). The second visual clue is the blue of Lalaing's robe. This color, which had long been popularized by writers such as Froissart as a symbol of chivalric fidelity,[28] can be understood here as a reference to the steadfast faithfulness that the hero demonstrated toward his family, companions, and sovereign, not least because it is often (though not exclusively) the color of the robes that he wears in court scenes and of the fabric-covered breastplates that he sports in combat. Even more importantly, however, his robe invites a rereading of the significance of Lalaing's chivalric achievements as a whole by virtue of its echoing the traditional color of the Virgin Mary's robe, as seen in the earlier miniature of the Pas de la Fontaine des Pleurs (fol. 124r), which Michelle Szkilnik sees as underlining the knight's commitment to "la mission sacrée de la chevalerie."[29] This interpretation of the final image is reinforced in the text itself. Shortly after narrating how the hero died, it reveals retrospectively that Lalaing had chosen to dedicate himself to the Virgin, for whom he took the motto "la nonpareille" [she who is without equal].

A further link between the episodes of the *pas d'armes* and the hero's death is provided by two important references to the role played by Carmelites at each of these two key moments in Lalaing's life. While the knight is described as emerging devoutly from the "esglise des Carmes" before every one of his jousts during the year-long event he had organized under the aegis of the Virgin, he is later given the last rites at Poeke by a Carmelite friar who rushes to his side and encourages him to reaffirm his faith in God and Mary (p. 550). These textual and visual allusions to Lalaing's piety highlight the extent to which he was motivated by a desire not just for worldly renown but also for eternal salvation, thereby putting the final seal on his status as an exemplary "mirror" of chivalric conduct.[30] In showing how the violence of Lalaing's unchivalric demise is transcended when the depiction of his last minutes on earth is visually recontextualized as an affirmation of his high social status, steadfastness, and piety, the narrative only adds further poign-

---

[28] See Peter F. Ainsworth, "Heralds, Heraldry and the Colour Blue in the *Chronicles* of Jean Froissart," in *The Medieval Chronicle: Proceedings of the 1st International Conference on the Medieval Chronicle, Driebergen/Utrecht 13–16 July 1996*, ed. Erik Kooper (Amsterdam: Rodopi, 1999), pp. 40–55.

[29] Szkilnik, "Mise en mots," 84.

[30] On the knight's mission as ideally being to pursue both a lasting reputation in this life and salvation in the next, see Stephen H. Rigby, *Wisdom and Chivalry: Chaucer's "Knight's Tale" and Medieval Political Theory* (Leiden: Brill, 2009), p. 272.

ancy and weight to its portrayal of the dead knight as a more than worthy recipient of literary commemoration.

Conclusion: Immortalizing Violence?

The relationship between text and image in the earliest of the extant manuscripts of the biography of Jacques de Lalaing involves a complex interplay between literal and symbolic levels of meaning as part of its project of immortalizing the reputation of this late medieval hero as an exceptional exponent of the violent art of chivalry. The eternally youthful appearance of the figure who is pictorially cast in the frontispiece in the role of author of the *Livre des faits*, Toison d'Or, and his subject, Lalaing himself, signifies the symbiotic link between them in their complementary roles as herald and knight, the two also being united as companions in the same endeavor, perpetuating the honor of Burgundian knighthood through the celebration of chivalric violence. The seeming monotony of the text and the undoubted conventionality of its accompanying images, with their common emphasis on the hero's observance of protocol in his dress, speech, gestures, and behavior, proffer the spectacle of how this exceptional knight lived his life under the approving gaze of his male peers. At the same time, by recasting the literal violence of Lalaing's exploits as a ritualized expression of chivalric community, this combination of text and image also serves a further purpose, that of encouraging the reader to turn himself into Lalaing's *semblable*. Reconfiguring a contingent moment of violence as the tragico-ironic culmination of an otherwise exemplary career, the *Livre des faits* presents the hero's death not as an ending but as a beginning – of the hoped-for salvation of his soul in the afterlife, certainly, but also of the translation of his life into a book whose beauty and brilliance will never die.

12

Coming Communities in Medieval Francophone Writing about the Orient

SIMON GAUNT

In the thirteenth and fourteenth centuries Christian Europe confronted two related problems in which history and violence were inextricably entwined. First, how was Christendom to turn back the frequently bellicose expansion of Islam, in particular its conquest of the Holy Land, to which many believed Christianity had inalienable historic rights? Secondly, was the vast, and in medieval terms global, empire of the Mongols friend or foe, a potential ally against Islam or another, potentially devastating, threat? From the brutal Mongol invasions of Russia, Poland, and Hungary in the early 1240s through the fall of Acre in 1291, Europeans felt beleaguered. Although the onslaught of plague from 1347 focused attention on problems closer to home, it failed to lessen anxiety about European Christendom being overwhelmed, even if Europe's ostensible enemies were also weakened by the Black Death.

There is certainly no shortage of texts that inscribe virulent xenophobia – and in particular Islamophobia – while also exploring the possibility that the Mongols might become allies against Islam. A case in point is the Armenian prince-turned-monk Hayton's *Flor des estoires* (1307), written first in French and then translated into Latin, which ends with a stirring appeal to the Pope to mount a new Crusade against Muslims so that "la Terre Sainte, que fu arosée du precieus sanc Nostre Seignor Jhesu Crist, soit delivrée du poer des ennemis mescreans" [the Holy Land, which was watered with the precious blood of our Lord Jesus Christ, may be delivered from the power of our miscreant enemies].[1] Hayton recalls the shedding of Christ's blood in the Holy Land here precisely to anticipate the shedding of far larger quantities of blood by the *ennemis miscreans* of Christendom, which implies a violent and confrontational model of history. Literary scholarship inspired by

---

[1] Hayton, *La flor des estoires*, in *Recueil des historiens des croisades: Documents latins et français relatifs à l'Arménie* (Paris: L'Académie des Inscriptions et des Belles Lettres, 1906), p. 252 (accessible at http://gallica.bnf.fr/). All translations in this chapter are my own.

postcolonial theory and many historians of Christian/Muslim relations have tended to pick up on this view, suggesting that medieval European culture had an essentially binary view of the world. On the one hand, there were Christians, taken to be white and either from northwestern Europe or at the very least from the Frankish diaspora; on the other hand, there was the rest of the world, made up of Muslims (also known as pagans or Saracens) and "idolaters," who were frequently assimilated to an undifferentiated category of non-Christian others. According to this view, the purpose of the copious tradition of medieval writing about the Orient was to represent "the exorbitant otherness of an 'outlandish' world."[2]

However, several key texts originally composed in French but with a pan-European dissemination in a range of other vernaculars and Latin – Marco Polo's *Devisement du monde* (1298), on which Hayton clearly drew, and Mandeville's *Livre des merveilles* (ca. 1356), which clearly drew on Hayton – do not bear out the claim that their main concern is exorbitant otherness.[3] In recent articles I have explored how these texts toy with the uncanny and hybridity, presenting a challenging view of the world that assumes neither the preeminence of European culture nor a stark, binary contrast between Europe and the rest of the world. I further suggest that whereas *Le livre des merveilles* wavers between commitment to Eurocentric and Islamophobic prejudices and a fascination with uncanny alterity, *Le devisement du monde* offers a challenging engagement with difference that troubles the European subject's cultural, racial, and linguistic identity.[4] This suggests an openness to difference that is more in keeping with the kind of cultural traffic that Sharon Kinoshita sees at work in a range of twelfth- and thirteenth-century French and Occitan literary texts: Kinoshita offers a view of medieval francophone literary culture that is as interested in crossing borders as it is in reifying them.[5] But many medievalists are loathe to accord the Middle Ages this kind of openness, so strong is the commitment to locating the perni-

---

[2] Syed Manzarul Islam, *The Ethics of Travel from Marco Polo to Kafka* (Manchester: Manchester University Press, 1996), p. 149, writing of Marco Polo. See also Geraldine Heng, *Empire of Magic: Medieval Romance and the Politics of Cultural Fantasy* (New York: Columbia University Press, 2003), p. 254. For Heng, Mandeville writes "in the face of the exorbitantly foreign."

[3] I shall cite from Marco Polo, *Milione: Le divisament dou monde: Il milione nelle redazioni toscana e franco-italiana*, ed. Gabriella Ronchi (Milan: Mondadori, 1982), and Jean de Mandeville, *Le livre des merveilles du monde*, ed. Christiane Deluz (Paris: CNRS, 2000).

[4] See my "Translating the Diversity of the Middle Ages: Marco Polo and John Mandeville as 'French' writers," *Australian Journal of French Studies* 46 (2009): 235–48; and "L'inquiétante étrangeté de la littérature de voyage en français au Moyen Âge," *Medioevo Romanzo* 36 (2010): 57–81.

[5] Sharon Kinoshita, *Medieval Boundaries: Rethinking Difference in Old French Literature* (Philadelphia: University of Pennsylvania Press, 2006).

cious ideological roots and preconditions of colonialism in medieval culture.⁶ Thus, and perhaps ironically, the violent and confrontational model of history exemplified by Hayton prevails, rather than the more open models found in other texts.

This chapter seeks to explore how *Le devisement* mediates otherness by examining two themes that turn out to be intricately connected: language and money. Considering the role of language and money in *Le devisement* can help us to understand why the text holds up the Mongol empire as an alternative model of government and community, one that has the potential at least to bypass violent confrontation between cultures. This in turn engenders an alternative view of history, one in which Europe's future lies less in its own past (Greece, Rome, Arthurian Britain, or the recapture of Jerusalem, for example) than in stories of another place.

Diversity versus Otherness

A key term in medieval vernacular writing about the Orient is diversity, as we see from the outset in the *Devisement*, which I cite from the earliest, Franco-Italian, redaction, for reasons that I hope will become clear: "Seignors enperaor et rois, dux et marquois, cuens, chevaliers et b[o]rgio[i]s, et toutes gens que volés savoir les *deverses* jenerasions des homes et les *deversités* des *deverses* regions dou monde, si prennés cestui livre et le feites lire" [Lords, emperors and kings, dukes, marquises, counts, knight and burghers, and all you people who wish to know about the *diverse* kinds of men and all the *diversities* of the *diverse* regions of the world, take this book and have it read] (I.1; emphasis added).⁷ What are Marco Polo's main categories of diversity? Primarily, he focuses on places, usually categorized as cities or provinces, as well as the peoples, animals, and products found there. But, given his insistence on diversity, one of the striking things about Marco's text is its uncanny knack for making places sound extremely similar. Even though *Le devisement*'s information is usually accurate in terms of the relative positions of different places, their political affiliations and main religions, and their surrounding terrain and economic base, its descriptions are often highly formulaic:⁸

---

⁶ See further my "Can the Middle Ages Be Postcolonial?" *Comparative Literature* 61 (2009): 160–76.

⁷ All citations refer to chapter and sentence numbers in Ronchi's edition unless otherwise stated. This earliest version dates from 1298 and survives also in the earliest MS (1310), though it is clearly corrupt. The text was quickly translated into standard French (ca. 1310–11), Tuscan (ca. 1310), Venetian (ca. 1310–17), and Latin (ca. 1310–17), with numerous subsequent translations, retranslations, and adaptations.

⁸ In the first three quotations, *lengajes* and *rois* might seem plural. However, the text's noun (and verb) morphology is highly erratic, which is not to say they are

Bangala est une provence ver midi ... ont rois e lengajes por elz; il sunt pesimes ydres, ce entendés ydules. (CXXVI.1–2)

[Bangala is a province to the south ... they have a king and language of their own: they are dreadful idolaters, which means they have idols.]

Cangigu est une provence ver levant, il ha rois. Les jens <sunt> ydules et ont langajes por elz; il se renderent au grant <kan> et li font chascunz anz treu. (CXXVI.1)

[Upper Tonkin is a province to the east, with a king. The people are idolaters and have their own language; they are subjects of the Great Khan and each year pay him tribute.]

Aniu est une provence ver levant, que sunt au grant kaan. Ils sunt ydules; il vivent de bestiames et des profit de la terre; il ont langajes por elz.
(CXXVIII.1–2)

[Lower Tonkin is a province to the east, which belongs to the Great Khan. They are idolaters; they live from livestock and the land; they have their own language.]

Suigiu est une tranoble cité e grant. Il sunt ydules et <sunt> au grant can et ont monoie de carte. (CLI.1)

[Suzhoi is a very noble, big city. The people are idolaters, subjects of the Great Khan, and have paper money.]

Et ceste Vughin est encore une mout grant cité et noble. Il sunt ydres et <sunt> au grant kaan et ont monoie de carte. (CLI.13–14)

[And this Quinsai is again a very large, noble city. They are idolaters, subjects of the Great Khan, and have paper money.]

Ceste cité de Ciangan est mout grant et rique. Il sunt ydres et sunt au grant kaan et ont monoie de carte. (CLI.15–16)

[The city of Ch'ang-an is very large and rich. There are idolaters, subjects of the Great Khan, and they have paper money.]

"incorrect," as some commentators have argued. In this instance, all translations and adaptations thought to be made directly from the Franco-Italian text (which is to say the standard French, Venetian, Tuscan, and one of the Latin versions) render *lengajes* and *rois* with a singular noun. On the language of the Franco-Italian text, see Valeria Bertolucci Pizzorusso, "Lingue e stili nel *Milione*," in *L'epopea delle scoperte*, ed. Renzo Zorzi (Venice: Leo S. Olschki, 1994), pp. 61–73; and Maria Grazia Capusso, "La mescidanza linguistica del *Milione* franco-italiano," in *I viaggi del "Milione": Itinerari testuali, vettori di trasmissione e metamorfosi del Devisement du monde di Marco Polo e Rustichello da Pisa nella pluralità delle attestazioni*, ed. Silvia Conte (Rome: Tiellemedia, 2008), pp. 263–83.

Significantly, the role of race in Marco Polo's taxonomy of diversity is negligible: he comments on the black skin of people living near the equator, but he seems more interested in their nakedness than their color, while he dwells hardly at all on the racial characteristics of Mongols, the Chinese, the Indochinese, Tibetans, Arabs, Indians, and so on. As Thomas Hahn notes, race is not always a key marker of difference in medieval culture,[9] and the main categories of difference and diversity that interest Marco are marked rather by other factors: religion, language, government, and money.

Thus there are three main religious categories – Christians, Muslims, and idolaters – and frequently Marco represents them as cohabiting: for example, "La provence s'apelle Tangut. Il sunt tuit ydres, bien est il voir qu'il a auques cristienç nestorin; et encore hi a saracinç." [The province is called Tangout. They are all idolaters, but it is also true that there are some Nestorian Christians and also some Saracens.] (LVIII.2–3). It is striking that there are few instances of overt hostility to Muslims,[10] particularly compared to Hayton and Mandeville's strident Islamophobia. It is also noteworthy that these instances are consigned to descriptions of parts of the world through which the Polos passed either at the beginning or at the end of their travels: it is as if the closer they are to Europe, the greater the risk of what one might call default Islamophobia. Be that as it may, the infrequency of Marco's few explicit anti-Muslim statements is not consonant with the "anti-Islamic paranoia" (with its concomitant undercurrent of violence) that some critics attribute to him, inscribing him as they do in a confrontational narrative of Christian–Muslim relations.[11]

This confrontational narrative also rears its head when it is alleged that the Polos were sent to Asia by Pope Gregory X so that they might negotiate a pact between Christians and Mongols against the Muslim world with a view to reasserting Christian control of the Holy Land.[12] *Le devisement* itself nowhere says this. In fact, the Polo brothers (Marco's uncle and father) returned from their first trip to Asia (ca. 1260–69) as ambassadors for Kublai Khan (VI–IX). When they set out for Asia again in 1271, this time with Marco, the Pope's ambassadors were in fact two friars, who, it quickly tran-

---

[9] Thomas Hahn, "The Difference the Middle Ages Makes: Color and Race before the Modern World," *Journal of Medieval and Early Modern Studies* 31 (2001): 8 [1–37]. See also Robert Bartlett, "Medieval Concepts of Race and Ethnicity," *Journal of Medieval and Early Modern Studies* 31 (2001): 39–56. Bartlett argues that because it was believed that all people shared common descent from Noah's three sons, environment (particularly climate) and culture were thought to be the main determinants of racial differences.

[10] See XXVI.3; XXX.8–9; CXCIII.41; CXCIII.46; CXCIV.3.

[11] See, for example Islam, *Ethics*, p. 155.

[12] See, for example, Antonio García Espada, *Marco Polo y la Cruzada: Historia de la literatura de viajes a las Indias en el siglo XIV* (Madrid: Marcial Pons Historia, 2009), pp. 103–4. Espada reads the *Devisement* in the context of *tratados de recuperación*, early fourteenth-century texts urging the reconquest of the Holy Land.

spires, did not have the stomach for the perilous journey and therefore turned back before Armenia, consigning the Pope's messages (which are unspecified) to the Polos (XIII), who were nonetheless still in the service of Kublai.

Scholars who see *Le devisement*'s main agenda as anti-Islamic or pro-Christian are perhaps reading the text in the light of subsequent writers, such as Hayton, who wish to see the Crusades relaunched. Yet this is not just a modern mode of reception, since there is evidence that the text has a tendency in transmission to absorb and elaborate on prejudices and expectations that were not prevalent in its earliest redaction. Consider the following passage in the standard French text (ca. 1310–11) from the end of the narration of the miracle of the moving mountain:

> En tel maniere [ala] ce fait comme vous avez oÿ, [de quoy] ce fut moult grant miracle. Et ne vous merveilliez se li Sarrazin heent les Crestiens, car la maloite loy que Mahoms leur donna, si commande que tous les maulz que ils pueent faire a toutes manieres de gens et meïsmes aux Crestiens que il [le] doivent faire, et d'embler le leur et de tous les autres maus, puis que il n'est de sa loy. Et veez con sanglante loy et com mauvais commandemens que il ont, et tous les Sarrazins du monde se maintiennent en ceste maniere.[13]

> [And the event took place as you have heard, so it was a very great miracle. And do not be amazed if Saracens hate Christians, for the cursed law Mohamed gave them commands them to inflict wickedness on all kinds of people, even Christians, and to steal from them and other kinds of wickedness, because they are not of their religion. And just consider what a bloody law and what wicked commandments they have, and all the Saracens in the world behave in this way.]

This episode, near the beginning of the text, narrates how the Christians of Baghdad are rescued from Muslim persecution by the power of prayer, and this enables them to move a mountain at the request of their persecutors. But the episode ends far more neutrally in the earlier Franco-Italian redaction with "en cele mainere ala ceste mervoile come il avés oi" [in this manner the marvel you have heard came about] (XXIX.10), instead of the Islamophobic lines I have just cited. In other words, some modern critics continue a trend found already among medieval readers and transmitters whereby they read the text as more committed to xenophobia and violent confrontation than it actually was in its original redaction.

---

[13] Marco Polo, *Le devisement du monde*, ed. Philippe Ménard et al., 6 vols (Geneva: Droz, 2001–9), 28.44–54; after XXIX.9 in the Franco-Italian text. This addition in the Old French text may have been inspired by XXVI.3 in the Franco-Italian text. See note 7 above for further details on the different versions.

Far from showing "anti-Islamic paranoia" or representing idolatry as "the other religion by excellence" (Islam, *Ethics*, p. 155), the *Devisement* demonstrates a striking sense of the relative value of, and similarities between, different religions. Examples are legion, but particularly compelling are Marco's account of Brahmins and Yogis (CLXXVII) and his life of the Buddha (CLXXVIII), in which analogies with Christianity as well as accurate observations about Buddhism abound. Interestingly, the standard French text effects some key alterations to the life of the Buddha, one being that it is claimed that the Buddha himself rather than his bereaved father was the first idolater, as if the redactor could not quite believe what he or she read and sought to bring it into line with more orthodox cultural prejudices.

Marco Polo's unorthodoxy is also apparent in his treatment of Oriental Christians. Unlike Mandeville he treats Nestorian Christians simply as Christians, not as schismatics. Furthermore, being a Christian is not sufficient to warrant his support. Thus, in his narration of Kublai Khan's Christian uncle Nayan's rebellion (LXXVII–LXXX), Marco sides with Kublai. Indeed, he is at pains to portray Kublai's magnanimity and political as well as theological astuteness when his Muslim and "idolater" subjects take advantage of the circumstances to mock the cross the Christians have carried before them in battle: Kublai (and implicitly Marco, too) condemns the rebellious Christians, but he defends the value of the cross nonetheless (LXXX.6–10). This episode, in which Kublai's regime becomes an uncanny model of ideal government,[14] suggests that a guiding principle of the Mongol empire was religious tolerance.

Language, Money, Community

Kublai Khan governed a myriad of different peoples, both in reality and in Marco Polo's account. If Marco comments often on religious difference, he also, as we saw above, frequently remarks that the people of a city or a province "have their own language." Indeed, this formula occurs no fewer than twenty-eight times. However, it is interesting to observe that it is never combined with another frequent formula applied to cities and provinces, which is, as we also saw above, that "they have paper money," a reference to the banknotes Kublai famously introduced in China and elsewhere, money that is also described as "la charte dou grant kaan" [the paper of the Great Khan] or "la monnaie du seignor" [the lord's money]. There is striking geographic and stylistic symmetry here in that variations on "they have paper money" occur twenty-nine times. There is no suggestion that Marco Polo

---

[14] For more detail, see my "L'inquiétante étrangeté," pp. 66–71.

thought that paper currency meant that everyone spoke the same language; indeed, at a number of points he shows awareness of the linguistic difficulties that faced Western travelers in the Far East, and we are told that he learned to speak, read, and write four Oriental languages (XVI.1). But there nonetheless seems to be an implication that the barriers that linguistic differences erect dissolve with a shared currency. Perhaps, therefore, we can better understand the implications of the role of paper money in the text by considering why the communities that do not use this currency are represented as constituted and defined primarily by having their own language.

One important question posed by theorists of community concerns the role of essence and/or identity in community formation. Jean-Luc Nancy, for example, suggests that modern philosophy has implicitly posited an idea of community grounded in an essential identity: "La communauté n'est pas seulement la communication intime de ses membres entre eux, mais aussi la communication organique d'elle-même avec sa propre essence" [Community is not only grounded in the intimate communication of its members among themselves, but also in its inner organic communication with its own essence].[15] But, as Giorgio Agamben argues, drawing on medieval philosophy, "Non vi è differenza di essenza fra la natura comune e l'ecceità" [There is no difference in essence between common nature and ipseity].[16] Whereas, for Nancy, "[la communauté] est faite avant tout du partage et de la diffusion ou de l'imprégnation d'une identité dans une pluralité dont chaque membre, par là même, ne s'identifie que par la médiation supplémentaire de son identification au corps vivant de la communauté" [community is formed above all by the sharing and diffusion, or from the saturation, of an identity in a plurality with which each member, through this very process, only identifies by the supplementary mediation of his or her identification with the living body of the community] (p. 30), suggesting that what defines community is a shared but singular essence, for Agamben "l'idea et la natura comune non costituiscono l'essenza della singolarità ... la singolarità è, in questo senso, assolutamente inessenziale" [a common idea and nature do not constitute the essence of singularity ... singularity, in this sense, is absolutely inessential] (p. 20). This leads Agamben to conclude that "il rapporto fra commune e singolare non è più allora pensabile come il permanere di una identica essenza nei singoli individui e il problema stesso dell' individuazione rischia di presentarsi come uno pseudoproblema" [the relation between the common and the singular is no longer then thinkable as the residue of an identical essence in singular individuals and the very problem of individuation risks becoming a pseudoproblem] (p. 20). Although the two approaches differ, there is none-

---

[15] *La communauté désœuvrée*, 2nd edn. (1982; Paris: Christian Bourgois, 1999), p. 30.
[16] *La comunità che viene*, 2nd edn. (1990; Turin: Bollati Boringhieri, 2001), p. 20.

theless common ground. Even if, for Nancy, common essence is only realized as a future potential, or indeed as a future perfect (because "community," he suggests, is often represented as always already lost), "community" thus conceived nonetheless relies on a common essence that requires exclusion as much as inclusion: notions of "community" can therefore lead to totalitarian, brutal regimes that institutionalize violence. Therefore, rather than assuming a common essence, perhaps we need to experience (or aspire to) a utopic *être-en-commun* (being-in-common), an alternative model of community, *la communauté désœuvrée*, or "inoperative community," that allows for difference and heterogeneity. Similarly, for Agamben, the aim should be "l'idea di una comunità *inessenziale*, di un convenire che non concerne in alcun modo un' essenza" [the idea of an inessential community, of an accord that does not concern essence in any way] (p. 20), which is to say a "coming community" yet to be realized, grounded in solidarity with being itself, one that might be likewise inimical therefore to totalitarian regimes.

With this in mind, it is striking that if, on the one hand, *Le devisement* represents the myriad of communities that do not use paper money (as evidenced by each having a language of their own) as therefore deriving their singularity from their language, on the other hand, each community having a language of their own is precisely something they share. Language is thus accorded a special status here, in that whereas multiple communities are represented as Muslim, or Christian, or idolaters, or a mixture of different religions, or as merchants, farmers, bandits, or dishonest or honest, for example, when a group is said to have *langajes por elz*, this apparently differentiates them absolutely from others, even though the language in question is never identified. Language per se thus becomes a marker of difference, decisive in the formation of the communities Marco Polo encounters, suggesting a world fragmented into atomized but similar units, with some individuals (like Marco himself) circulating among them. Yet if all these communities have in common is having a "language of their own," perhaps they have, at least potentially, structural similarities that mean they are not as divided as they might appear to be at first blush. Perhaps there is a "coming community" here yet to be realized. If so, what might this look like, and what could be the agent of unity?

This Babel contrasts with the vast array of lands and provinces that use paper money. As already noted, the two formulas "ont lengajes por elz" and "ont monoie de carte" are never combined. This thus marks the distinction between the lands directly controlled by Kublai Khan and the rest of the world, even though other peoples may pay tribute to him. The frequency of the two formulas and their contrasting usage are clearly purposeful, particularly when it is considered that in other texts that certainly used *Le devisement* as a source (Hayton and Mandeville, for example), paper money is mentioned only briefly and either language is rarely an issue (as for Mandeville) or different scripts are as remarkable as different languages per se (as for

Hayton).[17] In some senses, paper money is thus *the* distinguishing feature of Kublai Khan's government and of his sovereignty.

The production, function, and circulation of paper money are unusually accorded a whole chapter of *Le devisement* (XCVI), yet this chapter has received surprisingly little attention from an interpretive point of view. If Kublai Khan's prosperity surpasses that of all other lords in the world put together, this is directly attributable to his paper money, according to Marco:

> Or voç ai contés la mainere et la raison por coi le grant sire doit avoir et ha plus tresor que nuls homes de ceste monde; et si vos dirai une greignor chouse: que tuit les seignor de<u> siecle ne ont si grant richese come le grant sire a solemant. (XCVI.15)
>
> [Now I have told you how and the reasons why the great lord has to have and has more treasure than any other in the world; and I will tell you something even greater: that all the lords of the world put together are not as rich as the great lord by himself.]

On the one hand, this clearly contributes to the hyperbolic and utopian description Marco offers of Kublai's magnificence: his court is larger, more elaborate, and more wondrous than that of any Occidental lord, his hunts more extensive, his learning and appetites (for food, sex, power) more prodigious. On the other hand, is it just opulence that Marco admires here? Clearly the social order that paper money symbolizes is every bit as crucial for Marco's admiration.

For Marco is well aware of the symbolic value of paper money as opposed to coins, precious stones, precious metals, silk, or other commodities. First and foremost, its value is not grounded in the intrinsic or essential value of the material from which it is made: thus the equivalence of different notes to Occidental coins is carefully calibrated, and it is pointed out that value is not dependent on weight (XCVI.3, 6). Secondly, value depends on title (which is to say that value depends on a written and visual signification system) and more specifically is guaranteed by the authority of Kublai himself, since his seal goes on each note to show it is genuine (XCVI.11). Thirdly, value is explicitly defined as exchange value: it is not the notes themselves that are valuable, but what you can exchange them for (XCVI.5–8). The whole system works through a network of substitutions and exchanges, such that paper money becomes symbolic of the symbolic order itself, a symbolic order that Kublai's subjects are said to embrace "willingly": "Et si voç di que toutes les jens et regionz d'omes que sunt sout sa seignorie prennent voluntier cestes chartre en paiement" [And I tell you that all the people and

---

[17] For passing references to paper money, see Hayton, *Flor*, p. 121; and Mandeville, *Livre*, pp. 396–97. Hayton frequently remarks on different scripts, and Mandeville manuscripts often contain alphabets in different languages.

all the regions of men who are under his sovereignty willingly accept this paper in payment] (XCVI.5). Indeed, it is as if they would in fact rather have the paper money than the goods given up in exchange: "Et les mercaant le prennent moult voluntieres, por ce que il le metent puis en toutes les chouses qu'il achatent, por toutes les teres do grant sire" [And the merchants take it very willingly, because with it they are able to buy everything in all the lands of the great lord] (XCVI.9). This utopian vision of the effects of paper money is tempered, however, by the threat of violence: "Nulz ne le ose refuser a poine de pardre sa vie" [No one dares refuse it on pain of death] (XCVI.5). Paradoxically, Kublai's subjects are free to accept paper money but not free to refuse it. Although the better, more prosperous world instantiated by paper money is thus apparently instantiated as well by a subliminal threat of violence, as Slavoj Žižek argues of precisely this kind of *choix forcé*, "There is nothing totalitarian about it. The subject who thinks he can avoid this paradox and really have a free choice is a *psychotic* subject, one who retains a kind of distance from the symbolic order – who is not really caught in the signifying network."[18] The refusal of paper money is tantamount to enacting self-banishment.[19]

Paper money allows Kublai's subjects to buy things, but more importantly, as Suzanne Conklin Akbari suggests, it allows them to buy into a social network of exchange, a network that concerns the circulation of signs as much as commodities, binding individuals together in a symbolic community.[20] For, in Marco Polo's world, it would seem that communities have *either* a language of their own *or* paper money. As Yunte Huang suggests in passing, "Money may be a universal language,"[21] as if the circulation and acceptance of paper money in itself makes any linguistic differences unworthy of remark, or even as if paper money allows communities to transcend linguistic difference, to form a larger, more fluid, and yet peaceful and connected community, performatively constituted by the acceptance of the paper currency. Is this perhaps a kind of "comunità *inessenziale*" as envisaged by Agamben, one that "non concerne in alcun modo un' essenza" [does not concern in any way an essence] (*La comunità*, p. 20)? If so, it is interesting that Kublai's regime avoids the fragmentation marked by every town and province having

---

[18] Slavoj Žižek, *The Sublime Object of Ideology* (New York: Verso, 1989), pp. 165–69 ("The Forced Choice of Freedom").

[19] See Agamben's influential *Homo Sacer: Il potere sovrano e la nuda vita* (Turin: Einaudi, 1995), pp. 116–23, on the ban and its relation to violence and power.

[20] See Suzanne Conklin Akbari, "Currents and Currency in Marco Polo's *Devisement dou monde* and *The Book of John Mandeville*," in *Marco Polo and the Encounter of East and West*, ed. Akbari and Amilcare A. Iannucci (Toronto: University of Toronto Press, 2008), pp. 124–28 [110–30].

[21] Yunte Huang, "Marco Polo: Meditations on Intangible Economy and Vernacular Imagination," in *Marco Polo and the Encounter of East And West*, ed. Akbari and Ianucci, p. 276 [262–79].

"a language of its own" only with the threat that rejecting the symbolic order represented by paper money will lead to violence.

Fiction and History

In his discussion of Baudelaire's *La fausse monnaie*, Jacques Derrida argues that all money – whether counterfeit or genuine – depends on an "acte de foi,"[22] requiring both credit and creditability, which is constitutive of authority as well as guaranteed by it. Money, in other words, instantiates and yet is a product of belief. It is thereby a prototype for, as well as a form of, fiction (p. 113), profoundly analogous to both language and literature. Michel Foucault also underlines these points: "Dire que la monnaie est une gage, c'est dire qu'elle n'est rien de plus qu'un jeton reçu de consentement commun – pure fiction par conséquent" [To say that a coin's value is guaranteed is to say that it is nothing more than a token with commonly recognized value – and thus pure fiction].[23] Money, for Foucault as for Derrida, functions primarily as a sign (*Les mots*, p. 187), as a form of representation (pp. 191–92) that grounds reciprocity and mutual belief. As such, it also partakes of the economy of the gift as conceived anthropologically: it thus dissolves the distinction between giving and taking, as in the scene in which Kublai's subjects exchange their precious stones (offered to him as a "present" [XCVI.7]) for his paper money, which they take (XCVI.9). Who is giving what to whom here? Who is giving, who taking? The wealth may in some senses flow in only one direction, but there is no doubt that paper money is empowering for those who use it, that it binds them together.

Le devisement thus implies both an analogy and a contrast between language and currency that invites reflection. Both allow for exchange and both engender (while also reflecting) community formation, but the latter on a larger and more inclusive scale. It might be tempting to see Marco Polo's preoccupation with money simply as a reflection of his outlook as a merchant. Indeed, one influential reading of *Le devisement* sees it as an elaborate "merchants' manual" or primarily as a merchant's view of the world.[24] However, as many scholars have noted, *Le devisement* lacks the practical detail found in near contemporary merchants' manuals and also seeks to impart knowledge that greatly exceeds the strictly mercantile concerns of

---

[22] Jacques Derrida, *Donner le temps 1: La fausse monnaie* (Paris: Galilée, 1991), p. 124.

[23] Michel Foucault, *Les mots et les choses: Une archéologie des sciences humaines* (Paris: Gallimard, 1966), p. 194.

[24] See F. Borlandini, "Alle origini del libro di Marco Polo," in *Studi in onore di Amintore Fanfani*, 6 vols (Milan: Giuffrè, 1962), 1:107–47.

merchants' manuals.[25] Furthermore, any strictly "mercantile" interpretation of the text fails to account for the complex problems of interpretation posed by its indeterminate narrative voice, by its alternation of description and narrative, by the way it draws on the conventions of a range of disparate genres (prose romance, history, and encyclopedias, as well as merchants' manuals), and by its languages of transmission. The "coming community" Marco portrays in the Far East is not simply a protocapitalist paradise for merchants but rather an alternative symbolic order as interested in a new way of exchanging signs as it is in the traffic of objects. In other words, although Kublai's subjects submit to his sovereignty under the threat of violence, as a result of doing so they partake of a less violent, more tolerant, and more diverse community.

What might a language for this new symbolic order, one that is not just for a specific group, be or look like? What language offers the same kind of fluidity and exchange as paper money? Within the parameters of the text, one answer to this might be French. This is not the case in the sense that French is represented as a neocolonial lingua franca, one that functions in Asia as well as in Europe, like English in the modern world, but rather, on the contrary, in the sense that this text is composed in a hybridized form of French outside France by two nonnative speakers (Marco Polo and his amanuensis Rustichello da Pisa).[26] Previous scholarship has tended to attribute the text's use of French to the centrality and influence of French courtly culture, a marker, therefore, of Marco and Rustichello's cultural subordination to France and French literature, but this is to neglect the political and economic role of French in the Mediterranean (which is not necessarily focused on France), and also to fail to consider the implications of the use of a foreign language as a means of spoken and written communication.[27] The language of the text, particularly in the earliest form in which it circulated, the so-called Franco-Italian literary koine, is always already marked by one kind of strangeness or difference (in that it is laced with Italianisms) at the same time as it mediates another kind (the Orient).

One of the interesting things about this text's transmission, then, is that linguistic standardization often seems to go hand in hand with ideological normalization. The standard French redaction, for example, "translates" the text into a less eccentric literary idiom (without, however, completely succeeding in the eradication of Italianisms), and yet at the same time it

---

[25] See, for example, Jacques Heers, *Marco Polo* (Paris: Fayard, 1983), pp. 165–85 ("Marco Polo: marchand?"), and Marina Münkler, *Marco Polo: Vita e leggenda* (Milan: Vita e Pensiero, 2001), pp. 93–94.

[26] The first chapter (I.7) informs readers that the text was dictated by Marco to Rustichello (who is otherwise known for an Arthurian prose compilation) in 1298, while both were imprisoned in Genoa.

[27] See my "Translating the Diversity."

eliminates some elements and details that may have been found troubling, or, alternatively, it edits and/or expands others in such a way as to make the text conform to more banal Eurocentric cultural stereotyping.[28] So how Eurocentric is the Franco-Italian text itself? I would suggest hardly at all. In fact, it is striking that Europe is almost entirely absent from Marco Polo's *devisement* or mapping of the world; indeed, it is mainly just a point of departure without ever quite becoming a point of return. It is certainly not the point at which the perspective of the narrator(s) is always situated, which is in sharp contrast to encyclopedic taxonomies of the world, or to Mandeville and Hayton.

Indeed, there are two main centers to Marco's account of the world, one representing political authority, embodied by Kublai Khan and located in the Far East, the other representing textual authority, embodied by Marco Polo himself, making its perambulating presence felt whenever Marco's narrative voice emerges.[29] For Marco, as the prologue intimates, is a teller of tales and a purveyor of marvels not just to his European readers but also to Kublai Khan, for whom, the text claims, Marco worked while in Asia:

> Li jeune baçaler fait sa enbasee bien et sajemant et por ce qu'el avoit veu et oi plusors fois que le grant kan, quant les mesajes k'il mandoit por les diverses partes dou monde, quant il retornoient a lui et li disoient l'anbasee por coi il estoit alés et no li savoient dir autres noveles de les contrees ou il estoient alés, il disoit elz qu'il estoient foux et non saiçhan[ç] et disoi[t] que miaus ameroit oir les noveles et les costumes et les usajes de celle estra<n>jes contree qu'il ne fasoit oir celç por coi il li avoit mandé, et Marc, ke bien savoie tout ce, quant il ala en cele mesajarie, toutes les nuvités et tutes les stranges chauses qu'il avoit, met[t]oit son entent por coi il le seust redire au grant kaan. (XVI.4; cf. XVII.1–2)

> [The young man conducted his embassy well and wisely, and because he had seen and heard several times that the Great Khan, when the envoys he sent out to the diverse parts of the world returned to him and recounted their embassies but couldn't tell him anything else about the countries where they had been, said they were foolish and ignorant and that he would rather hear about new customs and the habits of strange countries than he would hear about the business on which he had sent them, Marco, who realized this, when he went off on a mission, strived to be in a position to relate to the Great Khan all the novelties and strange things he could.]

---

[28] See Marco Polo, *Le devisement*, 28.41–54, a portion of which is quoted above, or the revisions made to Marco's *Life of the Buddha*, analyzed in my forthcoming book *Marco Polo's "Le devisement du monde": Narrative Voice, Language, and Diversity.*

[29] On narrative voice in *Le devisement*, see Valeria Bertolucci Pizzorusso, "Enunciazione e produzione del testo nel *Milione*," *Studi mediolatini e volgari* 25 (1977): 5–43.

As Italo Calvino saw in his novel inspired by *Il Milione*,[30] the medieval Tuscan redaction of *Le devisement*, the figure of Marco Polo plays a pivotal role in mediating foreignness to East *and* West. He becomes, in other words, a point of symbolic exchange or translation with or for the other.

As a mediator of strangeness, does Marco Polo not hold out to his Western readers, in the form of the Mongol empire, a rose-tinted promise for Europe's future, a coming community to which we might aspire, provided we submit to Kublai Khan's sovereignty? Should we embrace its symbolic system, we too could partake of its riches, its religious tolerance, and its technical marvels. Our route to this community is Marco himself in the form of his text, in all its troubling strangeness. But so incredible and disturbing was this vision that some readers could not accept it, preferring the more fabulous – but by other measures more credible and familiar – account of the world offered by Mandeville (whose travels were nonetheless pure fiction), more credible, perhaps, precisely because it offered a more violent and confrontational account of the world.[31] How appropriate then, from a Derridean perspective, that truth and fiction, the authentic and the counterfeit, should become so confused. But how appropriate, too, from a medieval perspective, that when Columbus set sail looking for the Great Khan's riches, which he had read about in Marco Polo, that he should thereby have gone looking for the future in the past, and not just in Europe's past, but rather a past that was also quite literally another country. "Viaggi per rivivere il tuo passato?" [Do you travel to relive your past?] (p. 35) asks Kublai of Marco in Calvino's *Le città invisibili*, a question the narrator tells us is the same as asking "Viaggi per ritrovare il tuo futuro?" [Do you travel to find once again your future?], which suggests there is a risk of mislaying the future if you do not journey into the past – into history, in other words – by telling stories about it.

---

[30] Italo Calvino, *Le città invisibili* (Turin: Einaudi, 1972).
[31] On skepticism about the authenticity of *Le devisement*'s account of Asia, see in particular John Larner, *Marco Polo and the Discovery of the World* (New Haven, CT: Yale University Press, 1999), pp. 58–67, 114–15, 144–46.

INDEX

Abbey of Saint Bertin, 57, 59, 61–62
Abbey of Saint Denis, 61
Abbey of Saint Peter in Ghent, 56
Abbey of Saint Vaast in Arras, 57
Abbot of Vaux, 44–45
Abelard, Peter, 58–59
Adolphe de Clèves, 177–78, 184
adultery, 137–42, 144–46
Agamben, Giorgio, 194–95, 197
Ainsworth, Peter F., 4, 137, 185
Ancient Chronicle of Flanders, 62–68
Andrew Horn
    see Horn, Andrew
Angevin Empire, 10
Annales de Dunstaplia [Dunstaple Annals], 86–87
Annales Londonienses (Andrew Horn), 88, 92
anti-Semitism, 92, 102
Antoine de Bourgogne, 184
Archbishop Reginald of Rheims, 58
Armstrong, Adrian, 151
Arn, Mary-Jo, 156, 163
Arnold of Lübeck, 36–37
Arnold the Great, 55
Arnold II of Ardres, 71–72, 76
Arnold III of Ardres, 9, 55–58, 75, 80
Arnold II of Guines, 76, 78, 80–82
Augustine, 7, 35, 37

Baldwin I, 35–37, 48–49, 55
Baldwin II, 56–57, 72, 81
Baldwin V, 59, 62, 65–67, 69
Baldwin VI, 9, 55–57, 60, 65–67
Baldwin VII, 55, 59, 62–63
Barthes, Roland, 2
Battle of Agincourt (1415), 152
Battle of Cassel (1071), 56
Battle of Evesham (1265), 95
Battle of Hastings (1066), 96, 117, 119–20, 125

Battle of Stirling Bridge (1297), 93
Becket, Thomas, 85
beer, 71–72
Beer, Jeanette M. A., 41, 43
beheading, 83, 86–88, 91–92, 95, 139
Benjamin, Walter, 15
Benoît de Sainte-Maure, 10, 117–20, 122–32
Berbers, 20
Bernard of Clairvaux, 39
Bernard of Saxony, 57, 60, 64
"Bertinian" genealogy, 55–62, 67
Black Death, 187
Blanchard, Joël, 153
blasphemy, 86, 143
bloodlines, 120–32, 145
Boethius, 94
Boswell, John, 134, 139, 147
Bower, Walter, 94
Bowman, Glenn, 24
Buef d'Aigremont, 30–31
Braudel, Fernand, 2
Brenhinedd y Saesson, 85
Brown-Grant, Rosalind, ix, 11, 113, 169–86
Byzantine Church, 45–46

Cain and Abel, 7
Canso de la Crozada
    beauty of violence, 111–14
    clerics and crusaders in, 102–5
Continuator, 99, 102, 105–7, 109–12
    bias in writing, 101–2
    dismemberment in, 99–101
    evil of violence, 102–7
    good of violence, 107–11
    historical reality and, 99–100
    Occitan barons in, 102, 105–7
castration, 83, 135, 137–42
Cathars, 22, 109

Catholic Church
  see Roman Church
Céline, Louis-Ferdinand, 153
Champion, Pierre, 154, 156–57, 163–64
Charlemagne, 22, 25, 27–32, 43–44, 126
Charles d'Orléans, 11, 151–67
Charles Martel
  see Martel, Charles
Charles the Good, 62–63
Chartier, Alain, 152
Chastellain, Georges, 170, 177
chivalry
  biographical writings and, 11–12, 81, 169–72
  color as symbol of, 185
  companions and, 172
  Edward I and, 90
  Jacques de Lalaing and, 181, 185–86
  knight as "mirror" of, 177–81
  lack of, 184
  violence and, 113–14, 172–76
Christianity
  Crusades and, 35–36, 44–45, 47–48, 50–51
  Devisement du monde (Marco Polo) and, 191–93, 195
  Enéas and, 124
  history and, 187–88
  Islam and, 191–92
  Judaism and, 22, 191
  sacred and, 22–23
  violence and, 23, 102, 187
Christine de Pizan, 152
Chronicle (Langtoft), 89–91, 93–96
Chronique (Le Bel), 135–42
Chronique de Mathieu d'Escouchy, 173, 175
Chronique des ducs de Normandie (Benoît de Sainte-Maure), 10, 117–20, 124–25, 128–29, 132
Chroniques (Froissart)
  color imagery in, 185
  Hugh Despenser and, 11, 137–38
  Hundred Years War and, 133
  Roger Mortimer and, 140–41
  sexuality and, 140–42
  violence and, 135
  writing of, 135
churches, pillaging of, 36, 61, 102
color, symbolism of, 179, 185
comedy, violence and, 74–82

commemoration
  believability and, 9
  books and, 163–67
  history and, 5
  poetry and, 152–54
  power and, 11
  sex and, 144–45
  violence and, 4, 6, 56, 61–62, 172, 177–79, 185–86
  war and, 153
  see also memory
community
  chivalry and, 113–14, 172, 177–81, 186
  imagined, 40
  language/money and, 189, 193–99
  reciprocity and, 22
  violence and, 11–12, 113–14
La conquête de Constantinople (Villehardouin)
  Constantinople, conquest of, 46–48
  crisis in Venice, 42–44
  crusade histories, 50–51
  Franco-Venetian accord, 40–42
  Fulk de Neuilly, 38–40
  Latin Empire, 48–50
  overview, 35–38
  Zara, conquest of, 44–46
  see also Villehardouin, Geoffroy de
Constantinople
  La conquête de Constantinople (Villehardouin) and, 46–48
  conquest of, 46–48
  Crusades and, 9, 37
  Girart de Roussillon and, 26
Continuator (of the *Canso de la Crozada*), 99, 102, 105–7, 109–12
Council of Clermont, 107
Cowell, James, ix, 8, 19–33
Crusades
  Albigensian, 10, 22, 100
  as anti-Islamic, 187, 192
  atrocities of, 10
  Canso de la Crozada and, 99–113
  epics, 26
  First, 4, 22, 38
  Fourth, 9, 35–51
  Fulk de Neuilly and, 38–40
  Girart de Roussillon and, 26
  Hayton and, 87, 192
  histories, medieval and modern, 50–51
  Jacques de Lalaing and, 171

written accounts of, 22, 26, 35–51

Damian, Peter, 143
Dafydd ap Gruffydd, 85–87, 97
Dandolo, Enrico, 40–44
de Certeau, Michel, 3, 6–7, 15
De consolatione Philosophiae (Boethius), 94
de Grazia, Margreta, 14
Derrida, Jacques, 1, 198, 201
desire, sexual, 27, 34, 134–37, 147, 154
Devisement du monde (Marco Polo), 12, 188–92, 195–98, 200
dialect, 12–13
Diego Guzman, 179
dismemberment, 83–97
    constructing texts around, 88–94
    dismembered body as relic, 94–97
    Edward I and, 85–88
    law and, 10
    recording of, 4
    see also Wallace, William
d'Outremeuse, Jean
    see Jean d'Outremeuse
Dudo of Saint-Quentin, 77
Dunstaple Annals
    see Annales de Dunstaplia
Durkheim, Émile, 41

Edmond of Kent, 143
empires
    Angevin Empire, 10
    discontinuity and, 119, 132
    Latin Empire, 9, 13, 35, 37, 43, 48–50
    Mongol Empire, 12, 187–89, 193, 201
Enrico Dandolo
    see Dandolo, Enrico
Epic of Revolt, 8, 21, 23, 26
Eracles, 36, 39
executions
    Arnold II and, 80
    body and, 83
    Dafydd ap Gruffydd, 85–88
    historical accounts of, 4, 9–10
    Hugh Despenser, 11, 134–35, 137–39, 142
    public, 83–85, 95–97, 142–43
    Roger Mortimer, 140
    sexual violence and, 135
    torture and, 84, 87–88
    William Wallace, 88–97
    see also castration; dismemberment

fabliaux, 9, 78–79, 82
faidit (dispossessed knight), 105, 108
Febvre, Lucien, 2
Federico, Sylvia, 5
Fisher, Matthew, ix, 9, 83–97
Flandria Generosa, 59–62
Floris of Frisia, 56–57, 60, 64–65
Flors des estoires (Hayton of Corycus), 187
Folquet de Marseille, 99–101, 105–6
Foucault, Michel, 9, 84, 87, 97, 143, 198
francophone
    sources, 50
    world, 6, 12–13
    writers/writing, 133–35, 139, 145, 151, 187–201
Frappier, Jean, 41
French language, 3, 12–13, 22, 68–70, 72–73, 75, 163, 187, 188–90, 192–93, 199
Froissart, Jean, 11, 133–147, 185
    see also Chroniques (Froissart)
Fulk de Neuilly, 38–40

Gaimar, Geoffrey, 73, 119
Gaucher, Elisabeth, 170, 179
Gaunt, Simon, ix, 12, 187–201
gender,
    honor and, 24
    sexuality and, 10–11, 144, 147
    social identity and, 172, 177–78, 186
    sodomy and, 134–35, 142
    vice/virtue and, 61, 64
    violence and, 8
"Genealogy of Arnold I," 55
Geoffrey Gaimar
    see Gaimar, Geoffrey
Geoffrey of Monmouth, 73, 84, 119–20
Geoffroy de Villehardouin
    see Villehardouin, Geoffroy de
Gertrude of Aalst, 71, 76
Gertrude of Saxony, 55–57, 60, 64–65
Ghent War, 170, 181, 183
gift-giving
    competition and, 20
    honor and, 23
    reciprocal, 8, 19–21, 23–24, 28, 31, 198
    sacred and, 20–21, 29, 31
    violence and, 33
    see also reciprocity

Girart de Roussillon, 26–30, 33
Gower, John, 152
grace, 7, 20, 46, 49, 161–62
Gui de Cavaillon, 102, 110
Gui of Dampierre, 68
Guicciardini, Francesco, 3
Guilhem de Tudela, 99–101, 103–4, 107–9, 111
Guinevere, 97
gunfanun, 89–90
Guynn, Noah D., ix, 1–16, 35–51

Haidu, Peter, 8
Harrison, Ann Tukey, 160–61
Hayton of Corycus, 187–89, 191–92, 195–96, 200
Henri de Valenciennes, 50, 68
Herman of Hainut, 55
Herman of Tournai, 62–63, 65–67
Hermann of Mons, 56
Herodotus, 7
Hervé de Meriadec, 179
Hincmar of Reims, 57
Hirsch, Eric, 3, 6
historical intelligibility, 4, 6–7, 10
historicity, 6, 15, 118
historicizing, 5
history, failure of, 31–32
History of the Counts of Guines and Lords of Ardres
  Arnold III, 75
  background on text, 72–73
  comedy in a violent world, 74–76
  Gertrude of Aalst, 71, 76
  influences, 73
  intentional humor, 76–79
  Latin satire and, 78–79
  overview, 71–74
  Ralph of Guines, 74–75
  shepherd as chorus, 74
  social impact of comedy and violence, 79–81
homosexuality, 11, 134, 143–44
honor
  Canso de la Crozada and, 10
  Charlemagne and, 27, 30, 32
  Chronique des ducs de Normandie and, 125, 127
  death and, 113–14
  dismemberment and, 93–94
  Girart de Roussillon and, 27–29
  grace and, 20

identity and, 23–24, 111
masculinity and, 24, 146
nation and, 49, 91
reciprocity and, 20
Raoul de Cambrai and, 33
Renaut de Montauban and, 30, 32
Song of London and, 25
William Wallace and, 96
Horn, Andrew, 88–89
Hue of Lannoy, 153
Hugh de Cressingham, 93–94
Hugh Despenser the Younger, 11, 133–41, 144
Hundred Years War, 11, 133–35, 137, 145–46, 151
hystericizing, 2, 5

identity,
  authorization of, 24
  chivalry and, 172, 178–79
  community and, 194–95
  cultural, 13, 188
  dismemberment and, 87
  heraldry and, 90
  "kept" items and, 20
  knighthood and, 12
  linguistic, 188, 195
  memory and, 166
  sexuality and, 134, 147
  social, 23, 90, 172
  violence and, 24
Ilion, 119–20, 123
imprisonment, 11, 105, 109, 136, 152–59, 161–67
institutions
  history and, 1, 5
  sacred and, 20
  violence and, 9, 195
intercourse, sexual
  adultery, 141–42
  birth and, 131
  performative nature of, 143
  punishment and, 141–42
  speech and, 142–44
  treason and, 141–42, 145
  violence and, 131
  see also sex
Islamophobia, 187–88, 191–93

Jacques de Lalaing, 11–12, 169–86
  see also Livre des faits de messier Jacques de Lalaing

Jaeger, Robert J., 152
Jean de Boniface, 179
Jean d'Outremeuse, 11, 133, 135–42
Jean Froissart,
    see Froissart, Jean
Jean Le Bel, 135–42
Jean Le Fèvre, 170, 173–75
    see also Toison d'Or
Jean Regnier, 152, 164
Jehan Pitois, 179
Jerusalem, 22, 33, 35, 40, 48, 189
Joan of Arc, 152
John of Salisbury, 79, 82
John Pike, 92–93
Judaism, 22, 91–92
Judas, 75, 124
Justice, Steven, 37, 50

Kay, Sarah, 151
Kelley, Donald R., 3, 7
King Arthur, 97, 126, 189, 199
King Charles IV of France, 134
King Charles VI of England, 155
King Charles VI of France, 135, 145–46
King Charles the Bald, 55
King Charles the Straightforward, 77
King Edward I of England, 9–10, 83–90, 93, 95, 97
King Edward II of England, 11, 133–37, 139, 141, 143, 146–47
King Edward III of England, 133–35, 140–45
King Edward IV of England, 170
King Edward the Confessor, 119
King Emeric I of Hungary, 43
King Harold, 96, 118
King Henry II of England, 106
King Henry IV of England, 152
King Henry V of England, 152, 155, 159
King Henry VI of England, 155, 159
King Louis VII of France, 79
King Philip Augustus of France, 105
King Philip I of France, 60–61, 64–66
King Philip IV of France, 145
King Philip VI of France, 145
King Richard the Lion-Hearted, 106, 146
knighthood
    chronicling of, 169–72, 176, 184–86
    expected conduct, 11–12, 39
    faidit (dispossessed knight), 105, 108
    honor and, 10, 75, 82
    identity and, 12

loyalty and, 80, 109
as mirror of chivalric community, 177–81
violence and, 82, 111–14
    see also chivalry; Crusades
Kristeva, Julia, 153–54
Kublai Khan, 12, 191, 193, 195–96, 200–1

Lambert of Ardres, 9, 71–82
Lambert of Saint-Omer, 9, 57–61, 67
Langtoft, Piers, 89–91, 93
Lascaris, Theodore, 49
Lateran Councils
    Third, 102
    Fourth, 99, 101, 104–5, 109, 111
Latin Empire, 9, 13, 35, 37, 43, 48–50
Latin language, 24, 27, 38, 59, 68–70, 72–73, 78, 81–82, 92, 130, 187–90
law
    dismemberment and, 10
    Edward I and, 10, 84, 93
    Foucault on, 9
    violence and, 9–10, 81
Les cronikes des contes de Flandres, 68–70
Lévi-Strauss, Claude, 3, 19, 33
Liber Floridus, 9, 57
Lideric of Harelbeke, 55
Livre de la paix (Christine de Pizan), 152
Livre des manières (Stephen of Fougères), 81
Livre des mervilles (Jean de Mandeville), 188
Livre des faits de messier Jacques de Lalaing, 11, 113, 169–86
    death of Lalaing and visual incongruity, 181–86
    heraldic author as arbiter of chivalric violence, 172–76
    immortalizing violence, 186
    knight as "mirror" of his chivalric community, 177–81
Llywelyn ap Gruffydd, 85
Louis of Orléans, 160, 165

Mandeville, Jean de, 188, 191, 193, 195–97, 200–1
Mannyng, Robert, 90
Marco Polo, 12, 188–93, 195–201
Marie de Clèves, 160
Martel, Charles, 26–33

INDEX

Marvin, Garry, 24
Mathieu d'Escouchy, 173, 175
Mauss, Marcel, 19
McGrady, Deborah, ix, 11, 151–67
Melanesia, 20
"mémoire hystérisée," 2
memory
    Abbey of Saint Bertin and, 61–62
    fame and, 94
    Michelet and, 2
    poetry and, 151–55, 163–67
    reality and, 15, 151
    violence and, 4–6, 9, 56, 89
    war and, 11
    see also commemoration
Michelet, Jules, 1–3, 6–7
    "vie intégrale," 1–2
Moeglin, Jean-Marie, 55, 62–63, 67
money
    belief and, 198–99
    Judaism and, 92
    language and, 189, 193–98
    Marco Polo and, 191
    Mongol Empire and, 12, 190
Mongol Empire, 12, 187–89, 193, 201
Mortimer, Roger, 11, 133, 135, 140–41, 144
Mühlethaler, Jean-Claude, 153, 157

Nair, Rukmini, 151
Nazism, 102
Nicaea, 48–49
Nirenberg, David, 22
Nolan, Maura, 5
nomos, 23–34
Nora, Pierre, 2–3
Norman Conquest, 13, 96, 119
    see also Battle of Hastings

Occitan language, 10, 13, 22, 101, 188
Offenstadt, Nicolas, 152
Orosius, 7, 36, 37
Oseney Abbey, 86
othering, 3, 6, 22–23
Outremer, 40–41, 45

Peire de Castelnau, 103–8
performative/performativity, 23–24, 27, 34, 41–42, 50, 85, 143, 178–79, 197
Peter Abelard
    see Abelard, Peter
Peter Damian
    see Damian, Peter

Peter the Hermit, 39
Philip of Alsace, 62, 67, 69
Philip of Swabia, 44–45
Philip the Good of Burgundy [Philippe le Bon], 152–55, 159–65, 176–77
Philippe de Mézières, 133, 135, 145
Piers Langtoft
    see Langtoft, Piers
Pike, John
    see John Pike
Pizan, Christine de
    see Christine de Pizan
plague, 145, 187
poetry
    past poetry and book commemoration, 163–67
    peace/war and, 156–59
    poètes engagés, 153
    politics and, 153–55
    speaking truth in, 159–63
    violence and, 11, 152
    see also Charles d'Orléans
Polyxena, 120–24
Pope Boniface, 49
Pope Clement IV, 13
Pope Gregory X, 191–92
Pope Innocent III, 35–38, 44, 103, 105–6, 110
    see also Roman Church
Pope Urban, 58

Queen Isabella (wife of Edward II), 11, 133–44

Rachilda (wife of Baldwin VI), 55–56, 60–69
Raimbaut de Vaqueiras, 50
Ralph of Guines, 74, 80
Ramon IV of Saint-Gilles, 106
Ramon VI of Toulouse, 103–5, 109
Ramon Roger Trencavel, 99–101, 109
Raoul de Cambrai, 31–35
Raoul of Cambria, 25, 31–35
rape, 4, 10, 122, 125, 131
reciprocity
    gift-giving and, 19–22, 28, 33
    Girart de Roussillon and, 27–29, 33
    messengers and, 30
    money and, 198
    Raoul de Cambrai and, 32, 34
    Renaut de Montauban and, 30–31
    violence and, 22–26

INDEX

Renaud of Dammartin, 78
Renaut de Montauban, 30–32
resurrection, 171
rhetoric
   Canso de la Crozada and, 101
   Charles d'Orléans and, 157–58, 162
   Chronicle (Langtoft) and, 90, 92
   Chronique des ducs de Normandie and, 125, 132
   execution and, 86–87
   history and, 4, 6–9, 15, 39–40
   La conquête de Constantinople (Villehardouin) and, 35–46, 48, 50–51
   narrative and, 35–38, 157–58
   providential, 35–37, 42, 44–46, 50–51
   sex and, 147
   violence and, 35–37
Rider, Jeff, x, 9, 55–69
Robert I (the Frisian), 9–10, 55–69, 125, 127–28, 131
Robert II, 56–57, 59
Robert Bruce, 97
Robert de Beaumont, 113
Robert of Gloucester, 95
Roger II Trencavel, 105–6
Roger Mortimer
   see Mortimer, Roger
Rollo, David, x, 10, 117–32
Roman Church, 35
   Byzantine Church and, 45–46
   Girart de Roussillon and, 30
   Occitania and, 102–3, 109
   political power, 104
   Raoul de Cambrai and, 33
   reciprocity and, 22
   violence and, 102–8
   see also Lateran Councils; Pope Innocent III
Roman de Rou (Wace), 129
Roman de toute chevalerie (Thomas of Kent), 90
Roman de Troie (Benoît de Sainte-Maure), 10, 118
romance writings, history and, 89–90, 172
Rosenwein, Barbara, 19, 77

sacred closure, 30–31
satire, 9, 79–82
Saverio, Guida, 102
Scala, Elizabeth, 5
Scotichronicon, 94–96

Seigneur de Berzé, 36
September Massacres, 2
Sermo de Annuntiatione Dominica, 35
sex
   birth and, 131
   Chronique des ducs de Normandie and, 125, 128–29
   death and, 154
   desire and, 27, 78
   events and, 135–37
   illicit and licit, 144–46
   punishment and, 11, 134–35
   violence and, 121, 139–42
   see also intercourse, sexual
sexuality, history and, 10–11, 146–47
Shopkow, Leah, x, 9, 71–81
Simon de Montfort, 95–96, 101, 104–7, 109–10, 113
sodomy, 11, 137, 139–40, 142–46
Song of Roland, The, 25, 29–30, 32–34, 49, 112
Spearing, A. C., 153
St. Albans Abbey, 96
Stahuljak, Zrinka, x, 1–16, 124, 133–47
Statute of Rhuddlan, 84
Stephen of Blois, 119
Stephen of Fougères, 73, 81
Stewart, Charles, 3, 6
Stirnemann, Patricia, 163, 165
Strohm, Paul, 5
subversion, violence and, 8–9, 22–23
Sullivan, Karen, x, 10, 99–114
Szkilnik, Michelle, 171, 185

Taylor, Jane H. M., 160, 164
Theodore Lascaris
   see Lascaris, Theodore
Thomas Becket
   see Becket, Thomas
Thomas of Kent, 90
Thucydides, 7
Toison d'Or, 170, 173–78, 184, 186
   see also Jean Le Fèvre
torture, 4, 10, 74, 84–87, 91, 101, 135, 139–40, 143
Tower of London, 86, 88
translation
   linguistic, 68–70, 81, 89, 187, 189
   visual, 15, 186
trauma
   lyric voice and, 151, 154–55, 162, 167
   war and, 11, 151–54

treason
    castration and, 142
    dismemberment and, 10, 83–85, 90
    execution and, 87
    Hugh Despenser and, 138, 141
    memory and, 94
    Roger Mortimer and, 140–41
    sex acts and, 135, 141–42, 144–45, 147
    William Wallace and, 90–91, 94
Treaty of Arras (1435), 156
Treaty of Troyes (1420), 155
Trigald, Fulk, 86
Trojan War, 119–20

Usurpation of 1071
    Ancient Chronicle of Flanders and, 62–68
    early accounts of, 56–59
    Flandria Generosa and, 59–62
    historical significance of, 9

Villehardouin, Geoffroy de, 9, 35–51, 68
violence
    antireciprocal, 31
    beauty and, 111–14
    Canso de la Crozada and, 99–114
    chivalry and, 170–86
    comedy and, 72, 74–82
    Crusades and, 45, 50–51, 191–92
    evil and, 102–7
    gift-giving and, 19–21, 33
    good and, 107–11
    history and, 6–8, 187–89, 201
    honor and, 28
    institutionalization of, 195, 199
    memory and, 167
    money and, 198
    nonreciprocal, 8, 31
    poetic verse and, 151–52
    political, 117–20, 144, 147
    reciprocal, 28–29, 34
    religion and, 35–36, 45, 50, 191–92
    repressed, 131–32
    ritual and, 86–87
    sacred and, 22, 26, 28–29, 34
    sex and, 134–35, 137, 139–41, 143
    subversion and, 8–9, 22–23
    symbolic nature of, 93–94
    tyranny and, 56–70
    writing of history and, 6–8, 22–26
    see also dismemberment; executions; reciprocity
Virgil, 74, 120, 124
Virgin Mary, 171, 185

Wace, 118–19, 125, 129–32
Wallace, William, 85, 88–97
Walter of Châtillon, 79
Walter of Le Clud, 73
Walter of Thérouanne, 62
war
    against the king, 84–87
    just, 47, 51, 152, 158
Ward, John O., 4, 37–38, 51
Weil, Simone, 109
William aux Blanches Mains, 79
William Clito, 63
William, Lord Hastings, 170
William of Ardres, 81
William of Malmesbury, 118–19, 130–31
William of Orange, 22, 26, 33–34, 81
William Rishanger, 92, 96
William the Conqueror, 10, 24–25, 125–28
William (viscount), 64–65
William Wallace
    see Wallace, William

xenophobia, 187, 192

Already Published

1. *Postcolonial Fictions in the 'Roman de Perceforest': Cultural Identities and Hybridities*, Sylvia Huot
2. *A Discourse for the Holy Grail in Old French Romance*, Ben Ramm
3. *Fashion in Medieval France*, Sarah-Grace Heller
4. *Christine de Pizan's Changing Opinion: A Quest for Certainty in the Midst of Chaos*, Douglas Kelly
5. *Cultural Performances in Medieval France: Essays in Honor of Nancy Freeman Regalado*, eds Eglal Doss-Quinby, Roberta L. Krueger, E. Jane Burns
6. *The Medieval Warrior Aristocracy: Gifts, Violence, Performance, and the Sacred*, Andrew Cowell
7. *Logic and Humour in the Fabliaux: An Essay in Applied Narratology*, Roy J. Pearcy
8. *Miraculous Rhymes: The Writing of Gautier de Coinci*, Tony Hunt
9. *Philippe de Vigneulles and the Art of Prose Translation*, Catherine M. Jones
10. *Desire by Gender and Genre in Trouvère Song*, Helen Dell
11. *Chartier in Europe*, eds Emma Cayley, Ashby Kinch
12. *Medieval Saints' Lives: The Gift, Kinship and Community in Old French Hagiography*, Emma Campbell
13. *Poetry, Knowledge and Community in Late Medieval France*, eds Rebecca Dixon, Finn E. Sinclair with Adrian Armstrong, Sylvia Huot, Sarah Kay
14. *The Troubadour Tensos and Partimens: A Critical Edition*, Ruth Harvey, Linda Paterson
15. *Old French Narrative Cycles: Heroism between Ethics and Morality*, Luke Sunderland
16. *The Cultural and Political Legacy of Anne de Bretagne: Negotiating Convention in Books and Documents*, ed. Cynthia J. Brown
17. *Lettering the Self in Medieval and Early Modern France*, Katherine Kong
18. *The Old French Lays of Ignaure, Oiselet and Amours*, eds Glyn S. Burgess, Leslie C. Brook
19. *Thinking Through Chrétien de Troyes*, Zrinka Stahuljak, Virginie Greene, Sarah Kay, Sharon Kinoshita, Peggy McCracken
20. *Blindness and Therapy in Late Medieval French and Italian Poetry*, Julie Singer
21. *Partonopeus de Blois: Romance in the Making*, Penny Eley
22. *Illuminating the Roman d'Alexandre: Oxford, Bodleian Library, MS Bodley 264: The Manuscript as Monument*, Mark Cruse
23. *The Conte du Graal Cycle: Chrétien de Troyes' Perceval, the Continuations, and French Arthurian Romance*, Thomas Hinton
24. *Marie de France: A Critical Companion*, Sharon Kinoshita, Peggy McCracken
25. *Constantinople and the West in Medieval French Literature: Renewal and Utopia*, Rima Devereaux

26. *Authorship and First Person Allegory in Late Medieval France and England*,
Stephanie A. Viereck Gibbs Kamath

27. *Virgilian Identities in the French Renaissance*,
ed. Philip John Usher, Isabelle Fernbach

28. *Shaping Courtliness in Medieval France*,
eds Daniel E. O'Sullivan, Laurie Shepard